Samādhi

SUNY series in Religious Studies

Harold Coward, editor

Samādhi

The Numinous and Cessative in Indo-Tibetan Yoga

Stuart Ray Sarbacker

State University of New York Press

Published by
State University of New York Press, Albany

Printed in the United States of America

For information, address State University of New York Press,
194 Washington Avenue, Suite 305, Albany, NY 12210-2384

Production by Michael Haggett
Marketing by Michael Campochiaro

Library of Congress Cataloging-in-Publication Data

Sarbacker, Stuart Ray, 1969–
Samādhi : the numinous and cessative in Indo-Tibetan yoga / Stuart Ray Sarbacker.
p. cm. — (SUNY series in religious studies)
Includes bibliographical references and index.
ISBN 0-7914-6553-5 (alk. paper)
1. Meditation—Hinduism. 2. Meditation—Buddhism. 3. Yoga. I. Series.

BL2015.M4S25 2005
294.5'436—dc22

2004062626

10 9 8 7 6 5 4 3 2 1

To Sara, my *ḍākinī*

Contents

Acknowledgments

This work is, in part, the fruit of many academic connections and correspondences over a number of years. I believe it is a positive reflection of the collegiality of the academic community involved in the study of the religions of South Asia. Indira Junghare and Robert Tapp at the University of Minnesota provided a wealth of advice and encouragement that continues to inspire and inform my work. Professor Junghare's guidance, support, and friendship have been an invaluable part of my academic career, and I am profoundly grateful for her generosity. David Knipe, my mentor at the University of Wisconsin, initiated me into the History of Religions as a living tradition of scholarship, and I am indebted to him for his sage advice, patience, and friendship. Also at the University of Wisconsin, I received significant support from John Dunne, Charles Hallisey, Joseph Elder, Usha Nilsson, and Ven. Geshe Lhundub Sopa. John Dunne played a critical role in the development of many of the ideas in the manuscript and inspired within me the confidence to work more deeply and closely with primary texts. Charles Hallisey helped greatly to bring focus, discipline, and closure to my writing. Joseph Elder has served in many respects as a model for my development as a scholar and researcher throughout my academic career. Usha Nilsson helped fill my imagination with a panorama of religious imagery found in Indian literature as a necessary counterpoint to the analytic and philosophical dimensions of my study. Lastly, I am grateful for the many insights into the Gelukpa tradition of Tibetan Buddhism given to me by Ven. Geshe Lhundub Sopa.

In the early stages of this project, I had the fortunate opportunity to discuss many of my ideas with Winston King of Vanderbilt University. He provided helpful comments on my early work and numerous insights into his own work on the relationship between yoga and Buddhism. Professor King passed away before this manuscript was completed, but I am comforted by the fact that my work bears his imprint and influence in many significant ways. Two other scholars who greatly encouraged me in the early stages of the project were Edward Crangle of the University of Sydney and Alan Wallace of the University of California, Santa Barbara. Both provided valuable suggestions and encouragement during the early and formative stages of this project.

A great number of scholars on the topic of yoga provided significant interest, support, and encouragement during various stages of research and writing, including Ian Whicher of the University of Manitoba, Christopher Key Chapple of Loyola Marymount University, David Carpenter of St. Joseph's University, and Lloyd Pflueger of Truman State University. Professor Whicher in particular went out of his way on numerous occasions to provide guidance, encouraging me to engage myself fully in both traditional and contemporary issues in the study of yoga. Likewise, I have benefited greatly from the examination of the scholarly work of and from personal communications with Johannes Bronkhorst and Gerald Larson, whose correspondence at important points during the development of this manuscript proved profoundly fruitful for my work. All of these scholars provided both academic and moral support during the various stages of this project, and their influence can be clearly seen in the finished product.

The academic environment in Chicago has proven to be an outstanding one in which to pursue this project, and I have greatly benefited from my numerous discussions and interactions with many colleagues and friends. George Bond of Northwestern University spent a considerable amount of time discussing a number of key points of intersection between his research and my project. He provided countless suggestions that ended up shaping the text in profound ways, and I am particularly grateful for his support and encouragement. Sarah Taylor Rountree, also of Northwestern University, has been an outstanding supporter of my academic work and is deserving of much gratitude for her kindness. Tracy Pintchman at Loyola University Chicago provided innumerable insights into the writing and editing process that have helped considerably in completing the project. Conversations with David Gitomer at DePaul University provided a range of insights on the topic of yoga that brought much light to the ideas that I have endeavored to develop in the text.

The work as a whole is an expanded and revised version of my doctoral dissertation from the University of Wisconsin, entitled "The Concept of *Samādhi*: Method and the Study of Meditation in South Asian Religion," completed in December 2001. This work was greatly facilitated by the support and assistance of Harold Coward of the University of Victoria, the editor of the series in *Religious Studies*, and Nancy Ellegate and Allison Lee of the State University of New York Press.

I also would like to thank the copyright holders of two journals, who have given me permission to reproduce significant parts of two of my previously published articles—Enrica Garzilli, for granting me permission to reproduce material from my article "Traditions in Transition: Meditative Concepts in the Development of Tantric *Sādhana*," *International Journal of Tantric Studies* 6:1 (2002), which appears in revision as chapter 5, and David Chidester, for granting me permission to reproduce material from my article "*Enstasis* and *Ecstasis*: A Critical Appraisal of Eliade on Yoga and Shamanism," *Journal for the Study of Religion* 15:1 (2002), which is further developed in chapter 3.

I am most of all grateful to my wife, Sara, who has been my greatest supporter throughout this project. Her ability to bring out the best in my work and life is truly extraordinary, and I am truly thankful for her encouragement and inspiration.

INTRODUCTION

Method and the Study of Meditation

MEDITATION AND THE STUDY OF RELIGION

The primary goal of this work is to develop a new methodological approach to the study of yoga and meditation in the religions of South Asia, most notably in the context of Hinduism and Buddhism. This methodology attempts to establish a balance between psychological and sociological approaches to the study of religion by integrating them into a larger phenomenological model for interpreting religious experience. The foundation of this approach is the examination of the dynamic relationship of what can be termed *numinous* and *cessative* dimensions of yoga and meditative practice in the Hindu and Buddhist context. The notion of the *numinous* represents the manner in which a practitioner of yoga embodies the world-surmounting power of divinity, while the *cessative* dimension emphasizes the attainment of freedom through separation from phenomenal existence. This relationship between *numinous* and *cessative* orientations in yoga and meditation relates to philosophical and psychological understandings of the nature of meditative states and to the connection between meditative concepts and the religious and cultural contexts in which they have developed. The usefulness of this approach to the study of yoga and meditation will be demonstrated through its application in the context of the comparison of Classical Yoga and Indian Buddhism and in the development of conceptions of tantric *sādhana* found in Indian and Tibetan Buddhism. It will be shown that a significantly more sophisticated understanding of the relationship of Classical Yoga and Buddhism emerges through an analysis of the concept of meditative absorption or contemplation, *samādhi*, in light of this methodological orientation. This approach also will help illuminate a number of issues regarding the scholastic and ritual functioning of meditative concepts and texts and their relationship to broader historical and cultural contexts. Through application of this theory to the development of tantric practice, *sādhana*, it will be demonstrated how *sādhana* represents an extension of pre-tantric conceptions of meditation, presupposing the integration of numinous and cessative qualities and posing a challenge to mainstream religious ideals in both the Hindu and Buddhist contexts. This methodology and its subsequent application will thus provide insight into a number of crucially important issues in the study of yoga and meditation in the Hindu and Buddhist religious contexts.

MEDITATION IN CONTEXT

In the schools of Indian Buddhism, *dhyāna*, typically translated as "meditation," is often considered an indispensable part of the path toward liberation. It is a key aspect of the eightfold path, *aṣṭāṅgikamārga*, the conception of the threefold training, *triśikṣā*, and the six perfections, or *pāramitās*. The importance of *dhyāna* in the contexts of the Classical Yoga and *Sāṃkhya* traditions, in Jainism and Vedānta, and in Indian *bhakti*, in both contemporary and premodern contexts, demonstrates its continuing vitality within these other manifestations of the Indian religious heritage as well. It would, however, be overly simplistic to state that meditation is an *essential* element of the range of religious practices and traditions falling under the great variety of religious phenomena constituting the Indian religions. In the context of yoga and meditation, this is exemplified by the fact that even those textual and oral traditions that appear to emphasize the meditative dimension of religious life may be scholastic or second-order traditions that are as much characterized by doctrine and ritual as by contemplation or meditation.

In the context of the study of religion, the emergence of critical theory has helped clarify the problems of essentializing traditions with one type of religious practice and the danger of reifying words such as "religion," "mysticism," and so on.[1] However, beyond generalizations about these traditions, it is clear that in both scholastic inquiry and in ascetic discipline, conceptions regarding *dhyāna* or the closely related term *bhāvanā* have played important roles in much of Indian and Tibetan Buddhism and in the numerous ascetic disciplines that are referred to as "yoga" in the Hindu, Buddhist, and Jaina contexts. Ideas regarding meditation have developed in a plurality of contexts, often taking shape in both dialogue and tension between different sects and schools, reflecting a process of mutual exchange and interdependence. The multivalence of the term *dhyāna* in these contexts demonstrates the manner in which religious practices extend across traditional boundaries and are often redefined in terms of divergent soteriological ends. In much of Theravāda meditation theory, in the Pātañjala Classical Yoga system, in Indian Mahāyāna philosophy, and in Advaita Vedānta, the role of meditation in the development of ethics and soteriology is viewed as an extremely important one. Where these practices do not see application in a primary pragmatic sense, they often serve as a basis for scholastic contemplation and analysis and the establishment of scriptural authority. As a subject of intense scrutiny and technical elaboration, meditation as an object of intellectual reflection can be said to establish another realm of practice, one in which alternative methodologies or strategies for liberation are put to the test of rigorous logical examination and debate. This extended use of the meditation text is further demonstrated by the common ritual use of religious texts as a basis for making merit through recitation and for the embodiment of text through the faculty of memory. In many cases, the boundary between the application of meditative concepts in the primary and secondary senses is a fluid or dynamic one. As we will discuss at length, meditation plays many roles within Hindu and Buddhist communities and demonstrates the tension between adaptation and innovation in the religious thought and practice of these traditions.

Meditation and Contemporary Culture

The proliferation in recent years of Hindu and Buddhist religious organizations throughout the world has been fueled in part by popular interest in empirical or experiential forms of religion or spirituality that contrast with perceptions of mainstream religion as dogmatic and ritualistic. The core concepts of the enlightenment tradition have, in part, led to the development of an attitude of quasi-empiricism that is a foundation for much of this contemporary attraction for meditation as an "experiential" enterprise. The other side of the picture is that the ideals of empiricism and faith in science have led many to a crisis of meaning and a search for religious "answers" outside of their own cultural and religious traditions. As Mircea Eliade has argued at length, a common perception in the contemporary American and European context is that the cosmos has been desacralized, that our cultures have lost touch with those realities that informed and instilled meaning into everyday life for premodern or *archaic* man.[2] Searching for a sense of meaning or mystery that will fend off the encroaching and suffocating feelings of emptiness, meaninglessness, and loss may lead people toward sublimated forms of religious expression and alternative forms of spirituality and religion.[3] This might take the form of engagement with what Robert Ellwood has called "excursis religion," meaning a religious "flight," a concept that might be applied to many of the contexts in which meditation is practiced.[4] From both the perspective of searching for religious expression in line with contemporary scientific thought and from one that stands in opposition, meditation is often seen as an alternative to both the secular and religious dimensions of mainstream culture in Europe and America.

On the empirical level, the idea that there are methods for conditioning the body and mind that provide a foundation for ethical and spiritual development is a matter of great interest from both philosophical and humanistic standpoints. Having few "superstructures," to borrow a term used by Frits Staal, practices such as yoga and meditation are often presented as experiential, personal, and individualistic—not grounded in the same presuppositions of faith and obedience as would be found in mainstream religion, particularly with Judaism and Christianity.[5] Following from the lack of superstructure is the conception that one may not need to change one's worldview or become Buddhist or Hindu to meditate or practice yoga. This conception, that practice and theory can be separated from one another, is arguably another key conception at the foundation of much contemporary fascination with these disciplines. It can be argued that this space or opening in which people can participate in the practices without significant ideological or faith commitment operates like a doorway or an antechamber to greater commitment, an opportunity to test the waters.[6] It is interesting to note the fact that *praxis*, here referring to meditative practices, is understood in this mode of thinking as an expression of independence and empiricism—a first-person, experiential phenomenon, one that seems to fit into the empirical paradigm. However, as postmodernism brings to our attention, it should be recognized that even this "experimentation" is a concrete manifestation of beliefs, attitudes, and inclinations, presupposing some degree of commitment to a particular worldview. Informal instruction in yoga and meditation and the availability of a range of popular literature on meditation provide an entryway into deeper involvement in the cultural aspects of religious practice. The process of becoming part of a social and religious community can be seen to operate on a number of levels and through a series of stages of progression, from that of informal participation to deliberate and formal declarations of faith.

Another facet of contemporary interest in meditation can be described as the search for profound experiences and a sense of enjoyment in life contrasted with the mundane or rote reality of secularized life. In this context, Erica Bourguignon has argued that Hindu and Buddhist cults, such as those that grew exponentially in the American countercultural movement, promise a degree of instant gratification characteristic of consumerist culture, supporting an "ease" or "a pleasure-centered" religious attitude.[7] This would be complemented by the attraction that such traditions have for individuals who have used psychogenic and other types of substances to deliberately cultivate ecstatic states and who pursue religious interests as an extension of that dimension of their cultural or spiritual life. This connection between meditation and the ecstatic is developed in a different manner by Gananath Obeyesekere, who argues that yogic methodologies can be qualified on the psychoanalytic level on the basis of the degree to which they aim at putting life in accordance with the so-called pleasure principle.[8] Obeyesekere thus sees yogic practices, such as shamanic forms, as being forms of psychological adaptation that may bring transformation to the personality in profound ways, and not simply as a form of escapism. The sense of dissatisfaction with life in its mundane manifestations plays into a desire to transform day-to-day living and into the search for profound experiences of an ecstatic character. Meditation also may represent an attempt to establish a degree of mental and emotional strength or stability that will provide for coping with the inevitability of the painful realities of life and the psychological strength to pursue meaningful avenues of change. The development of many models of meditation that view it as therapeutic exemplifies how such practices are being adapted to address the realities of social and emotional life outside of the religious context. The steady integration of meditative models into the domains of psychology and psychiatry has furthered interest in this domain and provided further rationale for focusing upon yoga and meditation as a legitimate subject of academic and scientific study.

A study of the historical, linguistic, and cultural elements that compose and contextualize meditation practice is valuable for a number of reasons. The study of meditation is an important point of intersection between cultures, a place of coming together that has a vitality and an immediacy of relevance to our society and the development of its cultural and religious horizons. An important relationship can be developed between scholars and practitioners of yoga and meditative traditions that may help further develop dialogue and, by extension, mutual understanding on this subject. Practitioners may be in a position to offer the academic study of religion insight into the concrete manifestations of meditation practice and provide anthropological opportunities for the scholar that allow for a deeper understanding of the practical and cultural realities of meditation. This is particularly important to the degree that yoga and other contemplative disciplines are said to be rooted in experiences that provide key insights for interpretation and explanation presumably not available to the uninitiated. In the academic context, approaching the subject with a critical lens can provide historical and cultural insights that complement the philosophical perspectives that are developed within the traditions themselves. In turn, the advancement of such a methodology will be valuable in light of the splintering and polarization in contemporary scholarship between empathetic and critical approaches toward the study of religion.[9] Scholarly perspectives on meditation often have been fractured, breaking into different views, such as academic and critical methodologies, medical and therapeutic applications, and popular discussions of yoga and meditation as alternative forms of spirituality. This is further complicated by the influences that scholarship has had upon its objects of study, an issue that becomes of paramount importance for some scholars in understanding the self-representations of the cultures they study.[10] This has led to a rift within the academic community and between the academic and nonacademic communities in the study of religion that is unnecessary and even to some degree harmful to the integrity of religious studies and the culture it exists within.[11] The current study aims to overcome these problems through the development of an integrative and interdisciplinary approach to the study of religion, and thus meditation, that values a range of perspectives and approaches.

Our hope is that this study also may, by extension, provide a theoretical foundation for the development of contemplative studies as a subdiscipline of the History of Religions methodology. There is great potential for the development of mutual understanding and cultural renewal in the study of contemplation and *praxis* in the academic context. This may occur through conversations with representatives of a range of religious backgrounds and through investigation of traditional and academic sources on contemplative technique in the historical and contemporary contexts. Perhaps in time practical training in meditative technique might be offered as part of a philosophy or religious studies curriculum, one that is developed and explored in the academic setting. On this level, the study of religion can play a significant role in the development of progressive social ideals and the validation of cultural diversity. It also may provide alternative perspectives on contemporary culture that demonstrate the meaningfulness of endeavors that are not currently validated by market-driven culture.[12] The pursuit of the study of meditation and other contemplative methods may be an avenue for exploring the psychological, social, and ethical ramifications of alternative approaches to living and may bolster the ability of religious studies to act as a medium for social and cultural renewal. The application of such methods in the academic context must be limited by the fact that they are rooted in a plurality of worldviews diverging from one another in critical ways. However, a great amount of common ground exists within contemplative traditions that make them particularly suitable for comparison and dialogue in the academic context.

Poststructural, Postmodern, and Postcolonial Considerations

Poststructural, postmodern, and postcolonial thought has led to greater contextuality in the study of religion through the development of new approaches to text and to ethnographic and anthropological research.[13] However, it may be argued that the emphasis on the knowledge-power relationship that thoroughly infuses postmodern and postcolonial thought at times comes dangerously close to being the sort of "master narrative" that it claims to eschew. J. J. Clarke has noted that postmodernism may be thought of as more an extension of, or an attempt to come to terms with, a number of the central problems of modernism than as an outright rejection of the modernist enterprise.[14] Along these lines, George Kalamaras has recently argued that one of the problems with postmodern theory is that it forms a basic dichotomy between itself and other forms of discourse and in effect propagates the very type of binary thinking that it attempts to avoid.[15] Kalamaras argues that poststructuralist rhetoric leaves no space for the possibility of phenomena outside the realm of language, pushing all appeals to realities beyond language into the realm of the primitive or the oppressive.[16] Due to this, the liberating potential of questioning the relationship of language and power can be at odds with knowledge claims based in appeals to nonlinguistic forms of experience and understanding, such as silence and paradox.[17] Though presenting a somewhat simplistic image of Indian forms of yoga, Kalamaras rightly notes the importance of *praxis* and the generative nature of opposition in the yogic context.[18] The play of paradox, the coincidence of opposites, and the transcendent aspects of religious thought and practice are issues where scholarship on religion walks a tightrope. Appeals to nonlinguistic phenomena and the characterization of cultural traditions as respectively rational versus irrational, or scientific versus mystical, are often said to be the foundation of orientalist thought.[19] While ruling out appeals to any nonlinguistic forms of knowledge a priori would be equivalent to undercutting the truth claims of many of the different Indian philosophical and religious traditions, the idea that Indian traditions do not value discursive thought or scholasticism is plainly false, as much as the assertion that Indian religions are exclusively mystical.[20] Kalamaras's presentation of the role and nature of *samādhi*, for example, clearly gives the impression that *samādhi* has traditionally been the central practice or goal of Vedānta, an assertion that is problematic at best.[21] He is correct, however, in asserting that transcendence is often the primary object of meditative practice, posing a problem for interpretations that situate it purely in a social or cultural field of relationships.

While being a challenge to comparativism in its emphasis on rootedness and contextuality, poststructural and postmodern thought also brings to light the reality that knowledge and understanding are themselves the result of comparative processes. Gadamer's idea of the "fusion of horizons," which emphasizes the rootedness of all human discourse in tradition and culture and the interaction of such contextual views, is demonstrated well by the progression toward more sophisticated and complex models of Indian religion and culture.[22] This process is at work both within as well as among cultures, including the religious traditions that are the object of our study and the academic orientations that inform our scholarly work. In Gadamer's thought, it does not make sense to talk about rescuing the original intentions of the author, but rather one should speak of the negotiation of meaning between text and interpreter.[23] We might compare this to Eliade's conception of "creative hermeneutics," a methodology in which a scholar attempts to enter into the religious world of a text and emerge changed by that text and in a position to fruitfully communicate the content of such an encounter. Though Eliade's theory may well presuppose a degree of recovery of intention in myth, rite, and symbol that recent scholarship would consider unwarranted, the strong sense of encounter between worlds or worldviews resembles Gadamer's considerations about traditions and texts.[24] Furthermore, Eliade appears to have been suspicious of the ways in which scholars would try to explain their object of study in light of popular theories in philosophy, sociology, and so on, and the degree to which doing so obscured rather than made clear the ideas and experiences of other cultures.[25] As an extension of this understanding, the current methodological study is oriented towards an awareness of the intimate relationship between context and comparison in the study of meditation and the degree to which each is dependent upon the other. It aims to provide for an awareness of the broader context of underlying social and cultural relationships underlying these practices and for the pursuit of comparative insight and investigation into the lived experience of them. This study is thus based on this conscious recognition of the reflexive relationship between the method of study and the object of study, integrating them together in such a way as to create interpretive parity.

OVERVIEW

We will begin, in chapter 1, with an examination of key terminology and definitions in the context of meditation, developing a basic textual and contextual background in which to place our study of meditation. We will study the development of the paradigmatic concepts of *dhyāna* and *samādhi* in two representative Hindu and Buddhist texts, the *Yogasūtra* of Patañjali (YS) and the *Bhāvanākrama* of Kamalaśīla (BK). Having established the core concepts of meditation and their contexts, we will then provide a brief overview of scholarship on the broad development of the practices of yoga and of meditation in the Indian context. Through this process, we will provide an overarching framework for the study of meditation and a foundation of terminology upon which our approach to the study of meditation and yoga will be built. We will suggest that meditation is an area of the Hindu and Buddhist traditions that offers great insights into the soteriological visions and social structure of both ancient and contemporary practice, even if they are not considered "essential" to these traditions. We will suggest how meditation provides an exceptionally interesting range of issues for the study of religion, contemporary theory on religious experience, and more broadly cultural studies.

Having developed our terms and definitions, in chapter 2 we will turn to an examination of issues regarding the notions of "mysticism" and "religious experience" as they have been applied to meditation in the context of the Hindu and Buddhist traditions. In particular, we will draw out a number of theoretical issues regarding the nature of religious experience hinging upon questions of context and comparison, including questions about the virtues of "constructivist" approaches to the study of religious experience versus those that argue the case for unmediated or direct mystical experience. This will be further developed through examining a number of studies that have looked critically at the term *experience* and the role that it has, as a category, played in the development of the phenomenological model in the study of religion. It will be argued that models of religious practice and experience that have been applied to the study of Buddhism may provide insight into the nature of the relationship between conceptions of meditation found in Buddhism and those of the Classical Yoga system. The foundation for this is an understanding of what can be called the distinction between *numinous* and *cessative* conceptions of the nature of meditation that play out in both the Hindu and Buddhist contexts. It will be suggested that a methodology of "incomplete constructivism," one that recognizes the relationship between conceptions of mediated and unmediated experience, is most suitable for the study of meditation in this context.

In chapter 3, we will further expand upon our notions of the numinous and cessative through the examination of Mircea Eliade's analysis of the relationship between yoga and shamanism and his postulation of notions of *enstasis* and *ecstasis* as categorical types of religious experience. Through this process, we will develop a critical understanding of Eliade's phenomenology in order to bring clarity to a number of issues in the study and interpretation of meditation. We will explore in detail Eliade's analysis of the practice of *dhyāna* and *samādhi* as enstatic phenomena and demonstrate the relevance of this interpretation in our development of more satisfactory conceptions of the numinous versus the cessative in the practice of yoga. Eliade's model will be expanded through an examination of how the numinous dimensions of yoga in both the Hindu and Buddhist traditions demonstrate the importance of visualization and embodiment within the context of yoga and in shamanism. Based upon these observations, we will argue that *samādhi* is better understood as a composite of *enstatic* and *ecstatic* elements, a conception that is at the foundation of the idea of the numinous-cessative relationship. Eliade's phenomenology will be further expanded to allow for a greater contextuality in the interpretation of religious experience through its connection with sociological models of ecstatic religion. Following the work of I. M. Lewis, we will argue that the types of ecstatic states engendered through meditation have an intimate relationship with the social and cultural realities of the environment in which they occur. This integration of Lewis's and Eliade's work will help bring together the more psychological dimension of phenomenology in comparative religion and the key sociological concepts in the study of ecstatic religion, thereby developing an expanded and more holistic interpretive model. In principle, this juxtaposition allows for the recognition of the dynamic relationship between autonomy and contextuality in religious experience, thereby meditating empathetic and critical approaches, and the issue of mediated and unmediated experience. Through this methodology, it will be demonstrated that the numinous and cessative dimensions of meditation can be understood as having repercussions both with respect to human consciousness and to the social and cultural environments in which they are developed and utilized. This relationship further provides the basis for a number of insights into meditative theory and practice, most notably regarding liberation and a liberated person's relationship to the phenomenal world as a *kevalin*, *arhant*, *jīvanmukta*, or as a buddha, as both a spiritual and a social being. In recognizing the relationship between autonomy and environment and between psychological and sociological components in the context of religious practice and experience, this methodological approach will provide an expanded model of phenomenology that builds upon and expands the History of Religions methodology.

Having established this methodological foundation, in chapter 4 we will clarify and expand our understanding of the relationship between the Classical Yoga tradition as represented in Patañjali's *Yogasūtra* and the Indian Buddhist conceptions of meditation. This will begin with an examination of a range of scholarship that has dealt with the issues of the origin and development of meditative practices in the Indian context. This examination will in turn bring to the surface a number of issues regarding the role and function of *dhyāna* in the context of Hinduism and Buddhism demonstrating the relevance and applicability of the methodological approach developed in this work. The primary example of this is the parallelism between presentations of the stages of meditative development as demonstrated by Hindu and Buddhist conceptions of *dhyāna* and *samādhi*. This parallelism will be extended through the examination of the relationship between notions of *śamatha* and *vipaśyanā* in Buddhism and *samāpatti* and *nirodha* in Classical Yoga, and through the comparison of ideas of *nirodhasamāpatti* in the respective traditions. This discussion will be placed in the larger context of issues regarding the development of yoga and meditation in ancient India and questions regarding the influence that these traditions have had upon one another in their formative stages. It also will be argued that the boundary between these traditions is more fluid than has been previously thought by scholars of these religions. It will be shown that meditative concepts in Hinduism and Buddhism can be said to be reflective of larger pan-Indian traditions in a manner antithetical to the conception that Hinduism and Buddhism are autonomous entities.

Through the analysis of the Classical Yoga-Buddhism relationship, it will become clear how the application of the methodological approach developed in this work provides insights into both the cultural and philosophical domains of meditative practice in the Indian religious context. On the social and cultural levels, we will discuss important notions of what will be known as charismatic versus scholastic authority in meditative theory and practice. On another level, the understanding of the numinous-cessative distinction will lead to the investigation of areas of intersection between the Classical Yoga system and Indian Buddhism not significantly acknowledged previously, including that of the relationship of meditation to cosmology and divinity. In particular, it will be demonstrated how the development of a sequence of meditative states, the *samāpattis*, is founded on common conceptions of the relationship between meditative states and conceptions of divinity and cosmology in both Hindu and Buddhist contexts. It also will be demonstrated that conceptions of *nirodha* in Classical Yoga demonstrate an intimate relationship, if not identity, to conceptions of *nirodha* in Buddhism, down to subtle nuances regarding "false cessations." Through this process, it will be thoroughly established that research that recognizes the import of the numinous-cessative distinction may offer a range of new insights into the role and function of meditation in both the Hindu and Buddhist traditions.

In chapter 5, we will expand our focus to demonstrate the utility of this approach in its application to meditative concepts within the context of tantric practice, *sādhana*. Having discussed the role that ideas of the numinous and cessative play in the context of Hindu and Buddhist conceptions of yoga, we will discuss how tantric *sādhana* incorporates and expands upon earlier Indian meditative theory and practice. It will be shown how Buddhist *sādhana* incorporates the existing structures of *dhyāna* and *samādhi*, augmenting and expanding upon these paradigms. The dynamic relationship of *śamatha-vipaśyana*, representing the numinous and cessative aspects of meditation, will be compared at length to the tension between ideas of spiritual attainment, *siddhi*, and of liberating insight, *bodhi* in tantra. It will be argued that this conception takes the form of a concern with embodiment, a numinous quality, and the development of ideas of dissolution and spaciousness, the cessative dimension. On this basis it will be asserted that the idea of *siddhi* in tantra can be related to the *samāpatti* aspect in earlier conceptions of meditation, and the *bodhi* or *prajñā* element can be related to the *nirodha* aspect. This connection will be demonstrated in the image of the Buddha, which serves as the paradigm for the numinous and cessative qualities of *dhyāna* in

Buddhism. The development of *buddhānusmṛti* as a *śamatha* practice along with *devānusmṛti* will be shown to parallel the visualization of buddhas, bodhisattvas, and peaceful and wrathful deities in the tantric systems of late Indian Buddhism. Although it may be an overstatement that an exact identification is possible, the mark of earlier meditative systems, most notably the *śamatha-vipaśyana* distinction, can clearly be found in the elaborate practices of tantra. The role of the numinous or "embodied" image as a critical element of tantric *sādhana* will be further demonstrated in the context of the *sādhana* of a particular goddess, Vajrayoginī, who demonstrates the philosophical ideals of tantra and its liminal qualities in a social and cultural sense. It also will be suggested that the modeling of divinity found in the YS, such as that of Īśvara, and those free from attachment, *vitarāga-cittam*, as well as practices such as *svādhyāya*, recitation to self, hint at a relationship between practitioner and divinity that is analogous in many respects to tantric practice. Expanding upon this, it will be shown how in the Tibetan context the boundary between tantric *sādhana* and shamanism, particularly possession, can be a fluid one, demonstrating the ongoing utility of comparing notions of shamanic practice with those of yoga. Through this discussion, it will become clear how a phenomenology that incorporates both psychological and sociological approaches and that hinges upon the numinous-cessative paradigm is an effective means for understanding a number of different facets of tantra in theory and in practice, linking them to earlier forms of yoga and to other religious typologies such as shamanism.

The methodological approach to the study of religion proposed in this work is thoroughly interdisciplinary in nature, valuing a range of perspectives rather than one dominant perspective. It can be considered an expanded form of phenomenology, one that attempts to bring psychological and sociological orientations toward religion into a dialogic and complementary relationship. In this respect it also can be seen as an extension of the History of Religions methodology, with its emphasis on bringing together historical-critical and phenomenological methods and on balancing critical and empathetic approaches. This study does not claim to solve all of the difficult questions regarding the origin and development of yoga and meditative techniques in the Indian religious context, though it does offer insights into many of these issues. It is our hope that it will provide a foundation for more extensive and fruitful research in this domain by providing direction and orientation to the study of this fascinating dimension of the study of religion.

1

Sources and Definitions

DHYĀNA AND MEDITATION THEORY

An appropriate starting point for our study is to establish some basic definitions of the philosophical concepts that are foundational in the practices of meditation and yoga in the Hindu and Buddhist context. Primary among these are *dhyāna*, "meditation," and *samādhi*, "meditative absorption" or "contemplation." *Dhyāna* and *samādhi* are terms that are well represented in the literature of the study of religion, particularly in the Indo-Tibetan context, but are rarely used by scholars of these religions with significant precision. These terms play crucial roles in both the Hindu and Buddhist meditative systems and the soteriological or liberatory processes of which they are a part. The development of Hindu and Buddhist conceptions of *dhyāna* and *samādhi* demonstrates the ongoing effort within these religious communities to clarify different interpretations of what constitutes liberation and what means are necessary to bring about these ends. In other words, examining the role of these ideas across the Hindu-Buddhist boundary is particularly helpful in understanding how different schools and sects of these traditions have understood the practice of meditation in the context of an assumed plurality of viewpoints. Researching across this boundary clarifies the role of meditation practice in both traditions and weakens the common viewpoint that these traditions are autonomous entities that can be viewed in isolation. The relationship between the Classical Yoga tradition of Patañjali and the development of Buddhist models of meditation also demonstrates the tension between scholastic and ascetic tendencies with meditation that occur in both Hindu and Buddhist contexts. As has been noted by Gerald Larson, it can be argued that both Hindu and Buddhist conceptions of meditation are based in a pan-Indian "tradition text," a body of knowledge that extends beyond the boundaries of either tradition, into Jainism and other *śramaṇa* traditions such as the Ājīvikas.[1] This "tradition text" can be said to be nuanced by the polemics that these traditions have used to differentiate themselves from one another and by the degree to which yoga was integrated, or *not* integrated, into the soteriological vision that each tradition represents as its own.

For developing definitions, we now examine two paradigmatic texts that represent Hindu and Buddhist attempts to codify the religious path and the role of the practices of yoga and meditation in that liberatory path. These texts are Patañjali's *Yogasūtra*, representing the Hindu Classical Yoga tradition, a text that continues to be used for Hindu self-definition in contemporary practice, and the *Bhāvanākrama* of Kamalaśīla, a text that demonstrates an attempt to codify the religious path according to the Indian Mahāyāna Buddhist tradition, also of import in contemporary religious practice. These two texts are ideal for comparison for a number of reasons, including the fact that both are terse attempts to communicate the essentials of their respective soteriological paths that make descriptions of the role of meditative technique the centerpiece in the discussion of the religious path. The speculative aspects of these traditions are discussed in intimate relationship to the pragmatic presentation of the soteriological path. In this respect, both texts could be argued to be "yoga" texts, aimed at portraying the religious life in the context of the discipline of meditation. Both represent an attempt to validate and synthesize a pragmatic perspective with a scholastic and discursive understanding of the nature of liberation. Both also provide a root text that serves as the foundation for a more detailed exposition on the nature of the religious life that synthesizes and codifies the larger traditions they represent.

Throughout the history of the range of Indian religious life and in contemporary yoga practice, the YS has been reinterpreted in light of greatly varying philosophical and theological systems. The core notion is that the text demonstrates the totality of the path and its variations, and that extended oral and written commentary brings the text to life and reality, as well as specificity. This can be considered an extension of the conception that a *sūtra* provides the underlying "thread," which is the basis for the greater expanse of conceptions that develop around it from oral and textual commentary. Like the YS, which is a terse text that is to be memorized and supported by oral commentary by a teacher and which has been reappropriated by contemporary yoga organizations to introduce meditation, the BK is used by the Gelukpa sect of Tibetan Buddhism in contemporary Buddhism as a foundation for philosophical elaboration and practical instruction.[2] It is utilized by Mahāyāna to provide an introduction to the development of meditation in the Buddhist system, a guide for the Buddhist practitioner that is developed further by the teacher through oral commentary and through personal practice based upon that instruction. This in itself demonstrates the utility of the BK as a source text for understanding the Mahāyāna Buddhist path and the role of meditation therein. Paul Williams has noted that along with Atiśa's *Bodhipathapradīpa*, the BK serves as one of the most important foundations for Tibetan Buddhist conceptions of the stages on the path to enlightenment.[3]

Issues in Textual Composition

Whether or not these texts were composed for the purpose of instruction in meditation is related to a larger question of whether the YS was put together from another text by a Sāṃkhya composer for the purpose of arguing the Sāṃkhya position. Johannes Bronkhorst has recently argued that the attribution of the Yoga Bhāṣya (YBh) to Vyāsa is inherently problematic, and that it is likely that it was in fact composed by either Patañjali himself or by Vindhyavāsin.[4] The name Vyāsa, according to Bronkhorst, is ascribed to the text solely for the sake of establishing its authority, and it should not necessarily be taken to mean that Vyāsa is the literal name of the author or compiler. Bronkhorst also argues that the author of the YBh was likely the compiler of the YS and one who changed the root text of the YS to argue a view that may be inconsistent with the views of the original author or compiler. According to this theory, the *sūtras* themselves are a truncation and a rearrangement of the components of another text or set of texts that have been placed together to present the Sāṃkhya viewpoint most effectively. In this light, the text of the YS is simply a demonstrative tool for the Sāṃkhya proponent, and the text and commentary are thus not necessarily oriented toward practice, being instead an argument for a particular type of Sāṃkhya theory. This is arguably demonstrated by the fact that the Pātañjala-yoga tradition has no set lineage comparable to other traditions but rather has been adapted in different contexts to serve different traditional goals.[5] The malleability of yogic conceptions is particularly important in this regard, as the text is adapted to fit a range of circumstances and operates on the periphery of other established traditions rather than being its own autonomous tradition. These issues can all be said to be an extension of a long-standing question of whether or not the YS is a composite text, a question that has been of particular interest to a number of influential scholars of Indian philosophy and religion.[6] The question of whether to interpret the YS as a composite or as a unitary text is an important and a legitimate one that further contextualizes the discussion of its overarching structure and function.

It can be argued as well that Kamalaśīla's goal in writing the three *Bhāvanākrama* texts was to provide a concrete basis for arguing against a [illegible] as it was presenting a set of practical instructions. [illegible]n Buddhist meditation is often discussed as the division [illegible] and sudden methodologies, a division that was con[illegible] historiography as the "Great Debate" at the Samye [illegible] eighth century C.E., during the so-called "first propagation" [illegible] Tibet.[7] At this debate, Kamalaśīla is said to have represented [illegible]st" approach of the Indian Mahāyāna schools, whereas the Chin[illegible], Ho-shang Mahāyāna, represented the subitist Chinese Ch'an scho[illegible] thought. It is in this context that Kamalaśīla is said to have developed the series of *Bhāvanākrama* texts that elucidates, in abbreviated form, the Buddhist path and development of meditation, *bhāvanā* and *dhyāna*, within it. According to most Tibetan accounts, Kamalaśīla was successful in establishing a gradualist method that incorporated a system of stages on the path leading up to buddhahood, the *bodhisattvabhūmi*, and the meditative practices utilized on that graduated path. The gradualist interpretation of Buddhism has been characteristic of the approach of numerous renowned scholars within the Tibetan Buddhist tradition, including Atiśa and Tsongkhapa, who integrated a gradualist perspective into their "stages of the path," or *Lam Rim*, literature. While the Tibetan *Dzogchen* and *Mahāmudrā* systems can be said to embrace the language and *praxis* of a more sudden or natural typology of awakening, even these systems give credence to the *śamatha-vipaśyanā* distinction as demonstrating a dialectic of meditative development. In addition, to the degree that the final state of liberation is understood to be a nondiscursive awareness, these traditions are at least in partial agreement.[8] However, the scholastic Tibetan traditions, such as the Gelukpa, are at pains to demonstrate the validity and necessity of conceptuality on the lower and intermediate stages of the path.[9] The role of Kamalaśīla's text in establishing Mahāyāna conceptions of the Buddhist path and soteriology is therefore quite significant, demonstrating both the doctrinal and yogic character of Mahāyāna conceptions of the path, or *mārga*.

SOURCES AND DEFINITIONS: *DHYĀNA* AND *SAMĀDHI*

In the context of the YS, often considered the foremost authoritative text on the development of meditation in the "Classical Yoga" school of Indian philosophy, the *yoga darśana*, *dhyāna* refers to the process of meditation as a specific stage in yogic development and as a general notion of the process of yoga. *Dhyāna* is often referred to as being the seventh stage of the classical *āṣṭāṅgayoga*, or "eight-limbed yoga," defined by Patañjali in the context of the YS. These eight limbs include observances *(yama)*, restrictions *(niyama)*, posture *(āsana)*, breathing technique *(prāṇāyāma)*, sensory withdrawal *(pratyāhāra)*, fixation *(dhāraṇā)*, meditation *(dhyāna)*, and meditative absorption *(samādhi)*, and they are often appealed to as the definitive list of stages in the yogic path in the Hindu tradition.[10] This structure closely parallels that of the yogic path found in the *Maitrī Upaniṣad*, which postulates a system that contains key members of the *aṣṭāṅgayoga* series, including *dhāraṇā* and *samādhi*. In Patañjali's text, *Dhyāna* is used in the context of developing one-pointedness that prevents the arising of obstacles, *vikṣepa*, to meditation, *yathābhimatadhyānādvā*, "by meditating in the manner agreeable (to the practitioner)," and in the abandonment of the modifications *(vṛtti)* arisen from the afflictions *(kleśa)*, *dhyānaheyās tadvṛttayaḥ*, indicating the notion that the *process* of *dhyāna* is what is at stake.[11] It also appears in the context of describing the state of yoga-constructed minds *(nirmāṇacittāni)* as being without impressions, *tatra dhyānajaṃ anāśayaṃ*, a more technical definition that refers to the effects of *dhyāna* and their lack of residua.[12] Perhaps the most important *sūtra* with regard to the definition of meditation, however, is YS III.2, in which *dhyāna* is defined as *tatra pratyayaikatānatā dhyānam*, "in regard to that, meditation is the coherent continuity [i.e., extension of the unity] of cognition," referring to the previous *sūtra* describing one-pointedness and its referent. Vyāsa further adds the comment that this state is *pratyayāntareṇāparāmṛṣṭaḥ*, "unhindered by other cognitions."[13] This definition, which characterizes the state of meditation *(dhyāna)* as being the extension or continuity of placement *(dhāraṇā)* upon an object, is a clear technical definition of this term, meaning a continuous attentiveness to an object of concentration that does not fall prey to disturbance by other thoughts or ideas. It is not surprising in light of this technical specificity that Patañjali's definitions are used so often with respect to the technical meanings of *dhyāna*, particularly in the broader context of Indian and Hindu philosophy.

The work of Jan Gonda provides a number of insights into the broader development of the concept of *dhyāna* in the range of Indian literature. Viewing the term as being among the word group *dhyā*, developed from the verb *dhī* into the root form *dhyā*, Gonda argues that it is likely that this term is limited to the Indian linguistic context.[14] He notes that *dhyāna* is translated in a variety of ways, including "meditation," "meditative concentration," "méditation extatique," "höhere Beschauung," "deep absorption in meditation," "inward absorption," and "concentrated meditation leading to visualization," among others.[15] The relationship with *dhī* is particularly important for Gonda, as it relates in theory to the extension and reinterpretation of the quality of "vision" *(dhī)* that characterized the Vedic seers *(ṛṣis)* of the ancient Hindu tradition. According to Gonda, this notion of "special vision" is the foundation for a greater part of Indian religious theory and practice, including Jainism, Buddhism, and Hinduism. Gonda argues that the emphasis on the development of the ability not simply to infer but to experience transcendent reality directly that characterizes the Vedic *ṛṣis* is a key soteriological theme that underlies the significance of meditation and, by extension, philosophical theory in the Indian religious context.[16] This is demonstrated for Gonda by the progression of the usage of *dhyā* from simple and nontechnical applications to the more elaborate forms found in the context of the Vedas, *Aitareya* and *Śatapatha Brāhmanas*, the *Mahābhārata*, the *Viṣṇu Purāṇa*, *Śvetāśvatara* and *Maitrī Upaniṣads*, and numerous other texts.[17] However, Gonda notably suggests that the technical yogic usage of *dhyāna* is, in fact, best represented in the YS, in that its definition of *dhyāna* fits well into a broad range of soteriological contexts.[18] Rāmānuja and other Vedānta practitioners who followed the path of *bhakti* held that *dhyāna* was equivalent to *bhakti* and vice versa, a direct visionary experience that held the potential for liberation, and Śaivite thinkers saw *dhyāna* as a method to reach the absolute, which was in essence the intellectual state of Śiva.[19] Śaṅkara developed a conception of *dhyāna* that incorporated insights into the Upaniṣadic literature and the YS with respect to his own philosophical inclinations and interpretations.[20] Similarly, Buddhism and Jainism take up *dhyāna* both as a technical term for the development of stages of meditation and in the manner of defining a special type of direct vision into the nature of reality.[21] It can be added that these facts are complemented by the portrayal of yoga and meditation as a complement or a support for conceptions of ethics and renunciation as intermediate goals of religious practice and as the foundation for ultimate liberation.

In a manner that complements Gonda's work on the term *dhyāna*, Jonathan Bader has clarified the structure of the term *meditation* and its derivation from Latin in order to help bring more nuances to our understanding of both of these terms. According to Bader, "meditation" is derived from the Indo-European root *med*, meaning "measuring out," cognate with the Sanskrit verb *ma*, meaning "to mete out or mark off."[22] Following from this, the Greek term *meletao* also means "to mete out" and extends to signify "attending to, studying, practicing, and exercising" as does the Latin cognate *meditor.*[23] Meditation is thus derived in English from the Latin term, which had developed a denotation that referred it specifically to the exercise of mental or spiritual faculties.[24] And although *meditari*, a Latin cognate of *melete* and *meditor*, is used to indicate spiritual or mental as opposed to physical types of exercise, it is clear that they are terms of activity, thus more appropriately labeled *praxis* as opposed to *theoria.*[25] Bader also states that in the Judeo-Christian context the terms cogitate, meditate, and contemplate demonstrate a remarkable similarity to the notions of *dhāraṇā*, *dhyāna*, and *samādhi* that characterize the "internal limbs" *(antaraṇga)* that Patañjali proposes in the context of the YS.[26] The analysis of meditation as a precursor to contemplation, or the concept that meditation is the establishment of continuity and the foundation for the operation of contemplation, points comparatively to the heart of the *dhyāna-samādhi* relationship. Bader ultimately defines meditation as "the concentration of the mind on a particular theme or object in preparation for the direct intuition of truth," a definition that captures the broader sense of *dhyāna*, while perhaps hinting at its deeper nuances and viability for comparison.[27]

It also should be made clear that *dhyāna* shares much with another term, *bhāvanā*, which is often translated as "meditation" as well. *Bhāvanā* stems from the root verb *bhū* (to be) and often reflects the notion of bringing something into reality through imagination or contemplation. Patañjali refers to the term *bhāvanā* in several contexts. In YS I.28, *tajjāpas tadarthabhāvanam*, *bhāvanā* refers to meditation or contemplation of the meaning of *praṇava*, the sacred syllable *oṃ*, which was introduced in a previous *sūtra*. In YS II.2, *samādhibhāvanārthaḥ kleśatanūkaraṇārthaś ca*, it refers to the cultivation or establishment of *samādhi*, meditative absorption. YS II.33 demonstrates another context for the use of *bhāvanā*, that of the so-called cultivation of opposites or cultivation of antidotes: *vitarkabādhane pratipakṣabhāvanam*, "for the stoppage of [nonvirtuous] thought, there [should be] cultivation of antidotes." This particular *sūtra* is followed immediately by another one, YS II.34, which further defines the cultivation of opposites. This can be translated as "thoughts of harm and so on, done, caused, or rejoiced in, preceded by greed, anger, or delusion and [being of] mild, medium, or intense [degree], result in endless fruition of pain and ignorance, [and] thus there [should be] the cultivation of antidotes."[28] One last example is in YS IV.25, *viśeṣadarśina ātmabhāvabhāvanāvinivṛttiḥ*, "on the part of one perceiving the distinction [between mind and *puruṣa*] the cultivation of self-existence ceases." Though this last example strays from the meditative context, it demonstrates the extension of *bhāvanā* with the notion of cultivation.

In the Mahāyāna Buddhist context, *bhāvanā* plays a more extensive role in constituting what is considered to fall under the category of *dhyāna* in the Hindu context. This comes out in the notion that self-cultivation occurs in stages, such as the notion of *bhāvanākrama*, "stages of meditation," that play a formative role in Kamalaśīla's attempt to codify the range of meditative practice within the Mahāyāna soteriological framework. In the first *bhāvanākrama*, Kamalaśīla states "on account of this, the one who desires to perceive the nature [of things] should engage in *bhāvanā*," *tasmāt tattvam sākśātkartukāmo bhāvanāyām pravartate*.[29] In the third *Bhāvanākrama*, Kamalaśīla quotes the Buddha as stating *"nimittabandhanāj jantur atho doṣṭhulabandhanāt vipaśyanām bhāvyitvā śamatham ca vimucyate,"* "having cultivated tranquility *(śamatha)* and insight *(vipaśyanā)*, a person is freed from bondage to defilements and bondage to causes."[30] Similarly, Kamalaśīla quotes the *Āryaratnameghasūtra* as saying *sa evam apakṣālakuśalaḥ sarvaprapañcavigamāya śūnyatābhāvanāyā yogam āpadyate*, "in this manner, for the sake of eliminating all faults in order to escape mental elaboration, that person resorts to the yoga of meditation on emptiness."[31] Throughout Kamalaśīla's work, *bhāvanā* is used interchangeably with the term *dhyāna* and with the verbal form *dhyai*. *Bhāvanā* and *dhyāna* are close approximations, especially as we consider the connection of *śamatha* and *vipaśyanā* with *bhāvanā*, as they are also connected with *dhyāna* and *samādhi* in many Buddhist contexts, particularly with respect to *śamatha*. This notion of *dhyāna* presupposes the *samāpatti*, "attainment," scheme of the *dhyānasamāpatti* system, a Buddhist conception that the progression of meditative concentration results in a succession of states, entitled *dhyāna* and *samāpatti*, respectively. This notion of a step-wise progression of mental states is one of the key indicators that similar language is being used to talk about meditation in both traditions. The continuity between the terms *dhyāna* and *bhāvanā* is extended further in Vajrayāna Buddhist sources where *bhāvanā* becomes even more important in that it accommodates the notion of visualization as the heart of meditative practice. Meditation on the image of a deity *(devatā)* is a product of the origination of that figure through the power of recitation *(mantra)* and visualization, an extension of the powers of *dhāraṇā* and *dhyāna* in the sense used in the broader yogic context.

The culmination of *dhyāna* and *bhāvanā* is represented in both the Hindu and Buddhist contexts by the concept of *samādhi*. *Samādhi* is formed through the conjunction of *sam-ā-dhā*, having the sense of "placing together," "union," and, by extension, "meditation," "contemplation," and "completion."[32] In both the Classical Yoga and Indian Mahāyāna traditions, *samādhi* appears to represent the perfection of the process of meditation and even at times the supreme goal or culmination of meditation practice. In the YS, *samādhi* is the final member of the *aṣṭāṅgayoga* series, the culmination of the "internal" as well as the "external" limbs of yoga. *Samādhi* is characterized by Patañjali in YS III.3 as *tadevārthamātranirbhāsaṃ svarūpaśūnyam iva samādhiḥ*, "that particular object appearing alone, as if empty of its own form, is *samādhi*." Vyāsa goes so far as to state that yoga itself is *samādhi*, saying in YBh I.1 *yogaḥ samādhiḥ*, "yoga is *samādhi*," implying that the goal of yoga, *cittavṛttinirodha*, "cessation of mental fluctuation," is the product of *samādhi*.[33] The first of the four *pādas* of the YS is aptly titled *samādhipāda*, as it deals with the structure of *samādhi* and its relationship to yogic soteriology. It is thus associated with such terminology as *samāpatti* "attainment" and *nirodha* "cessation," *saṃprajñāta* "cognitive" and *asaṃprajñāta* "noncognitive," and *sabīja* "seeded" and *nirbīja* "seedless," representing roughly the domains of cosmology, perception, and the mental substratum. These represent the progression leading up to cessation, the shift of perception from mental faculty to basic consciousness, and the presence or lack of seeds of future affliction. The terms *samāpatti* and *nirodha* are remarkably similar in both the Hindu yoga and Buddhist contexts, bearing both technical definitions in the meditative context and more general significance in the social and cultural domain. *Samāpatti* will be translated here as "attainment," though others have suggested definitions such as "unification,"[34] "falling into any state or condition,"[35] or as being "identical with *samādhi*."[36] The three of *dhāraṇā*, *dhyāna*, and *samādhi* form the potent *saṃyama*, "binding together," that is the basis for the establishment of the *vibhūti*, or preternatural accomplishments, that are largely the logical subject of the third part of the YS.[37] Whicher has aptly suggested the dynamics of the use of the term *samādhi* as being characterized by what could be called *ecstatic* and *enstatic* characteristics, in contrast to the often used term *enstasis* to refer to *samādhi* as a whole. This is a crucially important distinction that will be explored at greater length later in this work, in that it parallels our own distinction of the functions of *samādhi* and being respectively numinous and cessative.[38] This viewpoint allows for the incorporation of the pairs of corollaries that the YS postulates as the field in which *samādhi* operates, that is, *samāpatti*, *nirodha*, *saṃprajñāta*, *asaṃprajñāta*, *sabīja*, and *nirbīja*. Whicher rightly stresses the rarified character of *samādhi* in comparison to the other "internal" yogic limbs, *dhāraṇā* and *dhyāna*, which culminate in *samādhi*.[39] As such, *samādhi* represents the height of meditative attainment, though within itself bearing various degrees of fruition and mastery.

In the context of Kamalaśīla's work, *samādhi* plays a pivotal role with soteriological concerns as well. The establishment of *dhyāna*, the stages of the four *dhyāna* states, is characterized by the term *samādhi*. On one level, *samādhi* refers to the subject of *śamatha*, or tranquility meditation, and on another level it refers broadly to meditative states that incorporate both *śamatha* and *vipaśyanā* and the assumption of particular Buddhist virtues or objects of concentration. The *samādhi* of Mahāyāna Buddhism is distinguished as a uniquely Buddhist soteriological practice, although it is noted that within the families of *śrāvakas*, bodhisattvas, and buddhas, all forms of *samādhi* hinge upon the development of *śamatha* and *vipaśyanā*.[40] Kamalaśīla states *śamathavipaśyanābhāṃ sarve samādhayo vyāptāḥ*, that "all *samādhis* [implying the variety of terms referring to this condition in the Mahāyāna context] are characterized by *śamatha* and *vipaśyanā*."[41] As the culmination of the meditative process, the development of *samādhi* is seen to represent the fundamental meditative accomplishment that is to be attained by Buddhists on the path to liberation, through the union of the dimensions of *śamatha* and *vipaśyana*, in what is referred to as the "yoking of tranquility and insight," *śamathavipaśyanāyuganaddha*. As will be discussed at length later, this distinction can be understood by the notion of the yoking together of numinous and cessative dimensions of meditation, and it is a critical concept in understanding how meditative traditions within Hinduism and Buddhism conceive of *dhyāna* and *samādhi*.

DEVELOPMENT OF MEDITATIVE CONCEPTS

The development of clearer notions of the concepts of *dhyāna* and *samādhi* benefits from the analysis of the historical development of their usage, making work such as Gonda's valuable in articulating the subtler details and the contextuality of these terms. Complementing Gonda's study of *dhyāna* from the Vedic to the Mahāyāna context are studies that deal more broadly with philosophical and cultural developments characteristic of religious life in the early Indian context. Mircea Eliade, for example, has extensively documented the development of yoga in relation to the ritual forms and practices of the Brahmanical sacrificial traditions. He traces the methodology of the *ṛgveda* ascetic types such as the *ṛsis* and *munis* through the process of "ritual interiorization" toward more recognizable forms of yoga in Hindu and Buddhist sects and traditions such as Theravāda, Mahāyāna, and Classical Yoga.[42] He characterizes several historical phases of yoga, including Brahmanical Yoga, Classical Yoga, Buddhist Yoga, and Tantric Yoga, which provide a foundation for understanding the many roles of yoga and meditation in the Indian context. Eliade and others were particularly interested in the issues regarding the possible origins of yoga in the ancient Indus civilization, which for many represents the possibility of a pre-Vedic substratum of Indian culture. The import of the so-called Indus "yoga" seal, and the implication that some type of yoga practice may have been present in the Indus context, is compelling to Eliade, to the degree that he largely accepts the pre-Āryan genesis of yoga.[43] Jean Filliozat, however, has argued in opposition to this that the lack of substantial evidence and insight into yoga in the Indus records, due to the lack of textual or scriptural support, provides little encouragement for pursuing such a grand theory of yoga's origins.[44] Thus according to Filliozat, its controversial nature and the lack of material and textual evidence make it difficult to do anything more than scratch the surface with regard to this ancient culture. Other scholars, such as Karel Werner, have argued that the *munis* and *ṛṣis* of the Vedas demonstrate the substratum of ascetic practices that would later emerge as yoga, making the Indus records, by implication, of little significance. Similarly, David Knipe, in examining the concept of *tapas* as related to symbolism of fire, light, and combustion, has demonstrated the formative nature of numerous Vedic concepts with respect to notions of yoga and asceticism of relevance in both the Upaniṣadic and Pātañjala Yoga contexts.[45] Edward Crangle's recent work on contemplative theory in the Indian context is in many respects representative of a "compromise" or "mainstream" position that argues that parallel yoga and Buddhist systems of meditation developed in a complementary fashion out of a linguistic and cultural substratum that was significantly, but not exclusively, rooted in the Vedic tradition, which likely drew inspiration from non-Vedic sources.[46]

Other approaches, aptly demonstrated by Winston King, have shown at length the common yoga heritage found between the Hindu philosophical and religious systems and those of the Theravāda Buddhist tradition.[47] A key point in this context is that the development of *dhyāna* in Buddhism has hinged upon the distinction between *śamatha* and *vipaśyanā* (Pali *samatha/vipassanā*), the "concentration and insight" dynamics of Buddhist meditation. In Theravāda, *samatha* meditation is considered a practice common to both Buddhist and non-Buddhist traditions that does not lead to the ultimate soteriological end of the tradition but rather serves as a complement to what is considered the uniquely Buddhist practice *vipassanā*.[48] This is mirrored by the Mahāyāna view that identifies *śamatha* with yoga and states that *śamatha* is merely a suppression of the afflictions, as opposed to *vipaśyanā*, which eliminates them completely.[49] The division of meditation into these two domains appears to be a common current of thought in the Indian schools of Buddhism. However, it has been noted at length that in many of the contemporary sects of Therāvada Buddhism, the practice of *vipassanā* has become central, and *samatha* has become largely a relic of the past, or even a term used to designate meditative practices not in line with the soteriological path of the Buddha. This issue, which hinges on the role of *dhyāna* (Pali *jhāna*) in the soteriological system of the Theravāda, has been addressed by a number of scholars, particularly with respect to the notion of "dry" or "bare insight." This refers to the idea that enlightenment can be attained without recourse to *samatha* meditation, through the development of a "momentary" type of *vipassanā* that analyzes phenomena from instance to instance.[50] Cousins and Griffiths, among others, have noted that the paradigm of the Buddha's own awakening experience as alluded to in treatises such as the *Visuddhimagga* does not appear to be at the heart of modern Theravāda practice.[51] Underlying this discussion is the assumption that these traditions became more scholastic as they moved away from the forest-ascetic *(śramaṇa)* model of religious practice and lost touch with the yogic character of early Buddhism. It might be argued that this situation is due to a combination of factors, including a polemical stance against Hinduism (following King), the development of a scholasticism that depended on analysis as opposed to meditative *praxis*, the socialization of the monastic community and its deepening connection with the "worldly" lay community, and the tradition that liberatory technique should suit the individual. It should be noted that, though it is less visible, *samatha* does continue to play an important role in the Theravāda tradition, both in the forest monastic setting and in the context of lay meditation communities.[52] Later we will explore ideas regarding the changing role of the monastic community and the possibility that changing views regarding meditation are related to a shift from *ecstatic* to *scholastic* authority and a subject of continued negotiation and renegotiation in both Theravāda and Mahāyāna contexts.

In the Tibetan tradition, *śamatha* is still considered an important part of the Buddhist path, yet it goes without saying that the *vipaśyanā* aspect of meditation is the goal of meditation practice and the key to liberation. Thus it is said that they are complementary, but not equal in importance, with the process of liberation. The Tibetan case is complicated by the fact that there seems to be a fine line between the scholastic representations of *śamatha* and more specifically pragmatic ones. In some cases, the knowledge of such states may be purely scholastic, and in other cases knowledge is seen as a precursor to the actual practice or attainment of such states.[53] On the one hand, there is an elaborate "phenomenology" of meditation that explains the progression of mental states in a manner far removed from the actual practice of meditation. On the other hand, practice lineages that involve these ideas, particularly the *śamatha-vipaśyanā* typology of meditative development, orient themselves toward the types of nonconceptual and nondiscursive conceptions of liberating knowledge highlighted in the textual and philosophical traditions. The manner in which scholastic perspectives on meditation exist in co-relationship with the more pragmatic interests in meditation demonstrates an ongoing dynamic relationship between text and practice in the Buddhist context, a topic we will examine at length later.

The current discussion can be further extended by noting the degree to which the *śamatha-vipaśyanā* distinction has been sublimated into Buddhist tantric practice. It is clear that the development of concentration and visualization characteristic of deity yoga *(deva-yoga)* and *maṇḍala* practice in the tantric context shares a great deal with practices characterized as *śamatha*, such as the recollection of the Buddha's virtues, an example that we will take up later. Tantric *bhāvanā* demonstrates factors characteristic of *śamatha*, such as the development of supernormal abilities of action and perception that are characteristic of the historical Buddha, bodhisattvas, deities, and other beings. As will be argued, this can be seen as an extension of the *samāpatti* conception of meditation and a foundational concept with respect to *yoga* and *dhyāna*. The attainment of profound concentration and the ability to direct it toward a particular object or virtue and thereby attain the power of a divinity is intimately connected to what will be termed the *numinous* dimension of meditation, or *yoga*. The complement to this is the idea that meditation also can lead to *cessation*, that these divine forms also are a pathway to wisdom and liberation through insight into the nature of reality and freedom from attachment and affliction. In the tantric context, this distinction can be termed that of "mastery" *(siddhi)* versus "awakening" *(bodhi)*. Thus the paradigm of attainment-cessation *(samāpatti-nirodha)*, or of the *numinous* and *cessative*, can be said to lie beneath the surface of tantric conceptions of *praxis (sādhana)* as well as within Hindu conceptions of *yoga* and Buddhist conceptions of *śamatha-vipaśyanā*. The development of this distinction, of the numinous and the cessative, as a means of interpreting religious experience, specifically those offered by yoga and meditation, will be the primary goal of the next chapter.

2

Reinterpreting Religious Experience

Meditation, Mysticism, and Religious Experience

The concepts of "mysticism" and "religious experience" have been particularly important and controversial with respect to how meditation has been interpreted in the academic study of religion. The notion that there may be a cross-cultural basis for asserting a common foundation for religious experiences found throughout the world has been an ongoing and a provocative aspect of comparative religion since its inception. The term *mysticism* has often been applied in such a way as to represent the idea of a "core" or foundational type of religious experience that serves as the basis for religious phenomena across the range of human cultures. Such a position has been found in varying forms within the work of a range of scholars in the academic study of religion, some key representatives being W. T. Stace, Ninian Smart, and Agehananda Bharati. Bharati, for example, has postulated the term *zero-experience*, which he believes indicates the most basic religious experience, one in which a mystic realizes union with the "universal matrix" that underlies all theological and religious speculation.[1] In other contexts, mysticism has been conceptually separated from the "numinous" expressions of religion in which religious realities manifest themselves in concrete forms and in dialogic relationship, as opposed to being an ineffable or a transcendent reality that is understood through union and identity and is inexpressible in nature.[2] Ideas of ultimate reality as being beyond language, ineffable, inexpressible, and so on characterize the focal point of this particular way of looking at religious experience and mysticism. Particularly important in yoga and meditation is the notion of a progression through a series of states that is understood to represent stages of spiritual development leading to an ultimate and unmediated state of knowing or being. This *perennialist*-type view that the "common core" theory represents has largely been supplanted in recent scholarship by what is often called the "constructivist" or "contextualist" model.

This alternate approach to the study of religious experience, constructivism, has arisen out of the work of a range of scholarship that has sought to demonstrate the manner in which all religious phenomena, experiential or otherwise, are rooted in their contextual settings. The notion that cultural, social, intellectual, and other factors all "condition" religious experience, and furthermore that there are no "unmediated" or "unconditioned" experiences, has come to be the dominant perspective in the current discussion of the notion of mysticism. Despite being one of the most outstanding critics of constructivism, Robert Forman has noted the sensibility of such a viewpoint, arguing that it makes perfect sense that people come to religious experience and practice with divergent backgrounds, behavior, philosophy, and so on.[3] This includes the idea that religious practitioners bring varied beliefs and values to their encounter with religious realities and grow in experience and understanding accordingly with interaction with their environment. However, Forman usefully distinguishes between what one would call "complete" forms of constructivism, such as that of Steven Katz, versus other modalities, called "incomplete" and "catalytic" forms of constructivism.[4] Such "incomplete" forms of constructivism have at least an intuitive sense to them as well. This is the idea that there is a *relationship* between the makeup of the religious practitioner and the external world that the practitioner encounters, and arising from that engagement, from that interaction, is the reality of the religious experience and its subsequent interpretation.[5] In this respect, Agehananda Bharati's notions concerning religious practice fit neatly with Forman's notions of incomplete constructivism, most notably the idea that religious practice is no guarantee of religious experience, that practice may facilitate it, but religious experience does not follow from necessity.[6] This also meshes well with the vision of the phenomenological approach that this current study is intended to develop, one that recognizes that there is an intimate and a dynamic relationship between practitioner and environment. This relationship is one that cannot be accounted for simply by reference to the causal agency of one member of the relationship or the other, to the inner makeup of the individual or to the social and cultural environment in which he or she exists. The notion of "incomplete constructivism" thus allows for a conception of religious experience that recognizes the constructivist nature of doing historical work while acknowledging the limitations inherent in a view that espouses a more complete form of constructivism.

The question of whether or not human beings can have "religious experience" without having a religious background is also an interesting case in point regarding the question of constructivism. In fact, it represents a challenge to the causal efficacy of religious *praxis* and clarifies the problems with characterizing religious experience entirely by context and not content. This is to say, could there not be experiences that would mirror what we would typically understand as "religious" occurring outside of the religious context, and therefore be unrecognized as such? To what degree is the distinction between religious and nonreligious types of experiences a valid one, and on what grounds should such a distinction be made, if it is made? Do we call an experience religious because it is interpreted within a tradition that has such a self-awareness of being "religious"? Ninian Smart, for example, recently commented that the concept of a *pratyekabuddha*, or "solitary buddha," in Buddhism might be intended to recognize this very possibility.[7] That is, according to Buddhism, the *pratyekabuddha* is an individual who has reached the spiritual insight of a buddha and yet does not have the opportunity or the means to share her or his insight with others. As such, the concept suggests that an individual may have profound insights into the nature of reality and yet never communicate the understanding or the description of the experience itself to others. Another option would be that there may well be cases where initial experiences of intensity or illumination lead people to pursue religious paths, to learn about context rather than the other way around, thereby finding a way to frame their experience. This would suggest that in some cases it is an experience that happens outside of the religious context that pushes people to *find* a tradition that will offer a meaningful interpretation. In the context of *dhyāna*, practice can be said to provide the conditions for an experience but in and of itself would not be the *cause* of the experience that arose out of that practice. This is an idea that Forman argues can be tied to an idea of the "innate capacity" of consciousness itself that is not created by the practice of meditation. Bharati ties these ideas into those of *karma* and grace, arguing that there are different ways of explaining why certain people do or do not have religious experiences, which are attributed to either mysterious forces beyond human comprehension, such as grace, or to conditions that are difficult to discern, such as the effects of karma from earlier in one's life or from former lives.[8]

Perhaps the strongest blow to a strict constructivist perspective, however, comes from the increasing recognition that constructivism itself can be argued to be a reductive interpretive system that undercuts the truth claims of the traditions that it is used to study.[9] A strict constructivism, in its assertion that all reality is mediated and that there can be no unmediated experiences, establishes a priori that there are no transcendent experiences or realities, effectively reducing the truth claims of a great variety of traditions to its own truth claims. Richard King has noted that these "epistemologies of limitation" do not take into account the complex traditions of speculation on the nature of nonconceptual awareness that have taken place in the Indian context.[10] This would include examples such as Dignaga's notions of "escaping the web of cultural and linguistic conditioning" and Dharmakīrti's ideas regarding how conviction arises from experience.[11] Another example is the work of philosopher Kamalaśīla, which we discussed earlier, where thought builds up to a direct, unmediated encounter. King notes how Kamalaśīla plays a particularly significant role in Mahāyāna with respect to arguing that conceptuality is an integral part of the Buddhist path, despite the fact that he does assert that it culminates in a nonconceptual perceptual state.[12] This notion, according to King, is found in a number of other systems, such as Sāṃkhya, Classical Yoga, and Advaita Vedānta, and it is characterized by the ideas such as those of practice *(abhyāsa)* and detachment *(vairāgya)*, found in the context of Classical Yoga, and by the ideas of mental development *(citta-bhāvanā)* and equanimity *(upekṣa)* in the Mahāyāna context.[13] These oppositional pairs represent the contrasting tendencies toward active cultural conditioning and detachment or deconditioning. These tendencies toward conditioning and deconditioning are part and parcel of the meditative traditions that Hinduism and Buddhism espouse, and they manifest themselves clearly in the numinous and cessative characteristics that are reconciled with one another within the framework of their different soteriological visions. With the larger issue of constructivism, King summarizes well the difficulties inherent in it, stating that just as perennialism can be said to be the "myth of the transcendent object," constructivism may be considered the "myth of the isolated context," and that in the study of religion to reject one, one does not necessarily have to accept the other.[14]

DYNAMICS OF MEDITATION: THE NUMINOUS AND THE CESSATIVE

Robert Gimello has extensively discussed how analysis of Buddhist meditation methods demonstrates that a "constructivist" type of thinking operates in the religious context itself as well as being a methodology found among scholastic interpreters. He notes how the process of Buddhist meditation in the Mahāyāna context is distinct in terms of its ultimate soteriological goals, and notably not "unitive," a characteristic that is often said to be at the heart of mysticism as a object of comparative study. Gimello notes how the development of *śamatha* demonstrates a deep resemblance to certain aspects of religious experience traditionally understood to be characteristic of mysticism. This, he argues, is despite the fact that the practice itself is not oriented toward the ends characterized or defined as "mysticism."[15] According to this view, the meditative experience in *śamatha*, tranquility or calming meditation, is a constructed experience, an arduous training involving the memorization of complex and systematic conceptual structures and their incorporation in practice through repetition and discipline. According to this argument, one learns to perceive or experience the world in the modality presented by the meditative system rather than perceiving something outside or distinct from it as a result of such practice.[16] Gimello is quick to point out that although *śamatha* is only *part* of the Buddhist path it is often mistaken by scholars as being the *essential* aspect of it.[17] This is in part due to the fact that *śamatha* bears many of the features that are characteristically seen as mystical, such as profound states of being, for example, as "nothingness," "neither consciousness nor non-consciousness," and profound forms of perception and transformation, such as clairvoyance and "magical creation."[18] These states are seen to be sublime, tranquil, and near a state of stasis, bearing therefore resemblance to other religious and experiential phenomena. Gimello's goal in discussing this is to point out that the concentrated states are not the absolute goal of meditation, but that these states and the experiences and powers that emerge from them are only preparatory for insight *(vipaśyanā)* meditation.[19] In this mode of understanding, then, *śamatha* and its states could be a type of "phenomenology" of mental life of sorts, one that both instructs in and describes the nature of the process of developing these highly refined mental states.

Gimello uses an example of a meditation on the Buddha *(buddhānusmṛti)* as demonstration of how meditation points out the fundamental impermanence of the Buddha. This has the effect, according to Gimello, of distinguishing meditation from a sense of mystical union or essentialism, denying rather than affirming the ongoing existence or essence of the Buddha. Gimello overstates his point here, in that though it is not mystical identity with the Buddha that is being sought, even in the Theravāda there is a strong sense of the Buddha as being paradigmatic and a source of qualities that can be legitimate objects of identification.[20] Gimello also goes too far by identifying the goal of insight *(prajñā)* as being the central and only true goal of Buddhism, at least in the fullest sense of the nature of buddhahood. Buddhahood is identified first and foremost by the degree of insight into the nature of reality that a buddha possesses. Nevertheless, a buddha is also characterized as having special abilities of perception and action, which are more related to the *śamatha* side of the equation than to the *vipaśyanā-prajñā* side. The faculties of a complete buddha are numerous, and buddhahood is founded on the establishment of a range of abilities of preternatural action or manifestation *(nirmāṇa)* and perception *(abhijñā)*, as well as *prajñā*. These are key factors that help differentiate different types of religious practitioners in Buddhism, most notably the primary categories of the *śrāvaka*, bodhisattva, and buddha. As Gimello states, the majority of Buddhist sources seem to agree that *prajñā* is the "proximate cause" of enlightenment, not *śamatha* or *samādhi*.[21] There are exceptions to this, however, where the state of *saṃjñāveditanirodha* is recognized as being equivalent to liberation, a state that is often seen as the pinnacle of the practice of *samādhi* and one that has an ambiguous relationship with the development of *prajñā*. Also, there are considerations regarding the degree to which the powers attainted through meditation are either a help or a hindrance to the soteriological path. Gimello himself notes that there are ambiguities in different Buddhist contexts to the degree to which *śamatha* is developed as a prerequisite to the practice of *vipaśyanā*. Perhaps most important, however, is the fact that the full attainment of powers of perception and action is one of the key factors that sets a buddha apart from other spiritual beings.

Gimello's argument can be further construed as implicitly stating that Buddhism distinguishes between numinous and mystical types of experience, a position reminiscent of the thought of Ninian Smart, who has postulated that manifestations of religious life characterized outside of the scope of the numinous are the inheritance of the mystical domain.[22] Smart attempted to distinguish what he considered mystical religious phenomena from nonmystical religious phenomena on the basis of this distinction. According to Smart, mystical phenomena can and should be differentiated from what he called "numinous" experiences. Smart distinguishes the "inner visions and practices which are contemplative" of mystical experiences from those which would be characterized by an "outer and thunderous" quality.[23] The "outer and thunderous" quality refers, in principle, to Otto's *The Idea of the Holy* and Otto's description of the numinous as *mysterium tremendum* and *fascinans*. In this distinction, then, religious experiences, such as "mystical unions, prophetic visions, psychic ascents to heaven, ecstasies, auditions, intoxications," can be categorized as numinous or as mystical, depending upon their content.[24] Smart appears to be making a distinction on the basis of inwardness of experiences versus externality, perhaps hinting that the role, or lack thereof, of sensory perception in religious experience is a fundamental distinction that can be made. According to this theory, it is a quite different religious experience to have what might be referred to as a "vision" or an "ecstatic" type of experience. For example, a Buddhist practitioner might have a vision of the *mahābodhisattva* (great Bodhisattva) Avalokiteśvara, white as milk, with eleven crowned heads facing in all directions and 1,000 arms reaching out toward all sentient beings in *saṃsāra*. This, according to Smart, would constitute a numinous experience, in that it is a perception of a sacred entity and is a relationship that demonstrates the characteristics of the numinous, those of force, majesty, and power. On the other hand, should a Buddhist practitioner attain a state of mystical union or attain the state of *nirvāṇa*, the experience would not be characterized by its perceptual content, but instead it would be characterized by the lack thereof, the going beyond or utter lack of perceptual content. Similarly, Gimello argues that enlightenment is not an experience but a mode of being, thus escaping the whole problem of how to deal with the transition from *saṃsāric* existence to that of *nirvāṇa*. Smart's analysis, as opposed to Gimello's, ties well into perennialism, in that the utter lack of specificity as to the mystical state pushes context into the background, providing a fertile ground for universal theories of mysticism. This paradigmatic theoretical move is one that has been thoroughly criticized, and Smart's theories have borne the brunt of much of the recent constructivist criticism. It should be mentioned, however, that Smart himself thought that the study of religious experience needed to be done in its "living contexts," and that comparative religion is a relatively new discipline and one in which much work needs to be done.[25]

The idea that the development of both *śamatha* and *vipaśyanā* is the product of conscious and deliberative processes with definitive stages that are communicable through teaching is a great strength of Gimello's presentation. Though it may not be an assumption that is universal in the Buddhist context, it is representative of much of Theravāda and Mahāyāna soteriological thought. In this respect, Gimello's theory, rather than contradicting Smart's view, can be said to be comparable to or compatible with it in a critical way. This is to say that Gimello's analysis of Buddhist meditation postulates a distinction comparable to that of Smart's, between what would be called "numinous" religious experiences and those of the mystical. We would argue that these terms can be adapted to more specifically suit Buddhist context as *numinous* and *cessative*. *Śamatha* and *vipaśyanā*, whether considered constructed or unconstructed, can be said to be complementary in this respect. In the Buddhist context, along with leading to states of refined consciousness, such as those characterized by "neither perception nor nonperception" and "nothingness," *śamatha* meditation is considered the source of the Buddhist *abhijñās*, or "higher knowledges," special forms of perception, such as the divine eye, divine ear, and so forth, and powers of manifestation, referred to as *nirmāṇa*. On the other hand, it is *vipaśyanā* out of which emerges the *prajñā*, or wisdom, that realizes the Buddhist truths about reality, and by means of that attains cessation, or *nirodha*. In other words, the division between the types of Buddhist meditation can be said to be characterized by the development of numinous power through *śamatha*, namely, *dhyāna* and *samādhi*, and the liberating drive of *vipaśyanā*. In *śamatha* one is approximating the qualities of a divinity, the very basis of the idea of the numinous. In theory, through meditative powers, the yogin ascends the very divine hierarchy, gaining along the way numerous experiences and ultimately a range of powers of perception and action. The historical Buddha, Śākyamuni or Siddhārtha Gautama, demonstrated his own miraculous powers on numerous occasions, such as reading others' minds, making multiple versions of himself, levitating, and rising up into the heavens. In *vipaśyanā*, we have the understanding or wisdom that breaks one free of the cycle of birth and death, *saṃsāra*, yielding the cessation of suffering and the state of *nirvāṇa* in all its ineffability.

This postulation of oppositional factors referred to as the *numinous* and the *cessative* is similarly operative in the context of both Buddhism and the Hindu Classical Yoga tradition. This opposition takes the form of the distinction between *samāpatti* and *nirodha* and *śamatha* and *vipaśyanā* and is further characterized in the Buddhist context as mundane and supramundane attainments. It is clear that in the YS the establishment of *saṃprajñāta samādhi* and, by extension, the *vibhūtis* (supernormal powers) that manifest out of it is seen as a possible impediment to the realization of the liberated state, or *nirbija samādhi*, in which the yogin emerges from *prakṛtic* experience into pure knowing as *puruṣa*. In III.37, Patañjali states *te samādhau upasargāḥ vyutthāne siddhayaḥ*, "they [*vibhūti*] are obstacles for [*nirbija*] *samādhi*, [but are] perfections of manifestation." Yogic attainments, then, are part and parcel of the process of manifestation, the process that counters the liberating movement of withdrawal *(pratiprasava)*, just as attainments *(ṛddhi, iddhi)* are seen as having the potential for disrupting the Buddhist path to liberation. On the other hand, just as in the Buddhist context, the establishment of the foundational levels of *samādhi* is often considered the foundation for further realization and the types of powers that characterize the liberated sage. This is not to say that there is one simple paradigm that all of these traditions follow that represents the ideal form of meditation for all traditions, but rather that this paradigm can be seen as the dynamic space in which different interpretations are developed. Depending upon the dynamics between these dimensions, the numinous and cessative, and the subsequent interpretation of these dimensions within greater meditative theory, different soteriological visions emerge.

In the Classical Yoga tradition, the idea that religious phenomena as exemplified by the mythic religious imagery of the Hindu tradition are all temporal and spatial manifestations to be transcended seems clear in the discussion of deities and religious practitioners of various types that are found in the YS and YBh. These beings are seen as powerful, yet not liberated in the fullest yogic sense (such as the *videhas*, *prakṛtilayas*, and the *sthāni*). Similarly, we should note that the expansion of Buddhist notions of *kleśāvaraṇa-jñeyāvaraṇa* in Mahāyāna, particularly in Yogācāra, also come into play in the soteriological descriptions of chapter 4 of the YS.[26] Both traditions share a common cosmological schema in which religious phenomena that are of a *numinous* character can be explained as being part of the world of mundane experience, and that this world is transcended by the liberated one through the *cessative* character of meditation.[27] It also is interesting to note that through this schema, these systems have an extremely useful way of explaining religious phenomena that are claimed to be the result of the practice of other religious traditions. Through reference to the aspects of phenomenal reality that are encountered along the way in the development of their respective meditation systems, the numinous dimensions of other religious traditions can be subsumed under the rubric of the *samāpatti* aspect of the meditative sphere. Thus this distinction is rooted in and has effects with respect to both psychological and cultural realities. Furthermore, in the Mahāyāna Buddhist analysis, it makes sense that the deep meditative experiences of yogis are not necessarily transformative in an ethical sense, because they are only oriented toward *śamatha* and not toward the truly liberating insight characteristic of *vipaśyanā*, which has an intimate relationship with ethics. The Classical Yoga tradition notes the tenuous nature of the *vibhūtis* and at the same time the completeness of the final transformation of *nirodha* that would preclude any sort of worldly attachment. Gimello refers to Bharati's assessment that religious experience does not confer existential status on its content and also, by extension, that there is no uniquely ethical qualities to meditation.[28] This idea that one type of religious practice is fundamentally ethical and the other is not is an issue that has strong parallels in the context of ecstatic religion, as will be discussed later. In examining the relationship between the *numinous* dimension of meditative practice and the *cessative* dimension, it is clear there are implications about the moral or ethical agency of the individual who has developed a degree of proficiency in these methodologies.

Conceptuality and the Foundations of Meditation

Another issue that is closely related to issues of mysticism and its interpretation is the relationship in Buddhism between mental development and the discursive understanding of the object and character of meditative states.[29] According to this theory, in a variety of contexts, including Theravāda Abhidhamma, Indian and Tibetan Mahāyāna philosophy, Chinese Hua-yen and Ch'an traditions, and Japanese Zen thought, the rhetorical formulation of enlightenment and its characteristics is formative of the types of experiences that manifest within these traditions. This is exemplified in cases such as Asaṅga's notions of doctrine as a "seed" that sprouts in consciousness as a counteracting agent *(pratipakṣa)* to defiled mental states, thereby leading to those of a liberative character.[30] This concept of *pratipakṣa* plays out significantly in the context of the YS as well, in demonstrating a methodology for stoppage of thoughts *(vitarkabādhana)*, particularly those that are "rooted in hatred, delusion, and anger, and which result in endless pain and ignorance."[31] A more polemical example of this type of thought is the argument, found in many schools of Buddhism, that postulates that though other yogic traditions practice similar means, they nevertheless are lacking the conceptual "map" that Buddhism provides and therefore ultimately go astray. This manifests itself in the idea that non-Buddhist yoga practitioners enter into profound states of meditation (*numinous* states), mistaking them for the liberated state, and as a result argue for soteriological goals and the existence of metaphysical entities that are not the ultimate realities that they claim them to be. As Theravāda might argue that non-Buddhist yogins enter into profound states, only to emerge later to be disappointed by their continued bondage, this argument is carried on further in Mahāyāna to indicate that the Hīnayāna path also is an incomplete map. The Hīnayāna map, according to Mahāyāna, is one that leads to profound understandings of the Buddhist path but not to the fullness of complete liberation. Therefore, the Hīnayānists are attaining a cessation that is inferior to Mahāyāna, and one that may demonstrate a lack of compassion for other beings and will lead to their rebirth and the need to progress further on the Mahāyāna path.[32]

Anne Klein has developed this subject extensively with respect to meditation in the Tibetan Mahāyāna traditions.[33] She argues that one of the problems with scholarship on Buddhism has been a lack of understanding of just how conceptual knowledge builds a foundation for religious experience.[34] Scholars of religion often speak of the problem of ineffability, the question of the relationship between religion and nondiscursive realities that cannot be reduced to conceptuality. According to Klein, the Tibetan Gelukpa tradition, though aware of the notions of inexpressibility and ineffability of ultimate reality, is clear in thinking that although words cannot convey the content of a direct perception of this truth, they can help orient one toward that experience and understanding.[35] This is to say that knowledge and symbolism can help lead one in the direction of the ultimate, even if they are incapable of fully communicating that reality to which they are directing. This leads to an understanding of the continuum between wholly conceptual understandings of reality and the radical and direct realization of ultimate truth in the form of a yogin's *pratyakṣa*, or the direct perception of emptiness, *śunyatā*. The importance of this vision is represented in the ideas of *śrutamayi-prajñā* (insight born of learning), *cintāmayi-prajñā* (insight born of reflection), and *bhāvanāmayi-prajñā* (insight born of cultivation) in understanding the Mahāyāna's approach to the relationship between conceptuality and direct experience.[36]

Klein also points how Buddhist conceptions of religious experience can be said to be in contradiction to the thought of such important scholars in the European and American traditions as Lacan, Kant, and Foucault, through postulating experience as being beyond language, unmediated, and free of cultural constraint.[37] In particular, she demonstrates how Gelukpa theory attempts to reconcile processes that respectively open the mind up in a spacelike fashion versus those that aim at inward absorption into the stages of *dhyāna*.[38] This presentation of the *śamatha-vipaśyanā* relationship is thus parallel to the *samāpatti-nirodha* scheme that we see in the YS, where intensive and cessative mental orientations are postulated as having a complementary but complex relationship. Another salient point is that the complementary nature of the *śamatha* and *vipaśyana* aspects of Gelukpa theory result in the direct apprehension of reality and the arising of wisdom that is nonconceptual but at the same time analytical.[39] It is natural to compare the *vivekajam jñānam* of the YS to this, the idea that there is a point at which the mind that has been developed in *samāpatti* comes to an end in the direct and nonconceptual apprehension of the reality of the distinction between *puruṣa* and *prakṛti*. Klein mentions the fact that "non-conceptual analysis" seems to be a contradiction in terms.[40] However, the discrimination that takes place in both Hindu and Buddhist contexts presupposes a state of consciousness that is knowing and discriminative despite being nondiscursive. In fact, the problems associated with dealing with a consciousness that perceives emptiness are remarkably similar to those that arise when talking about the nature of consciousness that is attributed to the *puruṣa*.

Klein further argues that in *śamatha* the development of *dhyāna* works to eliminate conceptuality and free the mind from material culture through withdrawal and quiescence, ultimately bringing the mind to an unconditioned state.[41] This issue is significant in determining to what degree meditative practice is a process of conditioning of perception versus that of deautomization or deconditioning. In the Mahāyāna Buddhist context, there is a sense that viewing the world from the viewpoint of a substantial self is part of the problem, due to the positive ignorance of the unenlightened state. This would imply not seeing the world through a new lens or a conditioned state as much as it sees itself as cleaning the lens, removing the obscuration, and seeing the world as it truly is. We can also ask to what degree the *śamatha* and *vipaśyanā* styles of meditation can be seen to be relatively constructed or unconstructed, to what degree each represents an active shaping of perception versus a sense of releasing conditioned modes of perception. It should be emphasized that as much as conceptual knowledge may be considered to be of assistance in pursuing the soteriological goals of the meditative aspects of Buddhism or Classical Yoga, it is clear that the traditions themselves believe that the goal itself is irreducible to the sociolinguistic context in which it is attained. Though these traditions recognize the need for discursive tools in developing their respective paths, they nevertheless see the truths that arise out of following the path as being anything but culturally relative.

Lloyd Pflueger's presentation of the process of liberation according to the accounts of Sāṃkhya-Yoga provides a number of insights into this discussion of religious experience, mysticism, and language.[42] Noting that yoga as rendered in the YS is a means of transforming knowledge into liberating direct experience, he contrasts yoga with the Sāṃkhya system's conceptual-cognitive approach to understanding reality.[43] Patañjali's YS thus makes meditative experience the means of salvation.[44] Through the disjunction of *prakṛti* and *puruṣa* is effected the separation of materiality from consciousness, a point that deals a blow to a constructivist analysis. According to Pflueger, the fact that the yoga system points to a reality that is by definition completely untouched by materiality or by cultural influence establishes a conception of a state that is in direct opposition to a constructivist understanding.[45] This being so, the process and content of *kaivalya* would then emerge out of the world of construction, *prakṛti*, into a state that is untouched by culture, society, and so on, analogous to Klein's analysis of Buddhist liberation. However, one might imagine that constructivists might respond in turn by stating that the idea of an untouched consciousness is also a constructed reality that suits the culture, society, and psychology of its time, that it "functionally" exists but is not evidence for a transcultural reality or a universal theory of mysticism.

Pflueger also emphasizes the *experiential* nature of Yoga and Sāṃkhya realization, a point that emphasizes the differences between this type of interpretation and prevailing attitudes.[46] Experience points here to the notion of individual verification, that the truth of the tradition is not to be abstractly realized but rather to be directly perceived and understood. This brings out the paradox of experience mentioned earlier, that experience could be considered, on the one hand, the strongest empirical basis for personal verification of a religious reality and at the same time could be considered nonverifiable in an empirical, repeatable, observable sense. Pflueger notes correctly that in the Classical Yoga philosophy, all experiences that are characterized by phenomenal content, such as auditions, visions, and the like, belong to the domain of nature.[47] This paradigm is shared in the Buddhist worldview, where the scale of religious phenomena, the *numinous*, in the conditioned reality of *saṃsāra* is juxtaposed with that which stands in opposition to the mundane world, namely, the unconditioned realm of *cessation*, in the form of *nirodha* and *nirvāṇa*. The *nirodha* side of the equation characterizes what both traditions see as the domain of soteriology, in contradistinction to that of the *samāpatti* realm. Up to the point of liberation, the *samāpatti* aspect of yogic practice is reconcilable with a constructivist position, holding that experiences are composite and constructed. However, the radically different mode of perception that is characteristic of liberation and cessation is much more difficult to reconcile with a constructivist viewpoint. Pflueger's translations of *saṃprajñāta samādhi* as "perceptive coherence" and *asaṃprajñāta samādhi* as "quiescent coherence" get at the literal definition of *samādhi* yet do not convey as directly the implicit senses of *saṃprajñāta* and *asaṃprajñāta*.[48] Gerald Larson identifies the respective states as "cognitive intensive" and "cognitive restrictive," as Frauwallner had identified them, with the addition of the idea that they are complementary rather than competing techniques.[49] Pflueger argues in an interesting way that rather than "building up" an experience via language, one "deconstructs" language and by extension all manifestations of phenomenal existence in order to dwell in the primordial and transcendent state of liberation.[50]

An overemphasis on "aloneness" may be problematic, however, in that even though *kaivalya* is literally "aloneness," it may be more appropriate to define it as "separation."[51] This definition, as "separation," can be said to be at least partially consistent with Whicher's postulation of *cittavṛttinirodha* as the "cessation of the *misidentification* with mental fluctuations" and emphasizes separation from affliction rather than isolation from the world. One problem, however, in postulating this is that it may be at odds with the notion of *pratiprasava*, which seems to imply that there is a return to the origin of the manifestations of *prakṛti*. On the other hand, *pratiprasava* as an absolute interpretation is problematic as well, as the world still exists for other beings, as well as, presumably, for the yoga practitioner that has not yet passed away. Could *pratiprasava* then mean something to the effect that one has withdrawn from identification with manifest reality, but nevertheless that one manifests a mind and body, one that dwells in the perfection of *viveka-jñāna*? The ambiguity of *kaivalya* and, by comparison, *nirvāṇa* is an important issue in this respect. Does a person who reaches *kaivalya* simply pass away, or is *kaivalya* dependent upon physical death or simultaneous with it such as the notion of *aloka* (nonworldliness) that contextualizes *kaivalya* in Jainism? What about the tension between Theravāda and Mahāyāna representations of Buddhist liberation that suggests a number of key distinctions such as those implied by the use of the terms *nirvāṇa*, *parinirvāṇa*, and *apratiṣṭha-nirvāṇa*? Such questions get at the underlying issue of how liberation is manifested in the world, if at all, and how it is characterized as being numinous or cessative, relating to both soteriological and mythical-cosmological attitudes.[52]

The Limits of Meditative Experience and Interpretation

Robert Sharf has recently noted a number of the problematic aspects of talking about meditation in the context of religious experience and its interpretation. He attempts to dismantle the notion of "religious experience" and even to some extent the term *experience* itself as a means for understanding religious phenomena. Claiming that this term has not been subjected to significantly rigorous analysis, he aims to demonstrate how "experience," like its cousins "mystical" and "religious," is a problematic term, often held to be self-evident in meaning, though only presumptively so.[53] Furthermore, the "privileging" of the term *experience* is understood to be a means of defending religion against a secular critique and establishing religious studies as an autonomous entity in the academic sphere.[54] Sharf also portrays the study of Buddhism as being uniquely concerned with meditative experience.[55] This argument hinges upon the idea that South Asian, Southeast Asian, and Japanese authors and religious leaders have adapted to orientalist discourses by presenting the Hindu and Buddhist traditions as uniquely experiential and meditative. Thus Sarvepalli Radhakrishnan, D. T. Suzuki, and others are understood to have reified and essentially created conceptions of Hinduism and Buddhism that catered to European and American audiences that were captivated by ideas about religion that meshed with their own ideas of empiricism, philosophy, and psychology.[56]

Sharf further argues that premodern Buddhist treatises on meditation, *mārga* literature, are prescriptive rather than descriptive in contrast to their portrayal as experiential texts. Buddhist texts such as the *Bodhisattvabhūmi*, *Bhāvanākrama*, *Lam Rim Chen Mo*, *Visuddhimagga* and others are understood to be far from descriptive accounts of meditative practice, being instead prescriptive and analytical accounts of such types of practice.[57] According to this argument, the discursive nature of these treatises demonstrates that they were meant to be understood on a conceptual level and were rarely put into actual practice. Sharf argues that scholars such as Paul Griffiths are wrong to assume that meditative states are concretely manifested in practice.[58] Instead, they are the products of reflection upon Buddhist philosophy and practice as presented in texts and in theory, without implying recourse to practical understanding.[59] Philosophies such as Yogācāra can be understood without the necessity of appealing to experience, especially since certain philosophers such as Dharmakīrti and Chandrakīrti were suspicious of truth claims based upon experience.[60] Meditation could be thought of as enacting a state rather than engendering it, meditation being the "ritualization" of experience.[61] A basic question that can be asked about Sharf's criticisms is to what degree this is simply trading one category, meditation, for another one, ritual, that is equally as vague. It may also be examined whether this distinction between enacting and engendering is one that Buddhist themselves would make, or whether this itself is a scholarly imposition from without. In tantra, for example, the relationship between meditation and ritual can be argued to be a fluid one, to such a degree that distinguishing between them proves counterintuitive. It is more accurate to think of meditation and ritual as existing on a continuum rather than standing in absolute opposition or contradistinction to one another.

Meditation in the premodern Theravāda context, according to Sharf, was limited to recitation of texts with a devotional attitude for the sake of accumulating merit and developing wholesome attitudes, and not meditative states.[62] Sharf's sources here, as he admits, are limited to studies on reform movements, a point that to some degree counters his argument that there has been an undue amount of attention paid to meditation traditions in the study of Buddhism. Nevertheless, he argues that due to the ambiguity of interpretations of the terms *samatha* and *vipassanā* in the modern religious context, there can be no common understanding of the consequences of meditation in terms of phenomenology.[63] This is further extended to discussions of stream-entry *(sotāpatti)* and to arguments over the best "place" for developing *samatha* meditation (the abdomen, the nose, etc.).[64] The idea that there should be competing claims regarding meditative technique seems absolutely commonsensical. What is furthermore not warranted, we would argue, is Sharf's conclusion that these discoveries prove that there are no useful ways of talking about such types of experience. Whether or not there is agreement of the role of technique and the interpretation of the states and conditions arising from them, as there is obviously not with the Mahāsī Sayādaw method, it is quite apparent that these techniques do result in particular psychophysical conditions. Whether or not these conditions are the same as "classical" accounts (though they clearly have a relationship with them), they are significant aspects of the religious lives of these practitioners and are not simply verbal constructions that can be explained away through recourse to notions of "interpretation" and "rhetoric."

That religious practices should at times be the topic of controversy and used in the interest of the legitimization of authority is not surprising. However, to take such a position to the extreme of stating that it somehow captures all of the dimensions of what religion is about is unwarranted and obscures the larger scope of interpretive possibilities. Accepting that enlightenment is only significant when it is recognized by a community and that firsthand knowledge is secondary to the realities that meditation engenders obscures a whole spectrum of Buddhist conceptions of religious attainment. The basic Mahāyāna division between *śrāvakas*, *pratyekabuddhas*, and *buddhas*, the division of levels of attainment in Theravāda and so-called Hīnayāna schools, and the development of elaborate *Bodhisattvabhūmi* stages all suggest the development of religious practice through a series of stages and states. From the viewpoint of particular critiques, such as the *ekayāna* theory, one might conclude that some Buddhists have had problems with the differentiation of stages and states in the development of the path. However, it should be remembered that the *ekayāna* theory is one among a range of interpretations found in the many different schools of Buddhism. Nearly every sect of Buddhism or Hinduism that contains a yogic or meditative component will agree that there are different levels or stages of the path, different levels of realization, and at a bare minimum a distinction, as least conventionally, between those who have realization and those who do not. In fact, an extraordinary power possessed by buddhas and by yoga practitioners is the ability to recognize the level of spiritual attainment of other individuals.

Janet Gyatso has brought some clarity to the issue of experience in the context of Buddhism in a study of Tibetan conceptions of meditation and so-called "meditative experiences." She states that although experience is a complex category in Tibetan Buddhism, it nevertheless is an important concept that was received from the Indian tradition in the transmission of Buddhism, long before the influence of European thought.[65] Noting Sanskrit terms such as *anubhava*, Gyatso argues that rather than being a concept superimposed upon Buddhism, several different notions of experience have functioned as important concepts in the development of Indian and Buddhist tantra. Beyond Gyatso's presentation, it should be further noted that conceptions such as *pratyakṣa* in both the Hindu and Buddhist context contain a sense of immediacy of perception that could arguably be put into the frame of a notion of experience. In the YS, for example, *pratyakṣa* is considered one of the forms of valid knowledge, *pramāṇa*, along with inference, *anumāna*, and scriptural testimony, *āgama*, and it is also one of the five types of *vṛttis* or mental modifications *(pramāṇa, viparyaya, vikalpa, nidrā,* and *smṛti).*[66] The philosophical analysis of liberation in Classical Yoga and in major currents of Indian and Tibetan Mahāyāna is centered upon a conception of a nondiscursive end, though the means to getting there are facilitated by conceptuality. Therefore, it is critical to do what Gyatso has done in looking at the traditions' own representations of epistemology before making blanket statements about the "imposition of foreign concepts."[67]

Although Gyatso notes that it is not her goal to argue that experience is the unique reality of Buddhist practice, particularly in the sense of some ultimately private form of experiencing, she is not afraid to affirm resolutely that meditative types of experience play an important, if not a key, role in Tibetan traditions.[68] This role is demonstrated by first-person accounts and descriptions of personal experience within autobiographical genres of Tibetan literature that inform the more scholastic traditions.[69] Despite the fact that mainstream Buddhist practice may not necessarily engender meditative practice, or may even discourage it, it is nevertheless an "option," one that has been, over time, consistently chosen by a significant body of Buddhist practitioners. For many such practitioners, the goal has been to personally realize the meditative paths that are the subject of Buddhist literature and the autobiographical accounts of previous *yogins* and *yoginīs*. Gyatso's intention is to argue for an expanded notion of experience, one that affirms the importance of notions of direct perception and the psychological dimensions of ritual while recognizing their cultural contextuality. Experience, then, is an important concept in the Indian and Tibetan Buddhist context but should be understood, sensibly, to have nuances that are uniquely characteristic of Tibetan and Buddhist presentations. Having considered practices found in the Mahāmudrā, Dzogchen, *rdzogs-chen*, and "unexcelled," *anuttara*, tantra traditions, Gyatso comes to the conclusion that cultivation of experience plays a key role in numerous conceptions of meditative *praxis*. However, she tempers this observation with the understanding that such experiences are mediated categorically.[70] Her analogy is that rather than meditative experiences being unconstructed and unrelated to conceptual thought, that they are "postconceptual." According to this theory, the direct perception of primordial reality arises out of a conceptual substratum.[71]

We would argue that parallel to this tension between so-called particularity and monism is the numinous-cessative paradigm, the conception that conditioned reality and unconditioned reality are ultimately related with respect to liberation, whether one sees one preceding the other or the two in an intimate and a simultaneous relationship. Gimello has asked whether liberation constitutes experience at all. This is a particularly good question if liberation is the *cessative* aspect that is in opposition to the *numinous* and would apply to the context of Classical Yoga as well as it would for Buddhism. If experience is characterized by phenomenal attributes and liberation is not, then how can liberated experience be talked about? If it is so radically different, then does not one have to start talking about different *types* of experience? Is a notion such as taking place in time separable from the notion of experience? Gyatso points out that certain Buddhist traditions do posit an experiential quality to enlightenment, although in some cases it is a tentative and an ambivalent aspect of the path.[72] Experiences arguably are aspects of *saṃsāric* phenomena and thereby are part and parcel of the world of bondage, to the degree that those manifestations are based in an ignorant perspective of the world. In other words, we should not forget that experiences of the fruition of meditative practice are seen at times to be impediments to the path, and therefore it should not be surprising that these traditions have mixed attitudes about their value.

Philosophical Psychology and Phenomenology

On another level, from a psychological or psychoanalytical standpoint, the integration of the modalities of *samāpatti* and *nirodha* makes a degree of sense regarding the complementary mental functions to which each appeals. A useful way of differentiating between them psychologically would be to say that *samāpatti* here could be called "cathexis," a conscious reduction of the field of awareness in order to simultaneously bring a particular object of attention to the fore, consciously suppressing or at least inhibiting all other content from conscious awareness. This process is in part intended to introduce a degree of selectivity over the contents of consciousness and thereby introduce a heightened degree of control over objects of consciousness for the duration of the meditation session and often beyond. The development of a more tranquil, subtle form of consciousness would then ensue, yielding progressively more and more subtle yet powerful states of mind. Cathexis is a process of conditioning, training the mind to do something specific, bringing the mind at will to a particular object, the mind presumably becoming more powerful as its energies become less scattered. This seems to make intuitive sense as well, in that ultimately a tranquil and focused mind would be more powerful and useful than one that is jumping about from object to object.

Complementing this would be the *nirodha* aspect of catharsis, characterized by the releasing of objects and the deconditioning of habitual processes of awareness. This is complicated, however, by the fact that *nirodha* can have a number of different senses, some that suggest an utter lack of any awareness and others that suggest that awareness has reached its full fruition in the liberated state. Cathexis thus would bring stability due to its condensing and habitual formation of energy, whereas catharsis would be destabilizing, due to the fact that awareness is scattered. However, to the degree that the catharsis of *nirodha* occurs, it is training the mind to remain in a state of *upekṣa*, or equanimity, thereby strengthening the person's ability to tolerate the unsettledness of a greater field of awareness and, by extension, mental chaos. Also, if we tie this meditative conception of catharsis to a psychological one, we would suggest that *nirodha*-oriented meditation methods allow for the arising of repressed materials and therefore lead to a greater degree of emotive stability over the long term. Eliade has argued that meditation could be construed to be a *regressus ad originem*, a "regression to the origins," that bears a resemblance to the psychoanalytic ideal of the return and elimination of repressed materials.[73] This conception could be expanded with reference to Gestalt theories that contain the idea that certain types of physical and mental phenomena become excluded from the field of awareness, yielding problematic physical and mental symptoms, and that reclaiming these dimensions is critical to physical and mental health. The tension between the focusing aspect and the awareness aspect of consciousness can be said to demonstrate the bifurcation between figure and ground, the tension between fixation and relinquishment. The relationship here between stability and instability is clear, and it is also clear why it would be important or liberating to "yoke" these two forces together. Stability in and of itself is not productive, and according to both Classical Yoga and much of Buddhism, it is a flight from the world that can only be sustained for so long. On the other hand, the catharsis or destabilizing type that is characteristic of a *nirodha* type of yoga has the tendency to scatter and become undirected. The force of these two activities can be considered catalytic in the goals of *dhyāna*, in that they are understood to feed into one another, ultimately culminating in the liberative process itself. These polar dimensions would be like two sticks rubbing together, bringing upon a catalytic response, such as the realization that *nirvāṇa* and *saṃsāra* are intimately related.

Another way of looking at this relationship is to talk about the distinction between the emotive qualities that would be characteristic of these dimensions. We can postulate the *samāpatti* type of yoga as being characterized by a more profound sense of rapture, as is evident in the Buddhist system of *dhyāna* states. In the series of *dhyāna* states, as meditators move up the scale of *samāpatti*, they encounter more and more subtle yet profound states of joy and bliss, culminating in the quality of *upekṣa*, which might be characterized as a blissful peacefulness. We may look at the *samāpatti* states as moving toward a sense of more subtle as opposed to a rapturous feeling, from an ecstatic state toward a buoyancy or lightness. The emotive characteristics of *śamatha* are clear, as are those of yogic *samāpatti*, exemplified by the *samāpatti* state referred to as bliss *(ānanda)*. One can make a strong argument that the liberated state characterized by *nirodha* in both the Mahāyāna and Classical Yoga contexts is approximated by the attainment of these subtle levels of bliss and equanimity. The intimate relationship in the yoga system between the higher levels of *saṃprajñāta* and the state of *asaṃprajñāta* and the common Buddhist assertion that the fourth *dhyāna* state approximates the equanimity of liberation testify well to this. In terms of the emotive quality, we might consider the *saṃprajñāta* state "intensive" and the *asaṃprajñāta* state "extensive." To further this spatial metaphor, this would lead, on the one hand, to moving toward "one-pointedness" in *saṃprajñāta* and toward "spaciousness" in *asaṃprajñāta*.[74]

Gananath Obeyesekere has commented that he believes meditation fits into the scheme of what he would call "hypnomantic states," a range of cognitive states that includes dream, vision, trance, ecstasy, and concentration.[75] Following Eliade's identification of such states as being closely tied to shamanism, and thereby "one of the most powerful and ancient forms of knowing," Obeyesekere sees the variety of hypnomantic states being a hybrid of different factors. These factors include the human propensity for engaging in hypnomantic realities through a variety of different means, the cultural substratum that informs or is informed by the potency of the hypnomantic states, and the conscious motivations of the person engaging in such practices.[76] Thus the preconscious or unconscious dimensions of the human psyche can be accessed through working with states of consciousness other than ordinary waking consciousness, such as dream, trance, ecstasy, and so on. Dreams would be a powerful example of accessing dimensions of consciousness that do not fit the logic or character of waking consciousness and serve as a clear model of consciousness in a different modality. Other than lucid dreaming, which is the exception to the rule, the active part of dreams is in the interpretation and rumination upon them that occurs in the waking state after the dream. We should note here that Patañjali states that *siddhi*, the development of profound abilities, can be attained through a variety of different means (birth, herbs, mantra, *askesis*), acknowledging that the fruits of meditative practice are not all unique to yoga alone.

Obeyesekere argues that states such as "dream vision" and trance may form a feedback loop whereby the engagement of hypnomantic states and imagery is consciously manipulated and ultimately provides the fuel for further hypnomantic meditations or states.[77] The ecstatic, according to Obeyesekere, who could be a yogi, a devotee, or a shaman, turns away from the mundane world and penetrates an inner world often inhabited by fearsome realities in order to restructure and thereby transform reality into a bearable, even pleasurable, one.[78] The development of *samādhi*, according to Obeyesekere, is not regression but *progression*, shifting from a state of being overwhelmed by reality to having a sense of control over important aspects of it.[79] Such manifestations of Indian religions are characterized by the "dethroning" of normal consciousness, the idea that waking consciousness is subordinated to a vision of life that presupposes deeper motivations and realities.[80] Psychoanalytically it ties into the pleasure principle's manifestation in ecstatic religion and its transformations. He argues that these religious phenomena had their *origins* in this context, that they establish both alternate and independent reality and idealize and sublimate mundane and unconscious enterprises. The tension between the pursuit of pleasure and the concrete demands of living in society is transcended through the mediating and ultimately sublimating force of the development of hypnomantic states.[81]

The polar factors of the numinous and cessative fit well into this scheme. The numinous dimension here is the penetration into successively intensive dimensions of consciousness and the unconscious. These have as their analogues the attainment of supernatural powers, such as the *vibhūti*, *ṛddhi*, and *siddhi*, and have cosmological correlation with divine and semi-divine beings. These might deal with the more basic impulses that drive both humans and animals that are outside the domain of conscious awareness, thus tying them to shamanic motifs in both a neurophysiological and a cosmological manner—or perhaps ecopsychological.[82] Staal has noted in his theories of ritual and mysticism that religious practice may be a means of getting in touch with more basic developmental functions of consciousness, ones that we can be said to share with animals.[83] This discussion also may be related to ecological theories that postulate that we share much more than we are aware of with animals and more basic forms of life, a point that should further encourage us to see the deep ecological connections between our environment and ourselves.[84] This ties into ideas that in the process of rebirth, one can take the form of an animal or another myriad type of sentient being. In the development of *dhyāna*, characterized by willful orientation of attention, it entails power over subsequent levels of concentration and awareness. This could be construed to mean that it comes to hold sway over the deep drives and motivations of the animal psyche and thereby can reclaim that power. Eliade speaks of *pratiprasava* in the yoga context as a reduction to a vegetative state, hinting at notions of *kaivalya* that emphasize the abandonment of the human body.[85] However, we must keep in mind that the yogin, in the process of meditative ascension, claims power over subsequent cosmological levels that are encountered, though he or she may not exercise those powers. In cases where liberation is understood in more numinous terms, such as in Mahāyāna conceptions of Buddhahood, to suggest a vegetative state is profoundly problematic.[86]

Although *samāpatti* demonstrates a tendency towards inwardnes and a move away from the realm of the senses, it can be argued that it is not approaching a state of catalepsis, as some would suggest. As Patañjali understands it, the higher levels of *samādhi* yield the perfection of supernormal powers of perception, *prātibha*, such as supernormal hearing, sensation, seeing, tasting, and smelling (YS III.36, *tataḥ prātibhaśrāvaṇādarśāśvādavārthaḥ jāyante*). Patañjali extends this idea by insisting that these are *siddhis* characteristic of *vyutthāna*, or manifestation, and impediments to further *samādhi*. This is to say that they are powers characteristic of worldly experience and attachment and not the end of the yogic path. This is a classic case of a yogic warning against the temptations of psychic powers. This leads us to the *nirodha* factor, where the goal is to reach this point of cessation of bondage and secure liberation. This could be construed again, as it has been by Pflueger, as the attempt to recognize the pure lucidity of unconditioned consciousness, the *puruṣa*, and thereby break the *saṃsāric* cycle of existence once and for all. In the Buddhist context, this is a basic attempt to change the orientation of perception or consciousness through a process of breaking down conceptions of substantiality and of permanence in the conceptual and perceptual fields.

MEDITATION AND REALITY TESTING

Practice in itself takes on a subtle form of reality testing as well, as meditation is applied directly and thereby proven through the experiences afforded by practice. The question of whether reality testing is really going on or simply a process of verification and interpretation of phenomena within a particular framework is an important issue here. Frits Staal has written at length on this issue with respect to yoga and mysticism, arguing that it is the person who is willing to pursue experiential study of practices such as yoga that will most likely bring insights into the academic study of such practice. According to this theory, only first-person study can truly inform our analysis of the subject and prevent the mistakes of dogmatic and theoretical types of study. Staal argues that yoga is an ideal methodology for the practical study of religious experience, due to its relative lack of "superstructural" beliefs.[87]

However, it should be recognized that this factor of superstructure is never completely absent. As one progresses in any yoga program or Buddhist meditation community, there is a natural point at which those superstructural elements begin to emerge. At the beginning one can often enter into examination and practice without the requirement of extensive faith commitments, but as one advances to more complex practices, there are few environments where deeper faith commitments are not involved. Staal's approach, characterized by "effort, doubt, and criticism," attempts to distinguish empirical elements of religious practice from the superstructural elements that root these traditions in their particular cultural substratum. The experiential approach is one that has risks, which include conversion, socialization, and more generally the compromising of a sense of detachment regarding the traditions being encountered. Furthermore, it can be argued that the "superstructural" elements, largely those that would fall under the category of the *numinous* and cosmological dimensions of yoga and Buddhism, are largely inseparable from the more *cessative*. The superstructural elements may be pushed into the background, but they ultimately are part of the context in which such meditative practices are developed, and they may naturally emerge even if they are not consciously pursued. This is not to deny the validity and import of participant observation, which is a profoundly valuable dimension of this field of study. It does, however, suggest that the situation is a complex one that engenders a range of issues regarding participation and religious identity.

A NEW APPROACH TO PHENOMENOLOGY

In this chapter we have examined a number of aspects of how meditation has been approached on the basis of ideas of mysticism and religious experience. It has been suggested that along with acknowledging the problems inherent in a perennialist theory of mysticism, we should also acknowledge the limitations of stronger forms of constructivism. Many theories that posit a notion of religious experience or mysticism that is at the center of all religious life sacrifice attention to detail for the sake of comparison. However, there is a middle ground where the interplay between the individual and environment is recognized, leaving open the possibilities of representing religious phenomena accurately and at the same time allowing for comparative understandings to emerge. In this context, it is particularly interesting that the argument can be made that sources in the Indian traditions themselves wrestled with questions of how language and liberation are related to one another and how liberation can be said to transcend context. What has been suggested is that an incomplete constructivism may suit the study of meditation more satisfactorily, allowing for both the recognition of context and for the possibilities of both autonomy and transcendence in religious experience.

Through looking at Robert Gimello's application of a constructivist model to Buddhist meditation, we have examined how the relationship between *numinous* and *cessative* elements can be applied across the Hindu-Buddhist boundary. Gimello rightfully acknowledges the fact that Buddhism sees the development of meditative absorption characterized by *śamatha* meditation as not being soteriologically efficacious. It has been argued that the opposition of *samāpatti* and *nirodha* elements in the context of the YS closely follows this paradigm, that Classical Yoga accepts the idea of a relationship between numinous and cessative elements. By extension, the qualities of a being such as a buddha or a *jīvanmukta* are characterized by both dimensions to the degree that a given tradition emphasizes either the numinous or cessative qualities of liberation. It also should be recognized that Buddhist sources both within and across traditional boundaries are not all in agreement as to how exactly the notion of the union of these dimensions in *nirodhasamāpatti* fits into the soteriological scheme. The numinous dimension plays out in a profoundly similar manner in both Hindu and Buddhist contexts with the association of the attainments, *samāpatti*, and cosmology. These issues also come to the fore later, when we discuss how discursive qualities of the religious life are reconciled with nondiscursive qualities, and how different interpretations of the liberated state hinge upon the relative proportion of numinous and cessative characteristics.

We also have made clear the problems in following Sharf's argument that religious experience, particularly the practice of meditation, is a fundamentally problematic category of interpretation. There is no question that meditation is one among a range of practices, and that to essentialize either Hinduism or Buddhism as being uniquely meditative is clearly problematic. However, to argue that meditative methodologies are not meant to be put into practice or that they are simply textualized and ritualized is to draw significantly unwarranted conclusions. Similarly, the idea that meditation and ritual, as well as discursive teachings, are completely autonomous dimensions of religious practice is a misunderstanding of both Hindu and Buddhist pedagogy. Instead we have postulated the idea that notions of experience are critical in understanding the meditative methodologies that are characteristic of Indian and Tibetan Buddhism and the Hindu yoga traditions. The interplay of conditioned reality and unconditioned reality that is postulated in the Buddhist context demonstrates the interplay between numinous and cessative elements. However, it also should be recognized that this distinction does not rule out the interplay of social and environmental context along with notions of personal experience. In fact, it can be said that the numinous dimension presupposes a relationship between practitioner and environment, one that is attenuated and transformed though meditative practice.

Examining the functionality of *samāpatti* and *nirodha*, or the numinous and cessative, from the viewpoint of the psychology of religion further yields a number of insights into meditative practice. One is the functionality on the psychic level of the polarized modalities of *cathexis* and *catharsis* and how they relate to mental and emotional functioning. It has been suggested that these practices create different psychic conditions of stability and instability that have important psychological attributes regarding one's adaptation to the world of experience. One example of this would be how the development of equanimity *(upekṣa)* facilitates the reemergence of repressed physical, mental, and emotional contents in consciousness in a cathartic manner, a process that is analogous to dimensions of both psychoanalysis and gestalt psychological theory. The complementary functionality of *samāpatti* and *nirodha* aspects demonstrates their roles in soteriological function and the extremes of mental activity and passivity. Similarly, these states may well suggest a comparison between the immediate intensity of rapture and the subtle coolness and blissfulness of the state of cessation. As Obeyesekere argues, there may be a deep connection between the ecstatic characteristics of meditation and other religious forms and a degree to which the development of ecstatic states is adaptive on the psychological level. Lastly, meditation happens in a cultural context; as such, it has an organic relationship with both the soteriological and cultural elements that inform it.

In the context of the range of physical and mental effects of religious practice, it is apparent that deep psychic responses are provoked in the religious context that transforms both person and environment, sometimes profoundly changing the relationship between the two. These liminal dimensions of human thought, emotion, and creativity provide insights into the relationship between religion and culture, particularly the role of the ecstatic in shaping religious and cultural worlds for themselves and others. The multidimensionality of religious practice provides for both social and psychological understandings of religion that communicate, among other things, ideas about reaching equilibrium with oneself psychologically and one's environment socially or ecologically. A more complete vision of phenomenology engages the particularity of individual, subjective experience and, to borrow a term from Gyatso and Dewey, the "stretching" of that reality on the social and cultural planes. Thus the psychology of religion in its mode as phenomenology and the discipline of sociology together may shed light upon the ways in which religious practices have repercussions both for the individual and the environment. The notion of mysticism is one that is problematic on a number of levels, first and foremost to the degree it presupposes an ultimately individualistic experience as being universal to religious practice. However, to strip all religious practice of individuality and transcendence, assuming that all experiences are merely the product of deterministic environmental conditions, undercuts an evaluation of a range of religious practices on their own terms.

In the next chapter, we will extend the current phenomenological analysis to incorporate this shift. We will examine at length Mircea Eliade's comparison of yoga and shamanism, a comparison that yields a perspective on his development of the idea of *enstatic* versus *ecstatic* forms of religious practice and experience. Our goal will be to bring further nuance to this distinction and to demonstrate that this distinction is intimately related to the relationship between *samāpatti* and *nirodha* and the *numinous* and *cessative* dimensions of meditative *praxis*. This discussion will be extended by examining how recent scholarship on shamanism, and more broadly on ecstatic religion, demonstrates the utility of looking at the social analogues of religious practice, and how this can be applied to the study of meditation. The integration of these methodologies will provide further insight into our discussion of the multifaceted relationship between the Hindu yoga traditions and those of Buddhism.

3

Yoga, Shamanism, and Buddhism

A New Phenomenology*

The *Enstatic* and *Ecstatic* as Categories in Eliade's Thought

In two of his most famous works, *Yoga: Immortality and Freedom* and *Shamanism: Archaic Techniques of Ecstasy*, Mircea Eliade attempts to elucidate the distinctiveness of shamanic and yogic typologies of religious belief and practice. Through this process, Eliade notes at several points what he believes is a fundamental distinction between shamanic and yogic practice and experience that can be understood as the difference between *enstasis* and *ecstasis*, or *enstasy* and *ecstasy*, respectively, "standing within" and "standing without." This distinction has become part of the foundation of scholarship in both the domains of the academic study of yoga and shamanism far beyond the sphere of Eliade's own work. The controversial issue of determining the primary characteristics of shamanism is framed by the context of Eliade's emphasis on ecstasy as the definitive component of shamanism as opposed to possession and other phenomena. In the study of meditation *(dhyāna)* in the Hindu and Buddhist contexts, the terms *enstasy*, *enstasis*, and *enstatic* have become an important part of the terminology of both Hindu and Buddhist studies. With its roots in the comparison of yoga and shamanism, Eliade's *enstasis-ecstasis* distinction has found its way into the language of the phenomenological dimension of the study of religion and into the language of religious studies more broadly. The goal of this chapter is to provide a closer examination of these terms that may lead to a more sophisticated understanding of Eliade's phenomenological theory and the question of its ongoing utility in the study of religion.

In particular, this chapter will explore Eliade's notion that the ultimate goal of shamanism is a type of visionary experience that involves the association of mythical beings and their realities, in contrast to the more abstract goal of release from conditioned reality that is characteristic of Indian forms of yoga, most notably Classical Yoga. As well as reexamining Eliade's theory in this regard, a number of other issues not found in Eliade's work will be considered that may further illuminate this relationship and demonstrate other important possibilities for the yoga-shamanism comparison. These include examples of initiatory types of phenomena associated with Buddhist meditation, the junction of *enstatic* and *ecstatic* modalities in the development of meditation in Buddhist and Hindu yoga, and the possibility of viewing the yogic practitioner as a sort of "psychopomp" akin to the shaman. It will be demonstrated that the *enstatic* and *ecstatic* modalities can be better seen as being dynamically related rather than mutually exclusive, and that Eliade's distinction is useful but in need of further elaboration and specificity. *Enstatic* and *ecstatic* phenomena have an intimate relationship with what can be called *numinous* and *cessative* modalities or conceptions of religious practice and experience, demonstrating both continuity and distinction in the yoga-shamanism relationship. These dimensions have a deep connection in how they tie together the psychological and social realities in the lives of religious practitioners and relate both to questions of cosmology and divinity. It will be suggested that Eliade's phenomenology may hold much promise when brought into dialogue with more recent sociological approaches to the study of shamanism and ecstatic religion more broadly.

Religious Specialization in Comparative Analysis

Eliade states that shamanism can be said to possess four primary elements. These include: an initiation in which the adept faces death, dismemberment, and possibly a descent into the underworld and an ascent into heaven; an ecstatic journey in which the shaman acts as healer or psychopomp; a "mastery of fire" in which the shaman proves himself or herself capable of withstanding some type of ordeal; and an ability to change form, to "become invisible," and to demonstrate other magical powers.[1] The primary factor among these, according to Eliade, is *ecstasy*, the ability to leave the body in order to journey to otherworldly realms, and to master the world of spirits, ultimately qualifying the shaman as a "specialist in the sacred."

> The essential and defining element of shamanism is ecstasy—the shaman is a specialist in the sacred, able to abandon his body and undertake cosmic journeys "in the spirit" (in trance).[2]

The idea of the shaman as a specialist leaves the door open for a broad range of comparisons for Eliade and presents the implicit idea of specialization as a cross-cultural phenomenon. Along these lines, I. M. Lewis, working in the domain of ecstatic religion, particularly shamanism, has commented on the significance of understanding and unpacking the notion of shamanism in order to come to a greater comparative understanding of what he calls "universal religious roles."[3] Although Lewis and Eliade differ substantially in defining exactly what constitutes the specialization of the shaman, it is clear that they both believe that "religious specialization" or "profession" has cross-cultural validity. Similarly, Birgitte Sonne has asserted that a shaman is a "professional ecstatic," recognized as such on the basis of his or her ability to carry out an ecstatic ritual that consists of entering into dissociative states that have cultural and traditional analogues.[4] Though this definition differs substantially from Eliade's in the interpretation of the ecstatic, it nevertheless shares much with Eliade in regard to the sense of religious profession and the validity of profession as an authoritative concept in both the religious and secular context.

The notion of religious specialization and its consequences provides the foundation for Eliade's comparison of the shamanic type of religious specialization and that of yoga. The yogin, or yoga practitioner, as a specialist in the sacred is akin to the shaman as a religious ideal, an example of how religious ideas are concretely embodied. According to this interpretation, the yogin, like the shaman, is understood to embody the truths of his or her tradition (Hinduism, Buddhism, Jainism, etc.) and therefore exemplifies the living reality of its philosophy, mythology, and so on. Both the shaman and the yogin are understood in their respective traditions to have unique powers of perception and vision, and therefore they are understood to play a role as specialists in their religious community, perhaps even as mediators between the mundane (profane) and supramundane (sacred) worlds. There is a sense of direct access to religious truths that may be at the heart of Eliade's curiosity in this domain, the notion of specialization perhaps being kin to Weber's conceptions of religious virtuosity and charisma. However, unlike Weber, Eliade's primary concern is the experiences of individuals, the object of his phenomenology, rather than the sociocultural context in which these individuals live and have such experiences. For Eliade, the fact that both the shaman and the yogin experience the truths of their tradition directly and with a degree of autonomy provides a basis for distinguishing them as specialists and for examining their religious experience as being prototypical or paradigmatic of their respective traditions.

Dimensions of Comparison: Meditation and Initiation

Eliade investigates similarities between yoga and shamanism on a number of levels, including initiation, mystical ascent, magical heat, and ritual intoxication. In the first case, the subject of investigation refers to shamanic initiations that include ritual dismemberment and death.[5] Striking examples of yogic practices that center on death that Eliade does not significantly address are present within Theravāda meditation practices, namely, those of *maraṇasati*, "contemplation of death," and *asubhabhāvanā*, "meditation on [the] foulness [of decaying corpses]."[6] In the contemplation of aspects of death and decay, the yogin establishes both an existential sense of the immediacy and reality of death and an image of the repulsiveness of the physical body in life and death. In Eliade's view of initiation, George Bond has stated that "although he does not discuss Theravāda Buddhism's meditations on death in this context, they seem in many ways to fit this model and to be analogous to the symbolism of initiatory death as Eliade describes it."[7] Bond also has demonstrated the strong resemblance in the contemplation of the skeleton that presents itself in Eskimo initiation and in Theravāda practices. He ultimately comes to the conclusion that the effects of the contemplation of death in Shamanism and in Theravāda Buddhism "are phenomenologically identical: transforming religious experience, attainment of wisdom and liberation."[8]

It also should be noted that meditations such as *asubhabhāvanā* have a strong numinous component in that they hinge upon the contemplation of images and not simply abstract truths, although faith or understanding of such abstract truths may be seen to arise out of such practice. The initiatory quality of such meditations is significantly different in character from the shamanic paradigm in that the contemplation of corpses does not lead the Buddhist meditator toward a sense of "mastery over spirits," which Eliade states is the paradigm of shamanic phenomena. However, it is clear that both Buddhism and shamanism utilize the power and psychological impact of imagery of death and dismemberment in the corporeal manifestation in service of religious ends. The embodiment of death lends concrete reality to religious conceptions and to the ability to see oneself or one's body taking on such a form. The impact of such embodied imagery is mirrored in the utilization of graphic embodied images as a basis for developing both liberating insight and temporal power in the Hindu and Buddhist tantric contexts as well. Liminal images, such as those that represent death, decay and pollution, characteristic of the cremation ground, bring about deep psychological responses suitable for evoking dramatic changes in consciousness and perception. In post-Aśokan Indian Buddhism and in the Theravāda tradition, we find the development of meditation methods that involve the engagement of powerful imagery of death and initiation ultimately oriented toward producing profound changes in the mental and emotional constitution of the practitioner.[9]

DIMENSIONS OF COMPARISON: ASCENSION MOTIFS

The notion of ascension is carried through several levels of investigation in Eliade's work.[10] The climbing of the ceremonial ladder in the performance of

Vedic ritual is said to represent the shamanic ascent of the heavens through the conquering of the "world tree," and it serves as a starting point for Eliade's analysis of ascension motifs.

> We meet the same symbolism again in Brahmanic ritual; it too involves a ceremonial ascent to the world of the gods. For the sacrifice, we are told, "there is only one foundation, only one finale . . . even heaven." "The ship fair crossing is the sacrifice"; "every sacrifice is a ship bound heavenwards." The mechanism of the ritual is a *dūrohana*, a "difficult ascent," since it implies ascending the World Tree itself.[11]

Eliade sees this ascent as being parallel to the mythical account of the birth of the Buddha—the infant Buddha's steps are said to represent the ascension through a sevenfold division of heavenly realms.[12] Eliade asserts that the Buddhist meditation system can be said to correspond to ascension through a progression of celestial realms. In this case, through the process of mastery, the Buddhist yogin acquires power over subsequent realms as a result of a higher rebirth, culminating in the attainment of *nirvāṇa*, or "liberation."[13] Here Eliade appears to be discussing Buddhist conceptions of the meditative sequence characterized by *rūpadhyāna*, "form meditation," *ārūpyadhyāna*, "formless meditation," and *nirodhasamāpatti*, "attainment of cessation." This identification is problematic in a number of respects, among them Eliade's apparent identification of *nirvāṇa* with *nirodhasamāpatti*, the association of rebirth with the soteriological process, and the absence of a discussion of the role of insight *(prajñā)* in the process of liberation.[14]

This is not to say that there is not a meditative ascension concept in Buddhism, but rather that the connection between ascension and liberation is much more problematic. In the development of *samādhi*, "contemplation" or "absorption" (Eliade's *enstasis*), and more generally *dhyāna*, "meditation," in the Buddhist context, there is an understanding that meditators who have attained a significant degree of progress in meditation approximate the consciousness of gods in higher cosmological realms. These realms in Buddhism are those of the *rūpadhātu* and the *ārūpyadhātu*, the "form realm" and the "formless realm," which constitute two of the so-called *traidhātuka* or "three realms" of Buddhism. The third realm, the *kāmadhātu*, is the "desire realm," in which there are successive levels of rebirth, including those of deities, human beings, animals, and hell beings, among others. The *rūpadhātu* and *ārūpyadhātu* contain only deities, and they are considered to have cognitive powers superior in many respects to the deities of the desire realm. As a result of attaining high degrees of refinement of meditation in one's life, a practitioner of *śamatha* or "tranquility" meditation may be reborn after death in the realm equivalent to that meditative state. There is clearly a sense in which the realms build upon each other, in that the higher realms imply that the beings have refined states of consciousness. The higher rebirths within the desire realm and, by extension, in the higher abodes of the form and formless realms, also are indicative of a high degree of religious merit. All of these states are considered part of *saṃsāra*, and they do not therefore constitute liberation or any permanent heavenly abode. Thus it is problematic to assert that the ascension through these cosmological and psychological states represents the soteriological path of Buddhism. The "attainment of cessation," *nirodhasamāpatti*, does not refer to a state of rebirth at all but rather to the cessation of all mental and physical functions, in some cases identified with liberation, but not in a locative or cosmological sense. It presupposes the action of *vipaśyanā* meditation, "insight meditation," the complement and partner of *śamatha* meditation. It is *śamatha* meditation that indicates the "ascension" and the *vipaśyanā* aspect that is considered the quintessential type of Buddhist meditation that brings about the cessation, *nirodha*, which is equivalent to liberation. It can be argued that there is a movement from gross to subtle implied in the movements of *dhyāna* that may have a deeper relationship with Vedic and Upaniṣadic conceptions of liberation. However, Theravāda and Mahāyāna conceptions regarding the role of *nirodhasamāpatti* in Buddhist soteriology make identification problematic.

As in the case of Buddhist *śamatha* meditation, where the yogin pursues *samāpatti*, "attainment," of the sublime levels of the *rūpadhātu* and *ārūpyadhātu*, the Pātañjala Yoga tradition embraces a series of levels of *samādhi* that leads to profound states of being, acting, and knowing. The Classical Yoga tradition presents a typology of yogins based upon the attainment of different stages of *samādhi*—such as the *prakṛtilaya*, "immersed in the phenomenal ground of material reality," and the *videha*, "bodiless one," who has developed a significant degree of skill in *samādhi* but not complete liberation.[15] In both cases, there is a set of stages that encompasses a notion of attainment through an ascension motif, which is placed parallel to a notion of cessation, *nirodha*, which is seen to be the distinct culmination of the soteriological process. Frits Staal has rightly noted that there is a strong distinction within yogic traditions between *nirodha* and *samāpatti*, similar to the *śamatha-vipaśyanā* distinction in Buddhism.[16] This fact may well suggest two trends rather than just one, possibly even the coexistence of ecstatic and enstatic techniques, establishing a dynamic between the ascension and cessation aspects. There is evidence that these *nirodha* and *samāpatti* aspects in the *Yogasūtras* have their origins in possibly separate texts and separate methodological approaches to yoga.[17] In this regard it makes more sense to follow Ian Whicher, however, who ultimately characterizes yogic experiences as both *ecstatic* and *enstatic* rather than seeing these aspects as being ultimately at odds with one another.[18] Gerald Larson also seems to be in agreement with such an interpretation in his criticism of Frauwallner's view that the tension between *saṃprajñāta*, "object-oriented," and *asaṃprajñāta*, "non-object oriented," forms of *samādhi* indicates that Patañjali's YS is a composite text.[19]

This tension is elucidated by examining distinctions between "introvertive" and "extrovertive" forms of religious phenomena and their relationship to the *enstasis-ecstasis* distinction. One of the ways this has been done is by developing a scale of religious experiences, depending on the level of arousal, or lack thereof, and the range of phenomena from the lower to the upper limits.[20] The extremes are understood as states of hyperarousal, or "ergotropic," and hypoarousal, or "trophotrophic," states. These represent the division between experiences and methods that aims at withdrawal and autonomy, similar to the *enstatic*, and experiences and methods that tend toward high degrees of cognitive, emotive, and perceptive stimulation, similar to the *ecstatic*. Forman notes in the study of mysticism, and notably in the work of W. T. Stace and others, that another parallel to this is the division of experience into "introvertive" and "extrovertive" types, again referring to the content of the religious experience. However, care must be taken to avoid oversimplification, for some shamanic and yogic practices may not be easily interpreted by such black-and-white terminology. For example, a type of cataleptic fit on the part of shamans during ecstatic performances may demonstrate outwardly *enstatic* elements at work in the context of shamanic practice, despite the inward *ecstatic* elements. As we have noted, the experience of the yogin may not be so easily separable or isolated from *ecstatic* elements, but rather the *enstatic* and *ecstatic* may well be at work together in the development of *dhyāna* and *samādhi*. Obeyesekere's theory of "hypnomantic" states is founded upon the notion that yoga and shamanism are, on one level, continuous with each other, and that shamanism contains a particular mode of knowledge hidden beneath the "superimposed ratiocinative speculations" of the traditions of Buddhism and yoga.[21] Louis de la Vallée Poussin similarly believed that Buddhism, among other Indian *śramaṇa* traditions, was initially founded upon a "pure yoga," an ecstatic technique later subsumed under broader scholastic and philosophical superstructures.[22] These cases demonstrate some of the ambiguity in a distinction hinging upon the outward appearances of *enstatic* and *ecstatic* manifestations of religious practice. In one example, it is the outward manifestation of tranquility (catalepsis) beyond that lies a postulated inner *ecstasis*. In the other, it is an *enstatic* inwardness (meditation) that is said to represent the adaptation of what were once external *ecstatic* modalities in service of a soteriological orientation toward cessation. A more consistent interpretation of such phenomena is that these dimensions are related dynamically, demonstrating the tension between cosmological-mythic considerations and soteriological and ethical concerns. In the context of Hinduism and Buddhism, these can be described as the tension between numinous and cessative tendencies found in the relationship between *samāpatti* and *nirodha* in the development of meditative *praxis*. In the broader context, it can be argued that the differing degree or relative degree of these factors may distinguish religious phenomena, such as yoga and shamanism, from one another rather than simply the inclination in one direction or the other.

THE DYNAMICS OF PRACTICE AND EXPERIENCE

Eliade does address the fact that "heavenly ascent" with respect to yogic attainments has been thoroughly interiorized—thus stripped of its ecstatic character.[23] The reversal of the function of the ecstatic is at the center of Eliade's notion of *enstasis* and *ecstasis*, which distinguishes shamanic and yogic practices on the basis of their teleology. "Yoga cannot possibly be confused with shamanism or classed among the techniques of ecstasy . . . the goal of classic Yoga remains perfect *autonomy*, enstasis, while shamanism is characterized by its desperate effort to attain the 'condition of a spirit,' to accomplish ecstatic flight."[24] According to Eliade, these two goals are seen to resemble one another in their hierophanic nature that provides for the abolition of history but are ultimately irreconcilable as modalities of religious experience. However, as has been argued earlier, a strong case can be made for the *enstatic* and *ecstatic* modalities complementing one another, even if we agree that they have different teleological functions. This characterization of shamanic and yogic experiences represents a fundamental dichotomy that is often made in the study of mysticism between types of religious practice and experience. The respective religious types are seen to differ in their ultimate aims, one of which is the experience of immanent mythical realities and the other an experience of complete cessation or suppression of all forms. This distinction is critically related to the idea of contrasting *samāpatti* and *nirodha* aspects, characterized by their numinous and cessative qualities. According to Eliade, the yogin is seen to escape the cosmic cycle altogether, whereas the shaman is forced to repeat his or her endeavor indefinitely. Though this points out a crucial distinction in the types of religious goals, the role of the *ecstatic* within yogic practice and its antecedents still remains unclear. This is complicated by that fact that Eliade argues differently when referring to the *enstatic* goal of autonomy versus that of *jīvanmukti*, "liberation in life," a yogic state that is characterized by *ecstatic* as well as *enstatic* qualities. In arguing the contrast between technique, he points to the *enstasis-ecstasis* distinction, whereas when referring to the *jīvanmukta*, "one liberated in life," and the shaman, he makes a different distinction, this time hinging on the relative permanence of the state.[25]

It can be asked here whether it is truly clear if the goals of *kaivalya*, the state of yogic liberation, and the status of *jīvanmukti* are in fact at odds with one another. Eliade seems to be construing *kaivalya* in its strictest sense, in which it means "aloneness," the complete separation between self and world in a radically dualistic fashion, such as in the Jaina context—a state that seems at odds with liberation in life. One of the most critical and problematic issues in discussing the soteriological path of the Classical Yoga tradition is the relationship or lack thereof between *kaivalya* and *jīvanmukti*.[26] Whicher has addressed what he sees as an overemphasis on the *kaivalya* aspect regarding the development of yogic practice, one that could perhaps be construed as an emphasis on the negative aspect of liberation as opposed to the positive side of *jīvanmukti*.[27] Vyāsa's commentary only seems to exacerbate this issue, as it seems to simultaneously support a strict Sāṃkhya (dualist) reading of *kaivalya* and at the same time provide greatly for the intersection between the philosophical concepts of the YS and mythological and the cosmological figurations of the greater Hindu tradition. As T. S. Rukmani has noted, the concept of the *jīvanmukti* is not found in the YS itself but only in commentarial literature, leaving the issue of the relationship of *kaivalya* to *jīvanmukti* problematic at best.[28]

Shaman, Yogin, and "Psychopomp"

Regarding apparent difficulties in reconciling the ecstatic elements of the two types of practice, Eliade asserts that little exists to support a connection regarding the "psychopomp" role of the shaman within the Indian tradition.[29] One finds scarce reference in Eliade of an attempt to discuss relationships between yoga and the shamanic role as healer. According to Eliade, the shamanic healer, through the initiatory experience, is able to understand the "drama of the human soul" and the causes of illness that are rooted in the "corruption or alienation of the soul."

> Everything that concerns the soul and its adventure, here on earth and in the beyond, is the exclusive province of the shaman. Through his own preinitiatory and initiatory experiences, he knows the drama of the human soul, its instability, its precariousness; in addition, he knows the forces that threaten it and the regions to which it can be carried away. If shamanic cure involves ecstasy, it is precisely because illness is regarded as a corruption or alienation of the soul.[30]

In Classical Yoga and in much of Buddhism, one finds a similar mastery, a knowledge and power that allows for the alleviation of another order of illness, metempsychosis, the problem of *saṃsāric* existence. In the YS, the "seer," or *puruṣa*, has become enmeshed in the material ground, *prakṛti*, thus causing a condition whereby suffering, sickness, and death fall upon the person.[31] The Theravāda system also suggests that *saṃsāric* existence is due to the clinging to the misconception of a self that exists in the phenomenal world as a distinct, unique, and permanent entity, as opposed to the reality of the process of dependent origination (Skt. *pratītya-samutpāda*, Pali *paṭicca-samuppāda*). The root problem in Buddhism is often referred to as *duḥkha*, translated as "suffering," but just as appropriately used as "illness" and "pain." The metaphor that the Buddha is a physician whose noble truths are the diagnosis and the Buddhist *mārga* the cure reifies the notion that illness applies to all dimensions of human existence.[32] Ultimately, physical illness can be seen as rooted in the contamination of ignorance and desire. This connection between conceptuality and numinous forces is concretely represented in the interweaving of impersonal forces into a shamanic-mythic substratum in Vajrayāna Buddhism and Hindu tantra. In this context, peaceful and wrathful manifestations of deities are identified as manifestations of the principles of *karma*, "action," *karuṇā*, "compassion," *śūnyatā*, "emptiness," *prajñā*, "wisdom," and so on, as well as negative emotional and cognitive attitudes and principles. Agehananda Bharati, reflecting on the scope of tantric religion, notes that one should be careful in assuming that a shamanic theology is somehow inferior to one based in a literary tradition.[33] The tantric engagement of fearsome and wrathful deities seems particularly well suited for comparison with the often-frightening aspects of shamanic initiation and may well demonstrate the surfacing of the numinous dimensions of yogic practice out of scholastic analysis and contemplation.

It also has been demonstrated that shamanic healing bears a striking resemblance in certain respects to the psychoanalytic method in terms of the physician-client relationship, the psychological constitution of the physician, and the alteration of consciousness, among other features.[34] As discussed earlier, there is much ground for reinterpreting cognitive and emotive dimensions of meditation in light of psychological and psychoanalytic principles. One can extend this comparison further by examining the parallelism between the physician-client relationship and the guru-disciple relationship and the relevance of ideas such as transference in these relationships. The idea that the Buddha was the "supreme physician," in that through his yogic powers he was able to provide the most effective form of treatment to a person based upon her or his psychological type, is one deeply rooted in the Indian notion of the *guru-śiṣya*, "teacher-disciple," relationship, as well as in Buddhist conceptions of *upāya*, "method." Inasmuch as one would grant "psychopomp" status to the yogin, it must be tempered to the degree that in Classical Yoga and in Indian Buddhism, an individual's own efforts toward realization or liberation are usually considered the most significant. On the other hand, we must not forget that the guru is often considered of utmost importance in pointing the student in the right direction, the tantric idea of the *sadguru*, or "true guru," the teacher who gives the priceless gift of a glimpse of realization, being the epitome of this idea.

REINTERPRETING THE *ENSTASIS-ECSTASIS* DISTINCTION

Within the realm of Hinduism and Buddhism few who have spent any time on the subject of meditation or yoga have not been influenced by Eliade's thought. His definition of *samādhi* (and also *dhyāna*) as *enstasis* as opposed to *ecstasis* has become part of the language of academic work on meditation in the context of both Hinduism and Buddhism. Beyond the *enstasis-ecstasis* distinction, Eliade's conceptions of "religious specialization," "religious virtuosity," and "mysticism" are ripe for further examination and elaboration. He "classifies" shamanism as being within the realm of mysticism:

> In other words, it would be more correct to class shamanism among the mysticisms than what is commonly called a religion. We shall find shamanism within a considerable number of religions, for shamanism always remains an ecstatic technique at the disposal of a particular elite and represents, as it were, the mysticism of a particular religion.[35]

Substituting "yoga" for "shamanism" here would seem coherent according to Eliade's definition. Similarly, Eliade elsewhere describes the shaman in terms that are applicable to yoga: "they transform a cosmo-theological concept into a *concrete mystical experience*."[36] Eliade here forwards a conception of *mysticism* that functions as a framework for his broader understanding of religious experience, albeit one not developed substantially. It is possible that through further examination of Eliade's notion of mysticism, we may be in a position to further understand the motivations behind his postulation of the *enstasis-ecstasis* distinction and other aspects of his theory. As noted earlier, Eliade's notions of "religious specialization" hinge upon ideas such as mysticism that suggest that particular individuals have special types of religious experience, a type of firsthand knowledge that gives them unique status and reputed powers.

Questions regarding the utility of the idea of mysticism and of typologies of religious experience and practice are currently at the heart of much controversy in religious studies. As we noted earlier, there are particular problems with postulating cross-cultural ideas of mysticism. Many difficult questions have been asked with regard to the need to contextualize religious phenomena and the degree to which privileging individual experience has ramifications for the study of religion. With Eliade's work in particular, recent studies by Douglas Allen,[37] David Cave,[38] Carl Olson,[39] and Bryan Rennie,[40] among others, have brought about a substantive reexamination of Eliade's theoretical position and its viability as part of the methodology of the discipline of religious studies. Some of Eliade's more ardent critics have ranged from social scientists who view his theory as a "proto-theology," such as Ivan Strenski[41] and Robert Segal,[42] to scholars who see Eliade's theory as an exotic "secularized Byzantine Christianity."[43] Other scholarship, exemplified by the work of Russell McCutcheon,[44] has brought to the surface questions regarding the ideological foundations of Eliade's theory. Common in all of these discussions have been questions regarding Eliade's phenomenological emphasis and the problems of relativity, verifiability, and ideology associated with it. Such discussions of the viability of Eliade's theory may well reflect questions of the viability of the History of Religions methodology and of comparative religion on a broader scale. Comparative theory that addresses postmodernism and critical theory has begun to emerge in such works as *A Magic Still Dwells*[45] and in a recent collection of essays entitled *Changing Religious Worlds: The Meaning and End of Mircea Eliade.*[46] Rennie's *Changing Religious Worlds* is probably the most representative of the range of contemporary scholarship trying either to move with or move beyond Eliade's theory.

Following Rennie's assertions of the ongoing utility of the History of Religions as a methodology,[47] it can be argued that a profitable direction in which to take this research is one that recognizes the valuable insights of Eliade's phenomenology while addressing the problems inherent in the individualistic and experiential focus that is characteristic of Eliade's History of Religions. Eliade's privileging of the subjective dimension of religious phenomena was based on an attempt to prevent the reduction of such phenomena to delusion, mental disorder, and ideology. While taking such an approach may have suited the academic milieu of Eliade's time, it is clear that the context and pretext of the study of religion have changed dramatically and as such are much better suited to accommodate both critical and empathetic perspectives. A new phenomenology may be developed that moves beyond the uniquely psychological focus of Eliade's phenomenology toward one that recognizes the tension between psychological factors and sociological and environmental ones. In the context of yoga and shamanism, recent research on shamanism and ecstatic religion found in the work of I. M. Lewis[48] and in the collections of Nils Holm, such as his *Religious Ecstasy*,[49] provides much promise for such a task. Lewis has noted Eliade's admission that a sociology of ecstasy needs to be developed, and it is this task that Lewis has taken up in his own work on shamanism.[50] Adaptation of the methodological approaches developed in the context of these more recent studies of shamanism and ecstatic religion can bring additional precision to our understandings of the psychological, social, and cultural effects of religious *praxis* in a manner that complements and expands upon Eliade's theory. Such an orientation leads to a balanced analysis that recognizes the utility as well as the limitations of Eliade's *enstasis-ecstasis* distinction and the ongoing usefulness of the comparison of yoga and shamanism. This in turn provides an expanded model of phenomenology that offers a more holistic view of religious practice. This model integrates the emphasis on the psychological and experiential dimension found in phenomenological approaches such as Eliade's with the sociocultural analyses found in sociological presentations on ecstatic religion. Together, the psychological and sociological approaches support a greater vision of phenomenology, one that has deep ramifications for both the study of shamanism and yoga. It provides a means for bridging the gap between what have been characterized as "experiential-expressive" and "cultural-linguistic" models in the study of religion.[51] It may also allow for greater balance in comparative religion between humanistic and social science models, thus resolving an issue that has been at the center of much debate with respect to the History of Religions methodology and religious studies more broadly in recent years.

Ecstatic Religion and Phenomenology

Noting what he observes as sociological ambiguity characteristic of ecstatic religion, Lewis points out the fact that ecstatic religious phenomena can be demonstrated in some cases to strengthen social realities and in others to "authorize innovation and change" in the cultural environment.[52] Bourguignon also supports the contention that ecstasy can be both integrative and challenging with respect to existing cultural conditions, bringing stability to psychological and social realities in ways that either affirm or challenge the status quo.[53] Lewis terms ecstatic cult groups that demonstrate ecstasy or possession and that are related to dangerous, foreign, or liminal beings or practices as "peripheral cults." These cults are characterized by the development of intensive types of ecstatic religious practice on the psychological and cultural levels and the status of being subordinate or peripheral to mainstream society or culture on the political level.[54] Ecstatic phenomena in this context represent a force of defiance in some cases and hopelessness among others.[55] "Central cults," on the other hand, represent the mainstream cultural center of society, being bound to types of ecstatic phenomena that reify existing social structures. Such ecstatic phenomena concretize and support social structure and are recapitulated in order to counter forces outside of mainstream society or culture that are seen as threatening to its own stability and integrity.[56] Another key distinction that is made by Lewis is between *possession* phenomena and *soul-loss* phenomena, of which Lewis believes possession is more broadly characteristic of shamanic phenomena.[57] With possession, Lewis, in association with the work of Bourguignon, argues that it can be characterized as "positive" (invited or benevolent) or "negative" (uninvited or malevolent), even within the same cult, according to different circumstances.[58] Lewis further criticizes Eliade and others who hold that shamanic phenomena are characterized by ecstasy as opposed to, or in contradistinction from, possession.[59] Lewis's theory rests upon the idea that possession phenomena are part and parcel of the shamanic, and the two modes can be seen as reinforcing one another (possession and ecstasy) or can be seen as examples of the same thing (possession alone).

Lewis also notes that possession cults can shift in status from peripheral to central and also may often carry or share the characteristics of the other, suggesting a continuum rather than a simple bifurcation between types.[60] The simple fact that ecstatic cults tend to lose their fervor as they become part of the establishment is a point that Weber was interested in at length regarding charismatic religion, authority, and the routinization of charisma in the religious context.[61] In this analysis, then, social and organizational stability relies on the development of religious practices that supplant the ecstatic with ritual modalities, a process that "suggests that enthusiasm relies on instability."[62] This is complicated in our culture by the fact that certain types of feelings that are associated in traditional contexts with the experience of religious realities are considered characteristic of mental illness and are therefore not allowed a traditional outlet.[63] Part of what distinguishes the shaman from the mentally ill, however, is the fact that the shaman is not at the mercy of his or her mental and emotional states but rather is able to connect with them in the proper context and on proper occasions.[64] The idea that in the context of ecstasy and possession individuals who are affected by psychological and social disequilibrium are the ones most prone to pursue such a calling is reminiscent of Obeyesekere's analysis of "personal symbols," the concept that religious phenomena are a means of negotiating the intersection of personal and sociocultural realities.[65] In this context, the manifestation of divine attributes is characteristic of the attempt to master different dimensions of the human personality that have been subject to chaos, disorder, or trauma.

The ecstatic modality makes sense as an interpretation of Indian contemplative techniques as well. First of all, we could characterize the *śramaṇa* traditions as being peripheral cults that saw themselves as a challenge to mainstream society and culture, particularly the Vedic Brahmanical culture. As opposed to the Vedic culture in its highly ritualized form, in which society was structurally based on a division of social function and reified and recapitulated through periodic sacrifice, the *śramaṇa* traditions operated on the fringes of Brahmanical society. For the Vedic Brahmin, at least in the middle to late stages of Vedic culture, social status and ritual observance were the foundation for religious authority. For the *śramaṇa*, authority may well have been more characterized by virtuosity, a stronger degree of charismatic authority.

The language and culture of the *śramaṇa* tradition shares much with that of the Vedic tradition, a conception that goes well with the situation of *śramaṇic* communities on the periphery of Vedic society and culture as opposed to its being completely separate or autonomous. We can expand on this analysis by pointing out the difference in attitudes about worldly life or worldly existence as well, in which Vedic society postulates a greater sense of cosmic order and worldly happiness, as opposed to a *śramaṇic* conception that sees the core reality to be *saṃsāra*, the world of sorrow and the ongoing process of birth and rebirth. We also can argue that *śramaṇa* traditions ultimately become central cults of their own, as is characteristic of the Classical Yoga, Buddhist, and Jaina traditions, and adapt considerably to suit their change from being peripheral to central in their respective cultures.

We can expand this argument even further by talking about the development of yoga in the *śramaṇa* context and how different types of meditation relate to these tendencies. The meditative endeavor as characterized by Eliade as *enstatic* is mirrored to a significant degree by the cessative and world-renouncing features of the *śramaṇic* traditions. On the other hand, the *ecstatic*, which can be characterized as being in the realm of the numinous and characteristic of the *samāpatti* dimension of meditation, is tied strongly to the idea that meditative methodologies are believed to be productive of special abilities of action and perception that presumably afford a degree of spiritual authority and power. The cessative dimension is notably similar to the sense of eliminating so-called negative possession, the affliction of *saṃsāric* existence, and the numinous dimension is comparable to the development of positive possession or the approximation of the consciousness of divinity through the development of meditative skill. On the other hand, the *samāpatti* dimension also presupposes a withdrawal from phenomenal existence, to the degree that it is characterized, or prepared for, by practices such as *pratyāhāra* and by limiting the field of consciousness, thereby containing *enstatic* as well as *ecstatic* features. However, the idea of shamanic catalepsies and thereby ecstasy can be said to be an approximation of the process of *pratyāhāra*, a prelude to an inwardly ecstatic process. To the degree to which cessation is the culmination of the *enstatic* qualities of the introverted meditation process or the application of it to the problem of existence, we also can suggest that it possesses outwardly *ecstatic* qualities.

Over and above all, though, the notions of attainment and cessation carry positive and negative connotations with respect to their objects, providing well for the connection of positive and negative possession concepts to the *samāpatti* and *nirodha*, or *numinous* and *cessative*, aspects of meditative *praxis*. Another way that this relationship can be described is through the notion of domestication versus exorcism, which gets at the idea that there are beings or states to be cultivated, brought under control, and others that must be uprooted or destroyed. Gerald Larson has similarly postulated that religious cults might be characterized as "experience-oriented ecstatic" versus "askesis-oriented enstatic" to delineate the outward manifestations of what he calls "mirco-communal" groups (analogous to religious cults), though making a much stricter distinction between these types than we have postulated.[66]

Another question that follows closely is that of the relationship between such practices and the ethical perspectives found in the traditions they inform. For Lewis, this issue is tied into the status of religious movements as central or peripheral cults. In his theory, peripheral cults are characterized by having an ambiguous moral status, with the spirits involved ranging from malevolent to benevolent, and as such, the religious practices do not have a central connection to a universal sense of morality. This seems to fit particularly well with mainstream Buddhism's analysis of yoga methodologies, in that they argue that the *śamatha* dimension of meditation is a carryover from the *śramaṇic* substratum that does not have an inherent connection to moral or ethical life. According to this interpretation, Hindu yoga forms do not contain the ethical component that Buddhist systems do.[67] This is to say that in portraying non-Buddhist traditions as containing only *śamatha* and not *vipaśyanā* types of meditation, Buddhism is stating that non-Buddhist traditions are inferior in methodology and with respect to the fact that *vipaśyanā* uproots all mental defilements, whereas *śamatha* only temporarily suppresses them. This is contingent upon the idea that the *nirodha* represented by the attainment of *nirvāṇa* and *prajñā*, or wisdom, is distinct from the *nirodha* of the non-Buddhist traditions, which is only a temporary state of stasis. This second type of *nirodha* could then be seen as separate from the transformation of liberation, in that enlightenment and moral perfection are intimately connected in the Buddhist sense of the functionality of yoga.

In Lewis's schema, the move from *śramaṇa* tradition toward mainstream tradition would presuppose that the ecstatic dimension would be, over time, replaced by a more ritualistic and scholastic tradition. Morality, according to this system, is critically connected to the idea that a tradition moves from being on the periphery of a culture toward its center, toward a sense of social integrity. This makes a significant amount of sense in thinking about issues of authority and identity in the *śramaṇic* context. To the degree that virtuosity in certain types of ascetic methodologies is seen as being the foundation for authority and spiritual development, there is a difficulty in bringing the tradition toward the mainstream. According to this theory the numinous dimensions of religious practice, such as the attainment of refined states of meditation, are difficult to place objective criteria upon and have an ambiguous relationship to ethics. This is the problem that Sharf mistakenly identifies as meaning that contemporary meditation practices are somehow inauthentic, the problem of the difficulty in determining who, if anyone, is practicing an "authentic" tradition. This tendency in Theravāda may have logically developed such that over time it moved toward a scholastic and ritualized central cult that abandoned the more numinous dimensions of meditation practice that were considered part of the external culture and a challenge to traditional ideas of monastic authority, or the splintering of the *numinous* off into the domain of spirit cults and possession ritualism.

In Mahāyāna traditions, we can argue that the greater willingness to incorporate and develop the numinous aspects of religious practice may have played a key role in its attempt to be more synthetic in its presentation of the traditional vision of the Buddhist soteriological path, and in its embracing of devotion to divinities within the bounds of mainstream tradition. The continuance of Mahāyāna's acceptance of the numinous dimension of meditation *praxis* is demonstrated by the Vajrayāna adaptation of *śamatha* or *samāpatti* forms and the reconnection to shamanic numinous phenomena, such as possession. This is exemplified in the lives of the *mahāsiddhas* and characterized by the older Tibetan lineages, most notably the Nyingmapa and Kagyupa, where yogic virtuosity and *śramaṇic* authority play a significant role in popular and monastic practice. To the degree that tantra represents the development of practice lineages as opposed to scholastic ones, it makes sense that the numinous dimensions should manifest themselves significantly. It also may have something to do with the moral ambiguity that seems so prevalent in the tantric context, and it can be further noted how such ambiguity is brought back into the fold in the central cult exemplified by the Tibetan Gelukpa sect.

In Classical Yoga, we have a complex situation where the tradition's status may well fit somewhere between a peripheral cult and a central cult. A critical point here is the question of to what degree the Classical Yoga system is a mainstream Indian tradition. As we mentioned earlier, Bronkhorst has demonstrated a number of significant points about how the YS may represent a tradition that does not have its own lineage, being instead a fossilized tradition that has been appealed to by a number of different systems.[68] As such, the Yoga system is seen as being a source of interpretation or materials for the presentation of the Sāṃkhya and Vedānta viewpoints rather than being an autonomous tradition of its own. However, one can arguably state that the Pātañjala Yoga system does contain oppositional elements of *samāpatti* and *nirodha* that demonstrate the qualities characteristic of numinous and cessative practices and experiences. Just as it can be adapted to suit the Sāṃkhya and Vedānta frameworks, it clearly stands on its own in a number of respects, at least hinting to some degree that it has its roots in the *śramaṇic* and, to some degree, the Upaniṣadic substratum of Indian culture. If we follow an interpretation of the YS that postulates that the text is a composite and that the yoga practices of *samāpatti* and *nirodha* have been brought together in a synthetic way, we can make an argument that the YS is a product of the attempt to bring a peripheral cult toward the center, or vice versa. More likely than this, however, is the idea that the Classical Yoga tradition bears a strong resemblance to the *nirodha-samāpatti* paradigm found in Buddhist texts, the idea that there is an ultimate experience of cessation that is the culmination of the numinous or the point at which the numinous reaches its end in the culmination of liberation. Through this interpretation, it is only when the cessative aspect finds expression as a uniquely ethical practice that the connections can be made to transform the tradition from its peripheral status as *śramaṇic* philosophy toward a central status in the context of being a *darśana*, or an extension, or a pragmatic tool in the development of another tradition. The status of action as "neither black nor white" for the yogin can be considered an argument for the peripheral status of the Classical Yoga system and the YS.[69] However, it is clear that the practice of yoga is understood to be supported by ethical action, such as the concept of *mahāvrāta*, or "universal vow."[70] Lastly, the status of the practice and the status of the practitioner in the state of *kaivalya* are problematic in any type of action. A common interpretation is that in the context of the YS it would signify the obliteration of the cosmos, the complete detachment from any social reality whatsoever, the ultimate sense of aloneness, suggesting an asocial soteriological state.

Both Hindu and Buddhist traditions posit ethical and social prerequisites for the practice of meditation, including preliminary moral instructions and environmental prerequisites that are considered important in establishing a meditation practice. The ramifications of practice on the ethical level can be considered another dimension altogether, one that may have a significant effect in terms of our discussions of authority and soteriology. Agehananda Bharati, for example, holds that religious experience and the range of experiences referred to as mysticism are not inherently dependent upon moral prerequisites and do not necessarily lead to any particular moral or ethical view or behavior. Sudhir Kakar has noted that Bharati's thesis has ramifications on a number of levels regarding the study of religion.[71] If religious experience is seen as being an autonomous dimension of human experience, it follows that there would be no connection between the experience and other facets of life. This means then that the experiences afforded by meditation would not confer any special knowledge about the world, such as technical knowledge or scientific knowledge, but would only confer an understanding of the religious state.[72] This has implications for ideas of religious omniscience, implying that religious awakening is the awakening of a special form of knowledge that may confer omniscience to spiritual states but does not confer any worldly knowledge upon the individual.

Such a view is counter to many traditional religious accounts that argue that religious experience causes deep changes in ethical agency. In the Buddhist systems, for example, the propensity to commit unethical actions is destroyed by liberating insight or knowledge *(prajñā, jñāna)* characteristic of the development of *vipaśyanā*. Buddhism might answer Bharati's criticism with the notion that he is correct about Hindu sects, which are understood to contain only the *śamatha* element of *dhyāna* and therefore can only lead to the temporary suppression of afflicted action. After a period of time, according to both Theravāda and Mahāyāna sources, the yoga practitioners who have immersed themselves in the heights of rapture eventually fall back to the phenomenal world with their defilements intact. This would be represented in the tradition as yogins who have reached high levels of concentration yet have not eliminated the roots of the mental defilements. Classical Yoga, however, notes that with the development of discriminating discernment, characteristic of the *nirodha* inclination, there is a cessation of afflicted action and ultimately the destruction of all defilements.[73] Also, both Hindu and Buddhist traditions, particularly in their tantric manifestations, suggest that beyond the ethical dimensions of meditation, there are numerous numinous effects. Ideas regarding the development of *siddhi*, *ṛddhi*, and so on testify strongly to the idea that along with the ethical dimension of action come special powers of cognition and action. One way of dealing with this problem would be to suggest a demythologized form of such powers, arguing that the divine eye, for example, is not literally a seeing but the ability to generalize from sensory stimuli what would be inferential types of understanding. However, it is clear that both in the numinous and cessative domains, there is a problem in interpreting these traditions themselves as not asserting the reality of the ethical and preternatural aspects that develop from meditative practice.

The socialization process that occurs in the context of meditation instruction, however, can be said to demonstrate the way in which the context of meditation shapes the experience as well as the character of the practitioner. Though no experiences may be guaranteed, nevertheless, the entrance of an individual into the context of group meditation requires that an individual learn new community behavior and abandon the old.[74] Practice-oriented settings, such as those of retreat, are psychologically intensive situations that often require attitudes uncharacteristic of normal monastic or lay life, such as silence, unusual hours, isolation, and the like. The context of practice, then, is a part of the conditioning process, involving learning a code of behavior that is to be held for the duration of one's practice or stay, which seems to be an important issue. The abandonment of material aims and the adoption of a code of behavior often strikingly different than the worldly one that one has left are crucial changes in the structure of one's relationship with society. However, the difference here may be that there is a question of whether certain types of religious experience cause conditions such that would in absence of any external stipulation cause one's behavior to be in line with a universal moral attitude.

For example, does the experience in meditation of interdependence necessitate acting in a manner consistent with such an experience? Is there a way of acting that is harmonious with such a perspective? Is this not made more problematic by notions that enlightened activity does not play by the same rules as unenlightened activity, as suggested by Buddhist notions of *upāya*?

NEW PERSPECTIVES ON YOGA AND SHAMANISM

The comparison of yoga and shamanism served as a fruitful source of ideas in the development of Eliade's phenomenological theory. The concepts of religious specialization and religious virtuosity are useful ways of talking about cross-cultural examples of how individuals strive to develop *ecstatic* capabilities. The attainment of such religious specialization has a number of facets, including the impact that spiritual development has upon the individual and upon her or his relationship to society and the environment. The idea that particular individuals embody the religious truths of their traditions, particularly in the manner of ecstatic states, has relevance both to our understanding of ancient and contemporary religious phenomena. As has been argued, a good example of how this comparison could be fruitful beyond Eliade's application is a comparison to numinous dimensions of Buddhist meditation practice that bear a significant resemblance to subjects of shamanic cultures. A primary example of this would be to follow George Bond in identifying the initiatory elements found in the Buddhist contemplations of death and decay, *maraṇasati* and *asubhabhāvanā*. Other examples from Theravāda include practices such as *buddhānusmṛti*, the contemplation of the Buddha image, and *devānusmṛti*, or the contemplation of deity images. Perhaps most demonstrative of the ongoing adaptation of numinous imagery that bears significant relationship in the Mahāyāna context is the development of graphic and embodied images representing the range of positive and negative mental states that are to be brought under control in the service of liberation and power in the Vajrayāna.

With respect to Eliade's notion that yogic soteriology shares similar ascension motifs with shamanism, we have argued for a more nuanced understanding of the *enstasis-ecstasis* distinction. First, it was demonstrated how it is problematic to identify the sequence of *rūpadhyāna-ārūpyadhyāna-nirodhasamāpatti* with the liberatory thrust of Buddhism, though it does fit with the numinous dimension of yogic cosmology. Similarly, it was argued that the Classical Yoga system incorporates a progressive system of *samāpattis* that is connected to the cosmology of the yoga system, and that this numinous dimension both describes the process of yogic ascension and the mythical relationships to that cosmology. Rather than seeing the numinous and cessative aspects as being opposed to one another, it is more appropriate to see them both at work in the context of the development of *samādhi* in both of these traditions. Ian Whicher is correct in stating that it is more accurate to see the development of *samādhi* in the context of Classical Yoga as being both *enstatic* and *ecstatic*. Doing so retains the thrust of much of Eliade's comparison, in that it allows for both the comparison and contrast of the yogic and shamanic religious practices, while more specifically getting at how this relationship works in the development of meditation. This argument works well in the Buddhist context as well, where *dhyāna* and *samāpatti*, the factors of developing *samādhi*, are characterized, on the one hand, by the ascensional gaining of power and, on the other hand, by their orientation and approximation of a state of cessation, *nirodha*.

This is complicated, however, by problems regarding the state of liberation, the states of *nirvāṇa* and *kaivalya*. A critical issue is the question of what the role of a liberated person is in life, if there is any. In *nirvāṇa* or *kaivalya*, a state of being completely separate from the world, a state of complete cessation of all phenomenal attributes, it is easier to distinguish the numinous from the cessative. However, there are numerous examples in the Indian tradition of liberated individuals having powers of a numinous type just as well as the cessative, as is apparent in the biographical literature surrounding the Buddha, an ambiguity noted by Obeyesekere.[75] The manifestation of such powers would seem to be *ecstatic* and therefore problematic regarding the ultimate opposition of *enstatic* versus *ecstatic* ends. The Mahāyāna conception of a buddha is even more close to a paradigm that asserts both dimensions as being characteristic of a fully enlightened being, to the degree to which a buddha is still "available," even after *parinirvāṇa*. On a more mundane level, the *ecstatic* character of yoga also can be demonstrated by the attribution of the status of "psychopomp" to the enlightened teacher, or guru, who helps in the "cure" of the "metaphysically ill" student, or *śiṣya*. Again, the reemergence of the numinous dimension finds great expression in the tantric context, where the philosophical principles that represent the understanding of the world of bondage become embodied in graphic form. The importance of the numinous as well as the cessative and the importance of initiation in the tantric context strengthens this comparison considerably.

We have argued for a new direction in the development of a phenomenology, based upon the impact of Lewis's theories of ecstatic religion upon the study of yoga and meditation. In doing so, we have attempted to bridge the gap between phenomenological-psychological and sociological perspectives, which also have been characterized as "experiential-expressive" and "cultural-linguistic" models. Following Lewis's model, we have demonstrated the utility of talking about the *samāpatti* and *nirodha* aspects as being comparable to shamanic conceptions of possession, as being positive invited and negative undesired. This notion fits neatly into the conception that through means such as *samāpatti*, a yoga practitioner develops the ability to both attain the status of and to embody the forms of the divine. In the *nirodha* component, there is a notion that there is a problematic reality in life, one that needs to be removed, whether that is considered *duḥkha*, *tṛṣṇā*, or *avidyā*. In association with this, we explored the idea that the *śramaṇa* movements are what would be called "peripheral cults," demonstrated by the fact that the *śramaṇa* traditions rejected both mainstream society and mainstream morality. *Śramaṇic* authority can be understood to be more deeply rooted in the development of meditation and *askesis* and the degree to which an ascetic embodied the numinous, as opposed to the degree to which he or she embodied ritual or scholastic authority. The peripheral domain, then, has continued to exist over time in a number of different contexts, most notably in the tantric context. This has logically been at odds with the tendency of these traditions to shift to central status, a move that changes the nature of religious practice in a logical fashion. This would be exemplified by the conception in Buddhism that the *śamatha-vipaśyanā* distinction incorporates the uniquely ethical component that is a Buddhist development and by the adaptation of a text such as the YS into mainstream Brahmanical culture.

We should keep in mind that the boundary between a central and peripheral cult is not necessarily a solid one but is rather subject to constant renegotiation. This is perfectly consistent with the greater range of arguments that has been presented thus far. At the foundational level, it is becoming clearer that boundaries between the Indian religious traditions may not be as solid as our disciplinary systems would seem to suggest. Similarly, the *enstatic-ecstatic* distinction, intimately related to the contrasting numinous and cessative aspects discussed earlier, also operates as a dynamic relationship that should be seen as being more fluid than solid. Rather than characterizing yogic phenomena on the side of the cessative, or the *enstatic*, dimension, it can be argued that both Hinduism and Buddhism demonstrate a tendency to try to reconcile or at least clarify the roles of these dimensions of religious *praxis*. This goal of this chapter has been to show that this tension is understandable both on the psychological and sociological levels, and that in fact these dimensions can be best understood through a phenomenological perspective that incorporates dimensions of each.

4

The Debate over Dialogue

Classical Yoga and Buddhism in Comparison

THE HINDU-BUDDHIST DIALOGUE IN THE STUDY OF RELIGION

Scholarship in religious studies over the past century has identified a great range of issues regarding the relationship between Indian forms of yoga and the development of Indian and Tibetan Buddhism. As we have demonstrated, this is a particularly important issue regarding the relationship between conceptions of meditation found in the Classical Yoga system and in Buddhism, most notably the *śamatha-vipaśyanā* distinction. In this chapter, we will examine a range of views on the relationship between Pātañjala Yoga and Buddhism. The foundation of this section will be an examination of the work of three pioneering scholars of South Asian religion, Emile Sénart, Louis de la Vallée Poussin, and Hermann Oldenburg, particularly their "debate" over issues in the development of Indian religion. This discussion of the Yoga-Buddhism relationship will be the background for our more contemporary discussion of this recurrent theme. Beyond the work of Sénart, de la Vallée Poussin, and Oldenburg, we will touch upon the work of a number of other critical scholars who have also dealt specifically with issues in the Yoga-Buddhism relationship, including Mircea Eliade, Winston King, L. S. Cousins, Johannes Bronkhorst, and Gerald Larson. It will become apparent to the reader that much can be learned simply by comparing the range of work that has been done by these scholars, noting the degrees of parity and disparity between their views of the Yoga-Buddhism relationship. Through this comparative approach, we hope to avoid the biases of entrenched disciplinary viewpoints and pursue a more integrative approach to this research, incorporating a range of scholarship representing numerous cultural situations and perspectives.

Although these scholars are in agreement in seeing close ties between these systems, they differ in significant ways in their analyses of the relationship.

Through this process, we will come to note the contrasting ideas of soteriology that emerge out of the Buddhist and Classical Yoga contexts, and how the meditative models present in these traditions demonstrate a degree of similarity not recognized previously. Having sketched out a broad range of comparative issues, we will discuss an issue that has been particularly noteworthy regarding the relationship between meditative practice, cosmology, and soteriology. This issue deals with the nature of *samādhi*, or the concept of *samādhi*, according to Classical Yoga and Buddhist sources. It is quite apparent in the textual and oral traditions of Classical Yoga and Buddhism that the development of *samādhi* is typically a key element of the soteriological process of meditation. As we will see, many scholars have noted that the concepts of *dhyāna* and *samādhi* demonstrate deep structural similarities between the conceptions of meditative *praxis* in the two traditions. Although it is not universal in the Hindu and Buddhist traditions to value *dhyāna* on the level that is given in the Classical Yoga system or in the meditation-oriented manifestations of Buddhism, these sources have left a mark on the broader range of religious culture, despite divergence on the practical and soteriological levels. *Dhyāna* and *samādhi* are valued throughout the Hindu and Buddhist traditions, despite the fact that they may not be considered as central of a practice in some contexts as opposed to others and are at times more connected to mythical figures than to human practitioners. Nevertheless, the notion of individual perfection, of developing fitness of mind, body, and spirit as characterized by yogic disciplines, is one that has been said to extend well across time and space and, most notably, cultures. These issues tie into a notion of *yoga pur*, or "pure yoga," as postulated by de la Valleé Poussin, the idea that yoga as a practical discipline is wedded to different philosophical systems but in itself is not dependent upon them. This would be consistent with the Buddhist notions of *dhyāna* and of *yoga* that suggest that the development of *samādhi* and other yogic techniques is not uniquely Hindu *or* Buddhist. A similar understanding in the Hindu context is that the Classical Yoga tradition is "Sāṃkhya Yoga," as a combination of a primordial yoga tradition with that of the Sāṃkhya philosophy, composing a *theoria-praxis* paradigm. This ties into the discussion of the notion of "superstructures" and the idea that some systems, such as yoga, do not have as great of a doctrinal element and therefore allow for engagement with a minimal degree of faith commitment. However, it is clear that the numinous and cessative dimensions characteristic of yoga contain the seeds of "superstructures," of conceptions of the nature of reality that are typically part and parcel of more advanced meditative practices.

When the term *yoga* is used, a number of possible references differ significantly in character and chronology. Classical Yoga, for example, is largely dependent upon a relatively late textual tradition, while Sāṃkhya is often understood to have a significantly earlier foundation as a systematic philosophy. Yoga bears a different character when we look at it as understood in the early Upaniṣads and in the greater Vedic corpus versus the more systematic and classical sense that it takes in the *Maitrī Upaniṣad* or in the *Bhagavadgītā*. Whether or not we believe in some purely practical and unadulterated form of yoga, we must acknowledge that when yoga is discussed, we should try to clarify to which "yoga" we are referring. Part of the difficulty in understanding the Yoga-Buddhism relationship has resulted from a lack of clarity as to which yoga is being discussed. One facet of this would be the relationship between the Classical Yoga tradition and the earlier stratum of yoga practice in the context of the *śramaṇa* traditions and Upaniṣads. Even if we follow scholars who date the YS in an early period, say 200 B.C.E., which is far from the consensus opinion that dates it more in the neighborhood of 200 C.E., we are looking at significant periods in which these traditions were informed and influenced by other philosophical and religious ideas. This is complicated in the case of the YS by the fact that many believe that the YS, like the *Bhagavadgītā*, is a hybrid text, composed of several texts that espouse competing views and practices. We also could ask about the role and nature of Sāṃkhya in this relationship, for if we follow scholars such as Larson and Oberhammer, it would appear that the Classical Yoga tradition is a subschool or an offshoot of the Sāṃkhya tradition rather than an autonomous tradition. The concrete nature of the Classical Yoga tradition is represented well in the YS and in oral and written commentaries and provides the foundation for developing a concrete vision of yoga, one that has been held as authoritative for nearly 2,000 years. Significant work remains to be done toward developing a deeper understanding of the relationship of Classical Yoga and Upaniṣadic yoga, as well as that of Classical Yoga and *haṭhayoga*, subjects that we will only touch upon briefly here.

What will emerge from our study are two objects of particular interest regarding the development of meditation in these traditions. The first is the question of the nature of the relationship between the Classical Yoga's system of *samādhi* and the concepts of *samādhi* in the context of Buddhist *śamatha* meditation. What we will see is that there is an intimate relationship between the concepts of *dhyāna* and *samāpatti* in both traditions that demonstrates a parallelism, if not an identity, between the two systems. The foundation for this assertion is a range of common terminology and common descriptions of meditative states seen as the foundation of meditation practice in both traditions. Most notable in this context is the relationship between the *saṃprajñāta samādhi* states of Classical Yoga and the system of four Buddhist *dhyāna* states (Pali *jhāna*). However, the relationship between these systems can be construed in a number of different ways, depending on how one "links" the comparison together. This is further complicated by the attempt to reconcile this comparison with the development of the Buddhist *samāpattis*, the *ārūpya-dhyānas*, or the series of "formless meditations," found in Indian Buddhist explications of meditation. This issue becomes even more relevant as we turn toward the conception of *nirodha* found in both the context of Classical Yoga and in the Buddhist systems, where the relationship between yoga and soteriology becomes an important issue. In particular, we will examine notions of *nirodhasamāpatti* found in Buddhism and the relationship of this state to the identification in Yoga of *cittavṛttinirodha* with *kaivalya*. Our goal is to demonstrate how our notions of numinous and cessative states and conceptions from ecstatic religion can be applied to interpret yoga and its relationship to soteriology in these contexts.

THE EARLY CONTEXT: SÉNART, DE LA VALLÉE POUSSIN, AND OLDENBURG ON YOGA

Looking at the yoga tradition as a cohesive unit that proceeded from the period of the *śramaṇas* to the Upaniṣads and eventually the Classical Yoga tradition, scholar Emile Sénart saw the Buddhist tradition as a development of the Indian yoga traditions that shared many of its characteristics. Among these characteristics are the philosophical foundations of the Classical Yoga system, notably concepts regarding the nature of *saṃsāra*, suffering, rebirth, the attainment of liberation, and the establishment of supernormal powers of action and cognition. Among these, Sénart noted a strong similarity to meditative practice and, in particular, the stages of *samādhi* between the Classical Yoga system and Buddhist meditation. Buddhism, in this context, is what Sénart terms *dans sa phase ancienne*, "Buddhism in its ancient phase."[1] The foundation for this comparison is in part the Buddha's statements in the Pali *sūtta* that he had surpassed but not rejected his own former teachers, such as Udraka Rāmaputra and Arāḍa Kālāma, who possessed the noble traits of *śraddhā*, *vīrya*, *smṛti*, and *samādhi*.[2] The Buddha's teaching was thus established on the ground of yoga, "in the mold of Yoga," and therefore is characterized, at least in its most ancient form, by its yogic character and, notably, by its morality (such as the *yamas* and *niyamas*) and notions of "internal vision."[3]

Sénart is quick to argue for a distinction between yoga and Sāṃkhya and against what he sees as a mistaken understanding that yoga is subservient to Sāṃkhya.[4] Though the most apparent difference is the Īśvara doctrine, he notes other significant differences.[5] This becomes most apparent as Sénart turns to the relationship between Buddhism and yoga, where his emphasis is on the practical nature of yogic discipline as opposed to the speculative nature of the Sāṃkhya system, a theory-practice split that is often attributed to the relationship between yoga and Sāṃkhyā. This is exemplified by reference to the *Bhagavadgītā's* contrast of yoga as action and Sāṃkhya as speculation.[6] His distinguishing yoga and Sāṃkhya parallels more recent yoga scholarship that is split into factions over the nature of this relationship, one side arguing that yoga is an extension of the Sāṃkhya tradition, the other arguing for the unique identity and philosophical distinctions of yoga. He forwards an argument that will surface again many times, that of the Buddha as "carrying on" or "crowning" the yoga tradition. This is often paired with the notion that in some Pali sources the Buddha does not seem as prone to polemical language. The fact that the Buddha's teacher, Arāḍa, is sometimes associated with the Sāṃkhya system notwithstanding, Sénart emphasizes the practical nature of the Buddha's yoga as being the core of what was transmitted to the Buddha, an idea that he shares with de la Vallée Poussin and later with Eliade. The "practical agnosticism" of early Buddhism, according to Sénart, was founded on a "proto-yoga" tradition, upon a foundation that had been laid by the earliest yoga practitioners, who developed the methods and theories that eventually would be codified in the Sāṃkhya and Classical Yoga traditions. According to this theory, "proto-yoga" laid the foundation for the Buddhist tradition, and the common language of Classical Yoga and Sāṃkhya was formative of the pragmatic emphasis of early Buddhism. Influence from more theistic sects, the early *Vaiṣṇavas*, was at the foundation of the propagation of Īśvara theory in the yoga context and the development of a *bhakti* element in Buddhism and eventually the more theistic adaptations of Buddhism over time.[7]

Sénart notes the remarkable similarity between the practice of meditation in the two systems, starting from the viewpoint of the traditional four-*dhyāna* system common to most of the descriptions of the Buddha's enlightenment experience.[8] Sénart argues that the four *dhyānas* of the Buddhist system are equivalent in structure to the twofold division of the Classical Yoga system of *samādhi* into the respective domains of *saṃprajñāta* and *asaṃprajñāta*. The fruits of *dhyāna* provide another level of comparison between the two traditions as well, on account of the common usage of such terms as *sarvajñāta, citta, dharmamegha, kleśa, karma, bhūmi*, and the *brahmavihāras (maitrī, karuṇā, muditā, upekṣa)*.[9] The development of *siddhis* (Pali *ṛddhi*) demonstrates the common foundation of yogic practices in the ancient substratum of magical practices, the supernormal abilities of perception and action characteristic of the Buddha in the Nikāya sources similar to those attributed to the advanced yogin in the YS.[10] Building further upon this is the notion of Īśvara as the ideal yogin in comparison to the Buddha as object of reverence and devotion *(praṇidhāna)*, the importance of ethical and practical emphases in opposition to the more speculative Sāṃkhya view, and common notions regarding the selfless nature of all external reality characteristic of the early religious communities of wandering ascetics.[11]

According to Sénart, the formulas for the *dhyānas* in Buddhism and yoga are both primitive due to their seeming identity.[12] Noting the structure of the *jhāna* system, including the foundation in *viveka* (discrimination), the factors of *ānanda, prīti, vicāra, vitarka, samādhi,* and the attainment of "calm interior," *ajjhattaṃ sampasādanaṃ* (as in YS I.47), he describes the sequence of the progression from the gross to the subtle states of meditation, the separation from pleasure and pain, and the elimination of concern for all things and memory.[13] The structure of the YS, based on notions of *vitarka, vicara, ānanda,* and *asmita,* allows for near identity, with *nirvitarka* and *nirvicara* extending the comparison for the higher levels, respectively, with their equivalents.[14] A key distinction, however, is that Sénart believes that the third level of the Buddhist *dhyāna* corresponds to the *saṃprajñāta* level in reference to the *saṃprajñāta-asamprajñata* distinction of the yogic system. He notes that the yoga system makes a distinction between conscious and unconscious forms of *samādhi* and that in that system it hinges upon the suppression of *asmitā,* which is absent from Buddhist sources.[15] Ultimately, though, he believes that there is equivalence between the levels of *dhyāna* characteristic of *asaṃprajñāta* up to the *asmitā* level of the yoga system with those characteristics of the Buddhist *dhyāna* system up to the level of the third *dhyāna.* The state of *asaṃprajñāta,* rendered here as "unconscious," is analogous to the fourth *dhyāna* level, due to the absence of all factors comparable to the yogic system's *dhyānas,* and due to its proximity to an unconscious state.[16] It is pointed out, however, that *upekṣāsmṛtipariśuddhi* is attributed to different *dhyāna* states, with *nirvitarka* in the yoga system and the fourth *dhyāna* in Buddhism, and that the notion of *viveka,* particularly *viveka jñāna,* is attributed to the preliminaries of Buddhist *dhyāna* versus being the culmination of the yoga system.[17] We might as well question whether these distinctions are hard and fast between the different levels of *samādhi* and their characteristics. Sometimes Buddhist sources refer to an "intermediate" *dhyāna* state between the first and second that eliminates *vitarka* but still contains *vicāra,* which would be comparable to a yogic *nirvitarka-savicāra* state. If the borders between these states are fluid, which is much more likely, then this is not a significant problem.

On the grounds of the ideal of *nirodha,* or cessation, Sénart does think that there is a stronger element of resemblance than difference between these two traditions. Noting the importance of *nirodha* as the means of eliminating or suppressing the *saṃskāras* in the context of Classical Yoga, Sénart goes on to point out the emphasis on *nirodha* in Buddhist sources, from the Four Noble Truths to the more technical notion of *saññāvedayitanirodha.*[18] Both aim at the elimination of the *saṃskāras* and refer to a state of release that hinges on identical notions of *karma* and *duḥkha.*[19] For Sénart, the issue ultimately comes down to a similar process and a similar goal for both traditions, for the yoga system, the *nirbija* state of *asaṃprajñāta*, and for the Buddhist system, the *saññāvedayitanirodha* state that emerges, according to him, from the attainment of the fourth *dhyāna*. The analysis of the structure of *dhyāna* and particularly his attempt to relate the Buddhist *dhyāna* states to the Classical Yoga *saṃprajñāta* and *asaṃprajñāta* forms of *samādhi* hits on some important technical distinctions that follow from looking at the progression in both systems from discursive thought to subtle states of absorption. However, his discussion of *saññāvedayitanirodha* does not address the *ārūpya-dhyāna* states that tend to play a prominent role in the attainment of cessation, or *nirodhasamāpatti*, according to Abhidharma sources. Although the attainment of cessation is more problematic, the *dhyāna* system consisting of both *rūpa* and *ārūpya* states is an integral part of larger Buddhist conceptions of *samādhi*. As we will see later, it has been argued that the *ārūpya* states are a part of the greater scheme that is characterized by *samādhi* in both the Hindu and Buddhist contexts. On the other hand, the recognition that *nirodha* is characteristic of the *samādhi* of both Buddhist and Classical Yoga systems is an important point of the relationship, perhaps more important than the *ārūpyas*.

De la Valleé Poussin, in a manner similar to Sénart, dwells on ideas of ecstasy and the dichotomy between direct experience and speculation, arguing that there is a *yoga pur*, "pure yoga," at the foundation of Buddhism and more generally the *śramaṇa* traditions of ancient India. Commenting that he does not claim to have unraveled the mystery of the relationship between yoga, Sāṃkhya, and Buddhism from a developmental standpoint, de la Vallée Poussin attempts to demonstrate further parallelisms between these traditions, particularly the contrast between contemplative tradition and practical instruction.[20] He states: "Yoga, by etymology, is an effort, a discipline; in fact, it is an ascetic morality, penitent, and particularly, ecstatic, adaptable for every purpose either mundane (magical) or supramundane (theosophical). . . . Yoga is indeed a method used by diverse eschatologies, controlled by diverse metaphysics."[21] With Sénart's position, he sees both positive and negative aspects, arguing that it is a valuable demonstration of the penetration of Buddhism by yogic types of practices but problematic in asserting that the basis for Buddhism was a Sāṃkhya or Vedāntic type of yoga.[22] De la Valleé Poussin turns this argument around, arguing that the YS owes a great deal to Buddhist sources, despite the antiquity of the Sāṃkhya metaphysics that informs it.[23] Buddhism itself is understood as a "pure yoga," oriented toward calmness and "silence of spirit and senses" via the "ecstatic" modalities of *samādhi*, *śamatha*, *mauna*, and so on, as opposed to the scholastic and contemplative tendencies that characterize the range of later Buddhist and non-Buddhist traditions.[24]

De la Valleé Poussin presents numerous points of conjunction with the YS with references to individual *sūtras*. These include the "means" *(upāya)*, such as *śraddhā*, the concept of *vivekaja*, the doctrine of *Īśvara*, and notions of *saṃsāra*, time, and epistemology.[25] He is particularly interested in noting the relationship between yoga and Sarvāstivāda, Sautrāntika, Vaibhāṣika, and Yogācāra sources, mentioning at one point that he believes Vyāsa was dependent on either Vibhāṣā or Vasubandhu for explication of Patañjali on at least one point.[26] He focuses largely on shared terminology, including such notable terms as *bīja*, *vāsanā*, *saṃskāra*, *ṛtaṃbharā*, *avidyā*, *mahāvrata*, *kaivalya*, *prajñā*, *janmakathaṃtā*, *saṃtoṣa*, *siddhi*, *manojavitva*, and *dharmamegha*, to name some of the more familiar ones. Having demonstrated the multifaceted nature of the yoga-Buddhism relationship, he ultimately asks the question of whether Patañjali and, by extension, Vyāsa combated the theories of Sautrāntika, Vaibhāṣika, and Yogācāra, or whether these doctrines may in fact be the same ones that were professed by the schools of antiquity.[27] With meditation, having noted Oldenburg's earlier reference to the doctrine of the four *dhyānas* being represented in the Mahābhārata, de la Valleé Poussin seems to largely follow Oldenburg's lead in asserting a pre-Buddhist origin of the *dhyānas*, but not one in the sense of the later codified Classical Yoga system. Having noted the Buddhist admittance that the four *dhyānas* were common to non-Buddhists, de la Vallée Poussin appears to agree with Oldenburg in the idea that there was an earlier tradition that Buddhism was built upon, that had yoga techniques but, as should be emphasized, is likely distinct from the Classical Yoga tradition as characterized by the Sāṃkhya-Yoga type of tradition.[28] He concludes that the Buddhist presentation of the *dhyāna* system as such is the oldest representation that we have of this "proto-yoga," and that it is problematic to determine what relationship, if any, this yoga had to the doctrine of Sāṃkhya.[29]

Like Sénart, de la Valleé Poussin mentions the parallelism with the four *dhyānas*, noting Patañjali's breakdown *(vitarka, vicāra, ānanda, asmitā)*, and the corresponding *dhyāna* states, particularly the first through the third *dhyāna* states.[30] With the exception of the rendering of *upekṣāsmṛtipariśuddhi* as the "perfection" of memory and indifference (equanimity), as opposed to Sénart's interpretation (following Bhoja) as "suppression," de la Vallée Poussin seems largely willing to accept Sénart's categorization. However, he never directly addresses the question of the nature of the fourth *dhyāna* and its relationship to the yoga system except for, again, the role of *upekṣānusmṛtipariśuddhi*, which he notes is characteristic of the fourth Buddhist *dhyāna* and the *nirvitarka* level of the YS. It is interesting to point out his emphasis on the "formless" meditations as demonstrating Buddhist originality in meditative technique, founded in his argument that these do not appear in non-Buddhist sources.[31] This is particularly interesting in comparison to the arguments of Bronkhorst, Vetter, and Griffiths, who all see the *ārūpya* meditations as either a foreign intrusion into Buddhist doctrine or at best late developments within the tradition, as we will see later.

The differences between Sénart's and Poussin's conclusions are interesting on another level in that they argue for separate origins of yogic methods, with Sénart leaning toward an origin that has proximity to the Classical Yoga tradition, versus Poussin who seems to see the origins in a nonsectarian type of yoga. This is only a slight difference but significant in that each argues that the Classical Yoga tradition has a relationship to Buddhism that has a developmental angle. It seems much easier to talk about the early Buddhist traditions than it does about the early yoga tradition, perhaps one of the reasons scholarship has long lingered upon yoga's relationship to Sāṃkhya, which has a more cohesive philosophical and literary tradition. One of the key elements of this discussion that would help clarify these issues would be an examination of the relationship between Classical Yoga and Upaniṣadic formulations of yoga. The *Maitrī Upaniṣad* has significant relationships in structure to Classical Yoga, yet it is relatively late in formation. Clearly this is a significant gap in scholarship, of which an important issue may be in finding possible proto-YS texts that would make a stronger connection to earlier *śramaṇic* or Upaniṣadic sources. Chakravarti has noted this type of text in the Ahirbudhnya-Saṃhitā of the Pañcarātra-Vaiṣṇavas, an exposition on the Sāṃkhya philosophical school.[32] The text, attributed to Hiraṇyagarbha, bears components that could be interpreted as *kriyā* and *nirodha*, suggesting an intimate relationship with the Classical Yoga system.[33]

Both Sénart and de la Valleé Poussin demonstrate a significant indebtedness to the work of Hermann Oldenburg and his highly synthetic and encyclopedic works. Oldenburg sees Upaniṣadic materials such as the *Śvetāśvatara* as containing some of the earliest references to yoga methods, largely related to the control of breathing, posture, and sense control.[34] He also stresses the intimate relationship between Yoga and Sāṃkhya, particularly in their development in the Upaniṣads. He asks the question of whether they are not both descended from the same root, in that the Upaniṣadic compilers sought to first bring about a synthesis and then later to separate them into conceptual and pragmatic disciplines.[35] With the Classical Yoga tradition, Oldenburg notes the "perceptible difference" between its terminology and that of Sāṃkhya and believes that the Buddhist sources confirm the antiquity of the Classical Yoga tradition.[36] The beginnings of Buddhist literature are considered to be significantly later than the older layers of the Upaniṣads, which informed the early Buddhist tradition philosophically and pragmatically.[37] Oldenburg argues that the Buddha himself was, like the Jainas, suspicious of speculative philosophy and "knowledge for knowledge's sake" and thus argued for a more practical path that abandons unprofitable views.[38] However, he demonstrates skepticism over the notions of Buddhism as a branch of yoga in the manner Sénart and Poussin may be interpreted.[39] He argues, rather, that yoga and knowledge came to an uneasy equilibrium in the Buddhist community due to the soteriological efficacy of meditation and the need to address an audience that extended far beyond the bounds of the small community of religious virtuosi.[40]

In his brief account of the Buddhist *dhyāna* states, Oldenburg mentions their equivalence to the Classical Yoga states of *saṃprajñāta samādhi*, with evidence in the Mahābhārata pointing to the common origin in the yoga tradition of both the Classical Yoga and Buddhist accounts.[41] As we mentioned before, the evidence here could arguably be used to demonstrate the antiquity of the Buddhist meditation system, as it is assumed that the epic account demonstrates what would be considered a Hindu viewpoint, despite its closer relationship to the Buddhist presentation.[42] He even attempts to correlate the plane of infinite space (an *ārūpya dhyāna*) to YS II.47, which seems problematic in that it is an isolated occurrence of the term *ānantya*, which falls in a *sūtra* on *āsana*.[43] More on the mark are his comments that the notion of *citta* plays a considerably similar role in both Yoga and Buddhism, as do other dimensions of the meditative path, such as the *brahmavihāras*, the so-called five virtues *(upāyas)*, and the development of particular *siddhis* through meditative *praxis*.[44] Ultimately, according to Oldenburg, it is the "pre-classical yoga" of the Upaniṣadic (and possibly the pre-Upaniṣadic) era that is the foundation for the yogas of both Buddhism and Classical Yoga, though the features of the pre-classical yoga are best represented in Classical Yoga. In the end he argues for an intimate, mutual exchange to take place upon even the subtlest philosophical levels.[45] Such a view is in line with a number of other influential European scholars concerned with the development of yoga in the Indian religious context. Friedrich Heiler, for example, argued that the Buddhist tradition contains a significant number of yoga doctrines and practices (including *dhyāna*, *siddhis*, the *brahmavihāras*, and so on), concluding that both traditions developed from the same root.[46] He noted the strong relationship of the Buddha's meditation and his prior teachers, and particularly the notion that *dhyāna* is an intimate part of the early Buddhist definition of soteriology.[47] Heiler was well aware of the relationship between the doctrines of Classical Yoga (primarily in *Yoga Bhāṣya*) and Buddhist scholasticism, arguing, along with Keith, that the fourth *pāda* of the YS criticizes the doctrines of Asaṅga and Vasubandhu, rather than a vague "Vijñānavāda," as other scholars had postulated.[48] Heiler subscribed more generally to the "common substratum" theory of the development of Classical Yoga and Buddhism, crediting the Yoga tradition with containing a more rich and detailed exposition of the technical dimensions of yoga practice.[49] More recently, Gerhard Oberhammer, noting the relationship between a number of yogic and Buddhist concepts, such as the five "powers," the definition of *samādhi* in the Milindapañha, and the use of meditative concepts in Vasubandhu's Abhidharmakośa, suggests, like Heiler, a possible "common root" to these yogic practices testified to in the early strata of Buddhism.[50]

A CHANGING TIDE: TOWARD A GREAT SYNTHESIS

Already at the time of the publishing of de la Valleé Poussin's important article, "Le Bouddhism et le Yoga de Patanjali," Mircea Eliade had made a considerable impact on the realm of scholarship on yoga, and even to some degree with the issues of the yoga-Buddhism relationship. At the beginning of his article, de la Vallée Poussin mentions Eliade and his teacher, S. N. Dasgupta, as being proponents of "official brahmanism," a view in which the "Yoga of Patañjali, otherwise known as the Yoga of the metaphysics and eschatology of Sāṃkhya," was considered as "serving as a model for Buddhism."[51] De la Vallée Poussin, on the other hand, argues that the Sāṃkhya-Yoga connection was just one among many that "yoga consented to," taking issue with both Eliade and Dasgupta. He singles out Eliade again at the end of his article to again differentiate his own view from what he apparently sees as the prevailing view. He argues that Eliade has understated the significance of this discussion, due to lack of attention to the apparent points of convergence with the range of Buddhist philosophical viewpoints (such as Sautrāntika, Vaibhāṣika, Yogācāra, etc.).[52] On the other hand, he makes it clear early on in his study that it seems unprofitable to try to determine the chronology of different *types* of practices, giving the impression that he does feel that there is a certain identity between Buddhist and Classical Yoga not found in other sources.

It is in Eliade's *Yoga: Immortality and Freedom*, or *Le Yoga: Immortalité et Liberté*, that we find the full flowering of his work on yoga in its many manifestations. Eliade tackles some of the more difficult issues regarding the YS, including those of authorship, such as the "one" versus "two" Patañjali issue and the question of the integrity of the original text. He summarizes discussions regarding the date of the YS, the question of whether Patañjali of the YS and Patañjali the grammarian are the same individual, questions regarding the relationship of the author of the *bhāṣya* to the YS, and questions regarding possible anti-Buddhist polemics, as raised by a number of scholars.[53] He appears to take a somewhat less aggressive approach to many of these issues, largely discussing them without giving a strong impression of his personal inclinations. He does, however, note de la Valleé Poussin's insistence upon the relationship between the YS and scholastic Buddhism, leaving one the impression that the issue has yet to be resolved.[54] Eliade's work is steeped in the work of his teacher and guru, S. N. Dasgupta, whose research is closely followed in many dimensions of Eliade's analysis.

Eliade deals with issues in the Classical Yoga-Buddhism relationship most definitively in his chapter "Yoga Techniques in Buddhism," in *Yoga: Immortality and Freedom*.[55] Eliade feels quite comfortable stating that the Buddha forged a path that was the "timeless way . . . of liberation, of nondeath, and it was also the way of Yoga."[56] Discussing early Buddhism through the eyes of an ancient Buddhism constructed from the Theravāda sources, he talks about the paradoxical position of Buddha of rejecting the ritualism of Brahmanism and the extreme asceticism and metaphysical speculation of the ascetics and of Upaniṣadic thought. Thus the Buddha developed a dangerous path that consisted of a type of understanding that had to be understood experimentally.[57] Eliade has no qualms in seeing the Buddha's approach to soteriology as being parallel, if not identical, to the negative formulations in the Upaniṣads, such as the well-known *neti neti*. The development of meditation for the Buddhist ascetic in early Buddhism constituted a "rediscovery" of the Buddha's truths in light of his or her own experience. The techniques of mindfulness are then seen as largely preliminary to the more esoteric practice of the Buddhist *dhyānas*. According to Eliade, the Buddha's practice and teaching of the *dhyānas* was representative of his inclination toward mystical experimentation and his distrust for the speculative systems and theistic practices of his day.[58]

The *dhyānas* and, by extension, the *ārūpya dhyānas*, which Eliade refers to as the *samāpattis*, are discussed in their phenomenological progression as culminating in *nirodhasamāpatti*. Using Rhys Davids's translation of the *Dīgha Nikāya* and referring to Śantideva's *Śikṣāsamuccaya*, Eliade demonstrates what he believes are scriptural bases for asserting that the attainment of cessation as a ninth stage of *dhyāna* is considered equivalent to liberation, showing the strong affinity between Buddhist and non-Buddhist yoga. He argues, however, that it was on the point of *saṃjñāveditanirodha samāpatti* that Buddhists distinguish themselves as having a unique doctrine that is liberating.[59] He notes the Buddhist claims that non-Buddhists have access to meditative states prior to *nirodha*, which are characterized by the *saṃprajñāta* and *asaṃprajñāta* classes of *samādhi*. It is clear that Eliade sees the modality of *samādhi* here as being the central point of the liberation process, that in comparison to the development of mindfulness and insight, it is a more advanced liberating process. The Buddha, then, can be characterized first and foremost by his yogic attainments, but if the ascetic is to follow in Buddha's footsteps, then he or she must know the path, and thus the primary danger in the yogic ascension is the danger of mistaking blissful heavenly states for the final goal.[60]

It is clear that Eliade's portrayal develops a dichotomy between the Theravāda presentations of the life and character of the Buddha and those of the Mahāyāna, which are seen as being much later compositions. The idea that the Buddha appears to be a "rationalist" in his representations by the Theravāda tradition is a perspective that many now see as a product of the imagination of early American and European scholars of Buddhism and an issue that may have had some impact on Eliade's work. However, Eliade does point out some crucial distinctions to the rationalist image of the Buddha that temper his analysis significantly. The most important of them is his strong awareness of the tension between what he calls "gnosis" and "mystical" experience, which he discusses subsequent to the *dhyāna* attainments. These are seen as being representative of two trends, namely, the "experimentalists" *(jhāins)* and the "speculatives" *(dhammayogis).*[61] This split is particularly important regarding conceptions of the nature of Buddhist practice, the differentiation of numinous and cessative types, and the shift or relationship between *śramaṇa* traditions as being either central or peripheral with the culture at large. This discussion elucidates the idea that Buddhism contains a tension between scholastic tendencies that is oriented toward Abhidharma-type pursuits and those of the more yogic character. Eliade believes that "there is sufficient evidence to prove that the Buddha always closely connected knowledge with a meditation experience of the yogic type."[62] This is further illustrated, according to Eliade, by the characteristics of the monks who constituted the Sangha and were distinguished according to their respective discursive and experiential knowledge. This issue culminates in the question of the possibility of *nirvāṇa* without recourse to the *enstatic* means of yogic meditation, a subject that is of great significance to conceptions of Buddhist soteriology but in which Eliade senses a "resistance to yogic excesses" as its basis.[63] The distinction between the experimentation and scholasticism also demonstrates one of the fundamental rifts in the interpretation of religion, between doctrine and experience, and it can also be compared to ritual, another dimension of religion that is often portrayed as being in a unique domain.

However, according to Leah Zahler, Eliade's view on this matter is problematic, due to the predominance of the "*śamatha* precedes *vipaśyanā*" model in Theravāda and Mahāyāna contexts, and due to the fact Eliade seems to want to split apart experience from doctrine.[64] Zahler, in association with Collett Cox, argues that there may well be a *praxis* to scholasticism as well that lies somewhere between the conceptions of "pure practice" or "pure scholasticism."[65] Zahler relates this to Gelukpa presentations of *śamatha-vipaśyanā* that serve only as scholastic subjects but are not formally put into practice. This is related to our earlier discussion, in that it hints at the idea that even "practice texts" can serve a more scholastic-ritual practice. Although there is significant evidence to argue for a "ritualized" aspect of scholasticism, a concept that scholasticism has a *praxis* dimension to it, there is still an important difference here. What makes more sense, rather than collapsing the whole distinction, which is what Sharf attempts to do, is to find the middle ground in the discussion. Scholasticism is not a "passive" endeavor and may well have a sense of "experience" or "experimentation" common with meditative enterprises. On the other hand, meditative *praxis* has a doctrinal, conceptual foundation, however few the "superstructures" may be, that provides for its development as a nondiscursive enterprise. Each shares in the other to some degree, but there is no question that there is a significant difference in the degree to which each dimension intersects the other. Just as you might not expect a scholastic to have a profound sense of what the fruits of *śamatha* are experientially, one should not expect the yogin, who has devoted a more significant amount of time to cultivating those states, to be able to situate his or her practices in the greater scope of doctrine in a defensible way. We have to be careful, however, in making this distinction too strict, and in postulating that a religious practitioner must be one or the other, when in fact he or she may well be both to a greater or lesser degree.

Speaking from the viewpoint of History of Religions, Eliade argues that the methodologies of liberation may well be understood to yield similar fruit. As with comparisons of different types of practices, such as are found in his comparisons of yoga and shamanism, Eliade argues that the different perspectives are nevertheless oriented toward the experience of the sacred through the "abolition of mundane life" and through a symbolic death and rebirth process.[66] In this vision of phenomenology, these different methodologies present different strategies for accessing the timelessness of the sacred in the midst of profane reality, a transformation that he believes lies at the heart of religious phenomena. He argues that the Buddhist monk performing ritual circumambulation entered into this alternate universe and "annihilated profane experience," just as the meditating monk did. This is a step farther, in some respects, from other arguments considering the range of Buddhist practices that has attributed the differences to either the development of the Buddha's thought, the development of the Buddha's doctrine by his community, or the intrusion of foreign ideas into the doctrinal foundation. On one level, Eliade's thought does not seem so problematic, in that both are arguing for, in general language, a transcendence that is a transformation or destruction of what would be considered the "mundane" state of affairs. But the question that arises is whether the experiences themselves share similar, concrete characteristics. It can be argued that this is close, if not identical, to postulating a universal theory of mysticism or religious experience, one that decontextualizes the practices that fall under its observations. Needless to say, Eliade's position raises serious issues regarding how to deal with these variations in practice, whether we see them as being questions of ritual, doctrine, or meditative practice.

A more pragmatic and less controversial examination of yoga in the Theravāda tradition can be found in Winston King's *Theravāda Meditation: The Buddhist Transformation of Yoga*. Unlike Eliade, whose work is a thoroughly comparative text that attempts to get at the nature of yoga in the pan-Indian, and even pan-Asian context, King's work is primarily an attempt to understand the role of meditation uniquely in the context of Theravāda's relationship with the yoga techniques characteristic of the early Buddhist context. The image that King develops is of a Buddhism that sees itself as an autonomous, non-Brahmanical tradition, one that grew out of an Indian yogic context but is nevertheless identified more by how it diverges from earlier tradition than how it converges. As an extension of the Theravāda's presentation of meditation, King's study appeals strongly to the Pali sources as a means of understanding early Buddhism. The Buddha is understood to have integrated the methods of his teachers, Ālāra and Udraka, with those that he discovered as a youth into a soteriological schema epitomized by his enlightenment experience.[67]

King's presentation mirrors Eliade's analysis in at least two important ways. The doctrinal foundations can be seen as "orienting" the meditative experience toward certain characteristics, in that the insight meditation process provides the context for the development of *śamatha*, and there is a sense of progression from external and ethical aspects of practice toward internal and meditative aspects. Acknowledging the viability of scholarship that discusses a common substratum of both Buddhist and Hindu systems of yoga based on a practical discipline as opposed to a superstructure of theory, King believes that finding the root of the *dhyāna* structure is a problem that may well be impossible to solve.[68] However, he is not afraid to note the similarities between Pātañjala-yoga and the Buddhist yogic system, stating in essence that both traditions develop a set of progressively subtle meditations, although yielding "different experiential and theoretical results."[69] He does, however, see a tension in the development of meditation theory in the Pali texts, particularly with regard to the formula of enlightenment as containing elements of *dhyāna*, the *ārūpya dhyānas*, and the attainment of cessation *nirodha-samāpatti*.[70] This is further complicated for King by questions regarding the nature and role of *vipassanā* in the liberation process and its character as distinguishing Buddhist and non-Buddhist meditation and soteriology. In the *nirodhasamāpatti* as well as the *ārūpyadhyāna* states, he demonstrates the uncertainty regarding the role of each with the attainment of liberation, or the lack thereof.[71] King, noting the lack of clarity on the issue in the Pali sources, nevertheless wants to follow Buddhaghosa's interpretation of the advanced meditative states as being secondary to the liberative process of developing insight, or even being unnecessary.[72]

Following the lead of Heiler, King wonders if the formless states were added to the Theravāda meditation system through a process of "reyoganization" that took place long after the development of the early Buddhist communities, or perhaps even the possibility of two variant Buddhist communities coming together.[73] Although he feels quite comfortable asserting the Theravāda's emphasis on *vipassanā* as being the Buddhist qua Buddhist practice, he nevertheless notes the marginal position of the more complex *śamatha* types of meditation that receive a significant amount of attention and emphasis in both canonical and noncanonical accounts.[74] King demonstrates an acute awareness of the importance of non-Buddhist yoga methodologies both in the early and later phases of the development of the Pali *sūttas*, as well as the importance of noncanonical sources such as Buddhaghosa's *Visuddhimagga*. Though briefly referring to Patañjali's system, including a reference to the statements of Stephan Beyer on the parallelism of Buddhist *samādhi* and Classical Yoga, King does not spend a significant amount of time discussing the possibilities of influence and development as extending from the Buddhist tradition into the Hindu and Jaina systems.[75] However, one of the stronger points he does make is that there are some ambiguities in the canonical sources about the role of yoga in soteriology, particularly the more complex yogic presentations of the formless realms and cessation. The role of *nirodhasamāpatti*, particularly in the modern Buddhist context, is problematic, in that *vipassanā* methods and the development of liberating insight are considered the essential teaching, and *dhyāna* types of accomplishments are either unimportant or forgotten methods. This has been a subject of considerable controversy in the realm of Buddhist studies, where there has been difficulty understanding why such an important part of Buddhist meditation theory *(samatha)* has become not only a marginal practice but one that might even receive ridicule by some practitioners.[76]

A point of particular controversy here is the problem of the sequence of insight and concentration methodologies. King suggests that one way of solving the problem would be to appeal to the presentation of alternate *vipassanā-jhāna* sequences where *samatha* and *vipassanā* precede one another respectively, are together, or contain only one member.[77] The difficulty of reconciling the different canonical views complicates the presentation, particularly if we allow for the possibility of multiple soteriological visions being presented under the rubric of a unified tradition. Nevertheless, a particularly critical point here is that there are a great number of variations in understanding the relationship between *samatha* and *vipassanā*, both in terms of the role of *nirodhasamāpatti* and in the sequence of meditation that is followed with the priority of *samatha* or *vipaśyanā*.

SAMĀDHI AT THE CENTER: DETERMINING THE STRUCTURE OF *DHYĀNA*

The specifics of *śamatha* and the development of *dhyāna* and *samādhi* as they are related between the Classical Yoga system and the Buddhist tradition have been discussed on a more technical level by Lance Cousins. Cousins notes that an "artificial appearance of difference" is often superimposed on this relationship.[78] Noting the tendency of scholars to see Buddhism and Brahmanical yoga as operating in separate realms, Cousins makes the case for their development in relationship to one another to different degrees in several phases of their development.[79] Noting the relationship between the Buddhist *dhyāna* series and the development of *saṃprajñāta samādhi* as portrayed in the YS, Cousins proceeds to demonstrate a number of points where the Classical Yoga system becomes more intelligible in light of Buddhist sources. He notes the primary significance of *vitarka* (Pali *vitakka*) and *vicāra* as primary elements in Buddhist *samādhi* as characterized by both Pali (including the *Nikāyas*, *Peṭakopadesa*, *Milindapañha*, *Vimuttimagga*, and *Visuddhimagga*) and Sanskrit sources (including the *Abhidharmakośabhāṣya*, *Abhidharmāvatāra*, *Abhidharmadīpa*, and *Abhidharmasamuccaya*), and he follows this with an analysis of these elements as represented in the Classical Yoga system. With Theravāda, a pertinent point he notes is the progression of *dhyāna* characterized by the absence of the mental factor of *vitakka* in the fivefold system of *dhyāna* practice, characterizing a fluid notion of *dhyāna* regarding mental factors.[80] In the Mahāyāna context, he points out the notion of "subtle" versus "gross" mental factors in the development of the stages of *dhyāna* and thus *samādhi*.[81] Cousins argues that the relationship between the mental factors constituting the yoga *dhyāna* system *(vitarka, vicāra, ānanda, asmitā)* is one of the modifications of the respective Buddhist list of factors *(vitarka, vicāra, prīti, upekṣa)*, a juxtaposition that Sénart and de la Vallée Poussin argue for as well.[82]

Cousins understands the yoga system to have shifted the psychological orientation of the movement from a gross to a subtle to a cosmological basis (i.e., Sāṃkhya), sharing in essence the Abhidharma notion that higher states of consciousness are more subtle, as are their objects.[83] This point needs to be taken with care, as the cosmological correlates of *samādhi* in Mahāyāna and Theravāda *śamatha* and in the Classical Yoga system are quite notable, as there is a correlation between meditative attainment and rebirth or manifestation in particular cosmological realms. According to Cousins, the notion of gross versus subtle states in the progression of *dhyāna* provides for a possible reinterpretation of the development of *samādhi* in the YS in a unique way. He argues that the designations of *nirvitarka* and *nirvicāra* may specify not separate or unique *samāpatti* states but rather subtle states to be attained through overcoming those factors, respectively, the *savicāra* and *sānanda* states.[84] This is particularly significant in that it would reconcile what appear to be conflicting views in the YS and YBh with the stages of *samādhi*.[85] In addition, although Cousins does not point it out directly, the Theravāda notion of a five-*dhyāna* progression in which there are separate stages characterized by the elimination of *vitarka* and *vicāra* from the mental continuum seems to be more in parity with the stepwise progression of the YS. However, this may be problematic in that it extends the Buddhist *samāpatti* system to include a range of terms that does not match with respective terms in the Yoga system. Also, this system only seems to work if the mental factor of *nirvicāra* includes both *sānanda* and *sasmitā*, which is not clear in the progression of *sūtras* at the end of *samādhipāda*, where this discussion is found. If the YS is viewed as a unitary text, then it would have to be assumed that the establishment of *nirvicāra* implies the development of those factors, otherwise it would contradict the earlier (YS I.17) description of all of these forms as unique entities.[86] Whicher, for example, argues for a fourfold classification of *samāpatti* states, in which *nirvicāra* contains itself, *ānanda*, and *asmitā* elements, a classification that would allow for the parallelism of the *ānanda* and *asmitā* terms. Furthermore, one of the limitations in Cousins's work, which may be more practical than theoretical, is his lack of attention to the *nirodha* aspect of the YS, most particularly *asaṃprajñāta samādhi*. As noted earlier, Sénart identifies the fourth *dhyāna* of the Buddhist system with *asaṃprajñāta samādhi*, thus eliminating the necessity of dealing with it as a separate scheme. Cousins seems satisfied to demonstrate the near equivalency of the Buddhist *dhyānas* with the structure of *saṃprajñāta samādhi*. This identification leaves open the possibilities of comparison of the *nirodha* aspects of the respective traditions with the *ārūpya* and *nirodhasamāpatti* states and *vipaśyanā* meditation. Cousins is apparently content to stay on the more stable ground of the lower levels of *dhyāna*, which is not surprising due to the fact that solid evidence for comparison is stronger in that domain.

Edward Crangle has recently worked more broadly on a number of problems presented in the Classical Yoga-Buddhism comparison. The foundation for his work is examining the range of meditative practitioners in early Indian history, including the *ṛsis*, *munis*, *yatis*, *brahmacārins*, *keśins*, *saṃnyāsins*, and *bhikṣus*.[87] Crangle endeavors to demonstrate the continuity between Upaniṣadic, Classical Yoga, and Buddhist sources and the influence and counterinfluence that these traditions have had on each other. Noting the structure of meditative practices found in key Upaniṣads, such as the Śvetāsvatara and Maitrī, and their relationship to the forms of Buddhism, Classical Yoga, and Vedic practices, Crangle argues for a continuous development throughout the ancient and classical periods.[88] This continuity has at its foundation the concept of *dhī* in the Vedic context and possibly an aboriginal yoga, which becomes the association of *yoga-upāsanā* in the Upaniṣads and the subsequent development of the *śamatha-vipaśyanā* distinction in the Buddhist context.[89] Influences are understood to have taken place at nearly every juncture, with possible aboriginal influences upon the Vedic tradition, and vice versa, yielding early Upaniṣadic doctrines that provided the context for the development of Buddhist techniques adapted in the later Upaniṣads and in the Classical Yoga system. Though noting, in affinity with Eliade, that Buddhist sources often criticize the non-Buddhist yoga practitioner's *samādhi*, Crangle feels comfortable asserting that these two traditions are sharing a common soteriological practice that leads to a common goal.[90] The goal, characterized by cessation, is arguably one in which there is physical continuity of the practitioner, apparently transitioning into the liberated state but not necessarily causing the destruction of the physical body (i.e., death) in the process.[91] The "ladder-like" progression of *dhyāna* and thus *samādhi* in the two traditions is seen to lead toward a similar goal, perhaps founded in the common basis of the two traditions or, as Crangle would likely argue, in the influence of Buddhism on the Brahmanical tradition. We would add that the *samāpatti* and *nirodha* elements in "tension" are notable, as are the cosmological correlates of these two traditions, implicitly suggesting that the attainments in *dhyāna* of refined consciousness have metaphysical and cosmological implications.

Crangle's orientation toward this discussion is that of looking at the relationship between *samādhi* in the YS and the Buddhist notions of *ārūpya dhyāna*.[92] He orients the Classical Yoga system with the Buddhist *dhyāna* series in a stepwise fashion but with a different structure than we have seen before. On the side of Classical Yoga, we have a progression of the elements of *samādhi* in characteristic groups formed of the *sa*-forms *(savitarka, savicāra, sānanda, sasmitā)*, a set of *nirvitarka* and *nirvicāra*, and individual sets of *nirānanda* and *nirasmitā samādhi*.[93] These groupings all fall under the characterization of *saṃprajñāta samādhi* according to this scheme and are placed parallel to the first, second, third, and fourth *dhyāna* states, respectively. The state of *asaṃprajñāta*, equivalent to *dharmamegha samādhi* and as a form of *sabija*, or "seeded" *samādhi*, according to Patañjali, is identified with the four *ārūpya dhyānas* of the Buddhist system, yielding an interesting comparison of *asaṃprajñāta samādhi* with the four "formless" levels of meditation. The progression is crowned by the identification of the liberated state of yogic *kaivalya*, *nirbija samādhi*, with the attainment of *nirvāṇa*, and, by extension, the identification of *cittavṛttinirodha* in the context of Pātañjala Yoga with the *nirodhasamāpatti* or *saṃjñāvedayitanirodha* of Buddhism. In this scheme, both the Buddhist and Classical Yoga systems are seen to have integral methodologies that lead through an organized and a logical meditative progression toward the ultimate state of liberation. This scheme also presupposes that the YS is not a composite text but rather is rather a unified soteriological vision based upon a progression of meditative states. Crangle does not, however, demonstrate why there should be such an intimate relationship, and what ramifications this has upon our understandings of soteriology in the Classical Yoga and Buddhist contexts, issues that we will address at length later.

Fluid Boundaries:
Cultural Currents and Tradition Texts

Johannes Bronkhorst has written as substantially as any other scholar on the relationship of Classical Yoga and Buddhism. His research involves many of the most controversial subjects in the study of South Asian religion, most notably the origins of Buddhism and the early *śramaṇa* communities in India, including the Hindu, Buddhist, and Jaina traditions. In his work *The Two Traditions of Meditation in Ancient India*, Bronkhorst ambitiously sets out to uncover the earliest strata of Buddhist scripture, differentiating it from what he believes are encroachments in Buddhist literature by Hindu and Jaina perspectives. He also focuses on the contrasting modes of knowledge and *praxis*, an issue that Eliade saw as being crucial in discussing yoga. Contrasting the practices of Buddhism with its contemporary "mainstream" rivals, Bronkhorst sets out to paint a picture of Buddhism that has been clarified by removing non-Buddhist perspectives. The picture he paints is a composite image of mainstream meditative tendencies and the more analytical tendencies represented by Buddhist meditation. In addition, Bronkhorst provides insights into the development of yoga alongside Buddhism, through an analysis of yoga as represented in the Mahābhārata, in Pātañjala Yoga, and to some degree in the Upaniṣads as well. He is quite clear in his assertions that the Pātañjala Yoga system is dependent theoretically and textually on the Buddhist tradition, offering numerous points of conjunction between the two.

The chief opposition that Bronkhorst sees in the meditative traditions of Buddhism, Hinduism, and Jainism is that of an introvertive, inactivity-based meditation where elements such as withdrawal of the senses, restriction of breathing, and stoppage of thought take precedence versus a more cognitive type of meditation that seeks a particular perception of the world and its character. In this analysis, Jaina meditation is contrasted to the meditation described by the Buddha, demonstrating the difference in orientation between the Buddhist and Jaina attitudes toward meditation, even to the degree of identifying the Jaina methods as "violent" versus the more "peaceful" and "cognitive" Buddhist meditation.[94] The characteristics of Jaina meditation include the stoppage of all mental and physical activity, mindfulness, peacefulness, nonclinging, and others.[95] In addition, Bronkhorst would like to argue that the Hindu yoga systems parallel this closely in their figurations in the Mahābhārata and in the Upaniṣads, emphasizing the significance of meditative practices involving breath control, remaining motionless, and fasting as a foundation for the stoppage of sensory and mental activity.[96] This form of meditation is understood as mainstream meditation, containing practices to some degree antithetical to the Buddhist tradition yet at the same time over the centuries exerting a notable influence upon it.

Bronkhorst's notion of "introvertive" yoga closely follows Eliade's interpretation of yoga as *enstasis*, ultimately culminating in a state of cessation that is a radical type of disjunction from the world. However, we also could argue that this dimension is signified by the cessative quality of yogic *kaivalya* in both the Classical Yoga and Jaina traditions. This follows closely with a Buddhist interpretation that would hold that the *nirodha* of such types of yoga is inferior to that of Buddhism. Where this becomes problematic, however, is in the question of the role and purpose of *nirodhasamāpatti* in the Buddhist context, and the degree to which we can correlate that with this possible "earlier strata" of *śramaṇa-yoga* thought based on suppression. Another aspect that needs resolution is the other dimension, the numinous, which is part and parcel of yogic development in the Hindu, Jaina, and Buddhist contexts. Whether we see this numinous state, characterized by the notion of *samāpatti*, on the same path as cessation or introversion, it nevertheless is characterized by a more purified form of awareness. Another question that we brought up earlier that is particularly significant as well is the role and status of the liberated individual and what, if any, relationship she or he has with the world, an issue tied intimately to notions of cessation that are characteristic both of so-called mainstream and Buddhist traditions.

According to Bronkhorst, Buddhist influences on mainstream religious practices are evident throughout the Hindu tradition, most notably in sources such as the Upaniṣads (such as *Maitrī*, *Yogakuṇḍali*, and *Muktikā Upaniṣads*), the *Mahābhārata* (MBh), and in the YS. The use of *dhyānayoga* in the MBh demonstrates a Hindu tradition appropriating Buddhist terminology and technique, yet in a manner that elides elements not consistent with their soteriological purposes.[97] With the YS, Bronkhorst notes the notion of *cittavṛttinirodha* as being indicative of the mainstream meditation tradition of Jainism and Hinduism, where thought is forcibly stopped as a liberative technique, a point that is illustrated in YS I.2–16.[98] He contrasts this to the other type of yoga being discussed in the latter portions of the first chapter of the YS, such as the identification of the *nirbija samādhi* state with *asaṃprajñāta samādhi*. The second type of yoga corresponds to the Buddhist system, being that point where the state of *asaṃprajñāta* is overcome through the application of *prajñā*, correlating with Buddhist thought regarding the notions of the destruction of the *saṃskāras* and the development of inner tranquility, *adhyātmaprasāda*.[99] In this system, the state of *asaṃprajñāta samādhi* becomes identified with what Bronkhorst calls the "five states added to the four *dhyānas* in Buddhist scriptures," the *ārūpya dhyānas* and the attainment of cessation, *nirodhasamāpatti*.[100] This system would then correlate with Crangle's presentation of the *dhyāna* system, where the yogic *samādhis* in the YS have direct correlates with those of the Buddhist system, as opposed to the presentations of Sénart and de la Valleé Poussin, who do not take the "formless states" into account. The development of the "ninefold" system of *rūpadhyāna*, *arūpyadhyāna*, and *nirodhasamāpatti*, or *saṃjñāvedayitanirodha*, would then correspond to the mainstream influences on the Buddhist tradition and therefore would demonstrate a significant parallelism to mainstream yogic practices.[101] However, the "original" Buddhist soteriology for Bronkhorst is composed of the development of the four *dhyānas* as the basis for the *prajñā* characteristic of the Buddha's enlightenment experience and the earliest sermons.[102] The meditation methodology ascribed to the Buddha is further characterized by its novelty among the ascetic communities of ancient India.[103] The YS is understood as a hybrid of the mainstream and Buddhist traditions, as are the soteriological descriptions characteristic of the sophisticated Buddhist meditation systems found in the late canonical accounts and in Buddhist Abhidharma philosophy.

With the YS specifically, Bronkhorst makes a number of points that are significant to the development of the Classical Yoga system. Like a number of other scholars, he questions the degree to which the Classical Yoga system should be understood as an autonomous entity. This is epitomized for Bronkhorst by the identification of the YBh as being *pātañjala sāṃkhyapravacana yogaśāstra*, "Patañjali's authoritative book on Yoga, expository of *Sāṃkhya*."[104] As opposed to the reading of "yoga philosophy" as referring to the *yoga darśana*, Bronkhorst points out the attribution of this notion in early sources to the systems of Nyāyā and Vaiśeṣika.[105] This is coupled with the ambiguity of the role of Īśvara in the YS and the YBh, which are often said to be "Seśvara Sāṃkhya," despite the fact that it is not altogether clear in the Indian philosophical context if the notion of Īśvara more broadly understood relates to the sense found in the YS.[106] Bronkhorst concludes from the available evidence that rather than viewing the Classical Yoga tradition as an autonomous entity, it is better understood as a complementary system connected to variety of different philosophies.[107] Such a position would seem consistent with presentations of yoga in the contemporary context, as we do not find a unique and an autonomous Classical Yoga lineage but rather see expositions on the *yoga darśana* from a range of different sectarian organizations.

The *Bhāṣya*, according to Bronkhorst, contains what appears to be a reinterpretation, and possibly even a reorganization, of an another yoga text or set of texts.[108] Bronkhorst argues that this point is apparent in a number of contexts, including notions of the degrees of yogins, in the discussion of omniscience, and due to ambiguities in the syntax and sequence of *sūtras* relating to basic versus advanced practices.[109] This suggests that through the appropriate means there is a possibility of reconstructing, at least in part, a proto-yoga text that lies in the substratum of the YS that is presented in the context of the YBh. In addition, the author of the YBh is understood to have accordingly organized and edited the proto-YS text to suit his own intention, and in doing so concretized the YS text in its current form. Noting evidence that weakens a case for identifying the author of the YBh as Vyāsa, Bronkhorst argues that it makes more sense to identify the author of the YBh as either Sāṃkhya philosopher Patañjali or Sāṃkhya philosopher Vindhyavāsin.[110] In both cases, there are textual as well as philosophical bases for asserting the plausibility of the particular author, apparently more than would support the more traditional appellation of the YBh author as Vyāsa.[111] Thus Bronkhorst concludes that the YBh was likely authored by a philosophical writer who was "no expert in practical yogic matters," who brought together the *sūtras* constituting the YS under the Sāṃkhya rubric to demonstrate the Sāṃkhya view.[112] This type of analysis is mirrored in principle by other scholars, such as Chapple, who have looked at the possibility of distinguishing the views of Patañjali and Vyāsa and of establishing an interpretation of Patañjali's YS as a text to be understood on its own terms.[113]

Through identifying the viewpoint of Vyāsa with concrete historical Sāṃkhya philosophers, Bronkhorst recognizes the context of the composition of the YBh and the YS in a concrete manner. This also allows us to understand how yogic terminology and philosophy were disseminated in the Hindu context and to some degree to non-Hindu, particularly Buddhist, sources. Vindhyavāsin, for example, clearly demonstrates a philosophical orientation that represents an engagement with Buddhist ideas. On the other hand, it is apparent that Buddhist philosophers were aware of his positions as well. It is indeed fascinating to consider the possibility of other texts from which the compiler of the YBh constructed the YS in order to demonstrate the Sāṃkhya view. One avenue of research that we touched on earlier that may bring this issue to further light would be to look at the yoga tradition text attributed to Hiraṇyagarbha as a possible "missing link" in the study of Classical Yoga, as suggested by Chakravarti. The fact that concepts such as *nirodha* and of *kriyā* were understood in contexts prior to the YS is illuminating from the viewpoint of both the theory and practice of yoga, and perhaps even more so regarding the dimension of practice. Though it may be clearer how the author of the YBh is representing the Sāṃkhya viewpoint, this position only deepens the questions regarding the nature of the YS, including its authorship, its integrity as a text, or lack thereof, and the formation of the practices characterized in the YS and their relationship to sources in Buddhist and other traditional expositions.

In this context, Koichi Yamashita has noted the deep relationships between the Classical Yoga system and the encounter between Sāṃkhya and Buddhist Abhidharma, particularly with notions of time and change found in the Sarvāstivāda school of Buddhist philosophy.[114] As we have noted, it is quite apparent that there is a strong relationship between the YBh and Abhidharma theory, to the degree that Vyāsa and even Patañjali are considered directly criticizing or reacting to particular Buddhist doctrines, such as the notion of a self-luminous mind. Particular doctrines that are of crucial significance in this sphere are the notions of the *dharma* and *dharmin*, that is, notions of manifest properties and the substratum of properties according to *pariṇāma* theory, and the notion of *citta*. It is apparent that the author of the

YBh propounded views regarding the nature of substances discussed and criticized at length by Vasubandhu in his *Abhidharmakośa*, primarily under the rubric of Sarvāstivāda philosophy.[115] This parallels the position of the YBh with regard to how change is to be understood from the viewpoints of substance and time.[116] Such parallelism includes numerous common arguments and phrases used by Vyāsa that are found in both the YBh and in the *Abhidharmakośa.* Although distinguishing itself from Buddhism through the criticism of the ideas of a self-luminous mind and of the unreality of the objective world (i.e., of the Vijñānavāda), the yoga system nevertheless propounds an understanding of the mind as the nexus of psychophysical activity that meshes well with Buddhist Abhidharma conceptions of mind.[117] It is clear that there is an intimate relationship between a number of Sarvāstivāda and Vaibhāṣika theories and those of the Sāṃkhya, indicating either influence of one by the other or a common foundation for the development of each theoretically.[118]

Chakravarti has suggested that this may be in part due to the conversion of non-Buddhist philosophers to the Buddhist tradition, thereby importing Sāṃkhya concepts into the Abhidharma fold.[119] As in the case of looking at the development of yoga as a religious phenomenon, and particularly as a practical discipline, it is difficult to determine the progression of ideas or how these ideas moved across traditional and sectarian boundaries. It is clear that on a philosophical level, the relationship between Sarvāstivāda philosophy and the YBh is an important one and would benefit greatly from further examination. Perhaps an understanding of the development of *dhyāna* in the context of the Sarvāstivāda would shed further light on that important dimension as well, as would an examination of the perspectives of Abhidharma and early Vijñānavāda on mind and meditation. Kalupahana has argued that Pātañjala Yoga can be considered a reworking of Upaniṣadic epistemology in an attempt to deal with Buddhist Abhidharma criticisms.[120] This assertion, however, depends on viewing the yoga trends in the Upaniṣads as being pre-Buddhist, which may be problematic.[121] Clearly, though, the doctrine of *anātman* suggests a rejection of a view of self, at the most basic level of selfhood in a conventional sense and on a more extended level the metaphysical notions of permanent and abiding selfhood that become part of the concept in the Upaniṣadic literature. Kalupahana also argues that the yogic processes out of which the Buddha developed his theory were freedom of thought *(ceto-vimutti)* and freedom through wisdom *(paññā-vimutti)*, which ultimately developed into the *śamatha-vipaśyanā (samatha-vipassanā)* distinction.[122]

Connections to the Abhidharma literature in terms of the meditative practice of *dhyāna* are plentiful, and the most important of these may well be the notion of the *acitta samāpattis*, namely, the development of *asaṃjñisamāpatti* and *nirodhasamāpatti*. Yamashita notes the intimate relationship between the concept of *asaṃjñisamāpatti* in the *Abhidharmakośa* and the concept of *asaṃprajñāta samādhi* in the YS, particularly the notion of the cessation of mind and its functions (*citta* and *caitta*).[123] Another point of significance is that *nirodhasamāpatti* in the Buddhist context can also refer to the restraint of *citta* and *caitta*, according to Yamashita's reading of the *Abhidharmakośakārikā*.[124] However, Yamashita problematically argues that the *nirodha* in this context occurs in the highest stage (the fourth) of the *arūpya* type of meditation, namely, *naivasamjñānāsaṃjñāyatana*. *Nirodha* should instead be considered a unique attainment due to the necessity of conjoining *śamatha* and *vipaśyanā*. Yamashita does, however, point out an interesting distinction between the attainment of *asaṃjñisamāpatti* by ordinary persons and the attainment of *nirodhasamāpatti* only available to Buddhist practitioners.[125] The question that this raises, of course, is whether or not the notion of an "inferior" *asamjñisamāpatti* is a reference to yoga practices such as those found in the YS in which *asaṃprajñāta* was considered the highest meditative attainment. Another interesting point to note is the connection of *nirodhasamāpatti* with the status of one free from passion, the *vītarāga*, which is the appelation of one of the stages of the Mahāyāna Buddhist *śravakabhūmis*, the *vītarāgabhūmi*, and also of a person or condition used to stabilize the mind in the *samādhipāda* of the YS.[126] Another question that arises as well, one that we have mentioned before, is the ambiguous place of *nirodhasamāpatti* in Buddhist soteriology, the question of whether it constitutes liberation itself or whether it is a complement to a more discursive type of perception, such as that of the Four Noble Truths.

The intimate connection between the philosophy and meditative discipline of the YS, the YBh, and Buddhist Abhidharma is an issue that has been summed up quite well by Gerald Larson in two articles on the formulation of the *yoga darśana*. Following in the tradition of Oldenburg, Stcherbatsky, Sénart, de la Vallée Poussin, and Frauwallner, Larson argues for a balanced perspective on the Yoga-Buddhism relationship, one that incorporates evidence for a multifaceted developmental scheme.[127] Like Bronkhorst, Larson is concerned with the notion of distinct philosophical schools being imposed upon data that do not support such a reality but rather a conglomeration of different viewpoints.[128] However, Larson is willing to consider the antiquity of Sāṃkhya and Yoga, beyond the bounds of the "classical phase," on the basis of fragmentary materials that provide for the possibility of an earlier systematic phase of Sāṃkhya, noting the validity of looking at the YS more in light of the *Abhidharmakośa* than the YBh.[129] His argument and agreement with Bronkhorst also deepens if we consider the emphasis he puts on Vindhyavāsin, whom Bronkhorst postulated as a possible author of the YBh, as conflating a "*vijñāna*-cum-*nirodha-samādhi*" from the correlation of the Sāṃkhya philosophical system and the Abhidharma's psychology and meditative techniques.[130] This is demonstrated most concretely in Larson's chronology of the development of the metaphysics of the Sāṃkhya and Yoga traditions, where Vindhyavāsin and Vasubandhu share a common time frame and context of philosophical development.

Using Deutsch's notion of a "tradition text," the idea of an aggregate of works and authors yielding texts considered constitutive of a particular tradition, Larson goes on to describe the YS as a "tradition text" that is the intersection of the earlier "tradition texts" of Sāṃkhya and Buddhist Abhidharma.[131] Noting the veracity of de la Vallée Poussin's research into the plethora of Abhidharma terms scattered throughout the YS, and not just in the fourth *pāda*, Larson demonstrates the solid foundation for such an assertion, ultimately seeing this conjoining as forming a "neo-Sāṃkhya" tradition that comes to its full fruition in the YBh as *"Sāmkhyapravacanabhāṣya."*[132] As in the case of Yamashita, Larson sees the relevant points of contention between Yoga and Buddhist sources as including the nature of *citta* and the notions of time and change *(pariṇāma)* from the viewpoint of the *kṣaṇa*, the *dharmin*, and the *dharmas*.[133] Particularly significant to note as well are issues regarding the subtle body *(sūkṣma-śarīra)*, the phenomenology of experience *(cittavṛtti/pramāṇa)*, god (Īśvara), and omniscience and the omniscients *(sarvajñās)*.[134] He criticizes Frauwallner's analysis of the *samādhi* typologies in the YS as being two types of yoga that have been patched together, what Larson calls the "cognitive intensive" *(saṃprajñāta)* and "cognitive restrictive" *(asaṃprajñāta)* typologies.[135] Larson argues for "a masterful synthesis" of these methodologies through adaptation of materials from Brahmanical and Buddhist sources, whereby a "revitalized Sāṃkhya" emerges, complete with a new and "sophisticated philosophical psychology."[136] The notion of Yoga as "neo-Sāṃkhya" is the foundation for Larson's conclusions regarding the success of the vision of yoga that is formulated in the YS and concretized by the YBh. As contentious as this may be, the synthesis of *samādhi*, or *dhyāna*, is one of the stronger aspects of Larson's theory, something that becomes clearer as we look at the YS from a comparative perspective. The emphasis on the Sāṃkhya element notwithstanding, there are arguably aspects of the YS that are much more strongly tied to its Upaniṣadic and Buddhist counterparts in which similar soteriological concerns are at work with *samādhi*.

A Reconsideration of Meditative Theory and Practice

At this point the deep structural similarities between the Classical Yoga system and a number of Buddhist interpretations of meditation should be clear. Whether or not we grant the possible existence of a *yoga pur* or the concept that the early Buddhist and early yoga traditions contained some notion of pure *praxis*, the numerous levels of comparison demonstrate an intimate and abiding relationship between the meditative practices of Classical Yoga and Buddhism. With the Classical Yoga tradition, it can be asserted that it offers insights into the *śramaṇa*-yoga practices in a manner that few other systems do. This is not to say that Classical Yoga in its contemporary formulations does not bear the impressions of the many transitional periods of Indian thought. Rather, in the form of the YS text and its commentaries, it bears the imprint of many changes in the philosophical and cultural environment of India. The fact that the YS is so encyclopedic regarding the concepts of meditation demonstrates its syncretic role in bringing together a great range of *śramaṇa* practices, and its engagement with more contemporary ideas. As has been asserted by Sénart, de la Vallée Poussin, and Oldenburg, the Classical Yoga tradition bears the imprint of influences from early Vedic, Upaniṣadic, and Epic religious concepts, from *śramaṇa* asceticism, in its mild and strong forms, and from early strains of Buddhist meditation and later trends in Abhidhamma and Abhidharma scholasticism.

The nature of the relationship between contemplative practice and religious scholasticism is an issue that emerges out of the possibility of a common yoga tradition shared by both Classical Yoga and Buddhism. This is an argument that Eliade has taken up in detail by noting the difference between the so-called *jhāins* and *dhammayogis* in the Theravāda context, the distinction between "experimentalists" and "speculatives."[137] This distinction, represented concretely in the early Buddhist community by the powers of Maudgalyāyana and the discernment of Śāriputra, demonstrates an issue that has been problematic for philosophers of religion throughout India's history as well as for contemporary scholars of these religions. We have argued here for the conception of a continuum between these dimensions of religious thought and application in meditation. This split might be considered a natural consequence of the division between the numinous and cessative dimensions of religious practice so critical within the practice of *dhyāna* itself. If we consider the shifting of the *śramaṇa* traditions from peripheral cults in nature to a central religious tradition or cult, it makes sense that there would be a natural inclination to move toward a scholastic-based system of authority, replacing virtuoso practice with scholasticism and ritual. It naturally follows that we would have the development of highly scholastic interpretations of the meditation systems, particularly represented by attempts to reconcile varied interpretations of such practices and their role in soteriology. Rather than the sense of charismatic authority arising out of the development of meditative practice, instead there would be the arising of a scholastic-based authority that relies on memorization and conceptualization of critical issues, and the ritual exchange of authority within the religious community. As Martin Stuart-Fox notes, it is also quite possible that meditative practice has continued to exist in the context of more esoteric forms of transmission communicated by adepts, while in

Theravāda and Mahāyāna scholasticism, there was a concerted effort to systematize and concretize analytically the different soteriological threads in the *sūttas* and *sūtras*.[138] This would suggest parallel traditions that respectively propagated central and peripheral practices with meditation and yoga, which would fit well with the scheme of village versus forest monastics in the Buddhist context.[139]

This may explain the propensity for the Theravāda to dismiss *śamatha* practice in the context of its scholastic traditions. Following Winston King, who argued that Theravāda slowly left *śamatha* behind due to its Brahmanical associations, it is quite possible that in such a scholastic atmosphere it would make sense to shift attention toward delineation of the nature of cessation, which affords a uniquely Buddhist analysis of the nature of reality and the nature of liberation. In the Southeast Asian context, the numinous dimension and perhaps even the cessative dimension, if we extend the analogy to hostile possession, exist in practical terms in the context of spirit cults, and in the context of forest monastic life.[140] In the context of Mahāyāna, the *śamatha-vipaśyanā* system is largely intact, in part because of the greater role of the numinous dimension throughout its history, in particular, its embracing the *bhakti* model of devotionalism. Also, we can consider the attempt to codify and reconcile the *śamatha-vipaśyanā* system within the Mahāyāna as one to accurately portray the Hīnayāna path in a coherent and unified fashion, as a precursor to the Mahāyāna and Vajrayāna. The attempt to do so, as Paul Griffiths has noted, is difficult for even the great philosopher Vasubandhu who, according to Griffiths, struggled to deal with the tension between Abhidharma speculation and the complexity of the *śamatha* system in its most extensive formulations.[141] This is not to say that such Buddhist scholars and practitioners did not or do not cultivate the *śamatha* system, or the traditional *vipaśyanā* for that matter, but rather that systematic codification implies a scholastic desire to create a unified sense of the Buddhist path that would provide stronger conceptions regarding what was considered authoritative doctrine. This can be argued quite reasonably with respect to the Kamalaśīla's work that was cited earlier, the *Bhāvanākrama*, where a sense of a unified Buddhist path served and still continues to serve as a source of doctrine and as a representation of the Buddhist *mārga* and its methods.

One of the problems with the views of Eliade and King is that they do not accommodate the changing nature of both Hindu and Buddhist interpretations and applications of meditation theory. Whether we talk about philosophical currents or greater tradition texts, it is clear that, over time, significantly different interpretations of meditation appear, three trends of which are the *śramaṇic* type, the Abhidharma type, and the tantric *sādhana* type. As we will examine in the next chapter, the meditative dimensions of Mahāyāna are characterized by the adaptation of the *śamatha-vipaśyanā* model in the development of tantric *sādhana*. Even in the contemporary context of Tibetan Buddhism, the tension between the central and peripheral religious dimensions of Buddhism is apparent in the Gelukpa insistence on the import of a reformed sense of *vinaya* and the more exotic and esoteric dimensions of Nyingmapa meditation, ritual, and possession. As we have noted earlier, Collett Cox and Leah Zahler are correct in stating that there is a subschool of meditative practice that would fall under the rubric of scholasticism. The conception that scholastic education and ritual have their own numinous and cessative characteristics is a powerful one. The ritual recitation of texts, it should be remembered, often is seen as a merit-producing activity, as well as being transformative in the sense of the development of conceptual understanding. This would hint at a theory-practice continuum, where the recitation of texts and the knowledge conferred are seen as being transformational in a manner analogous to meditation on these concepts. We would suggest that there is a sort of *jñānayoga* operating in this frame of reference, that scholastic study is seen as its own end, and that meditation practice is not really considered practical or necessary. This implies that at least some Indian Hindu and Buddhist scholastics were not the types of "believers" that we tend to assume they were and did not feel the compulsion of the philosophy to the degree that they felt liberation was a reasonable or perhaps even a desirable goal.

Beyond postulating a purely ritualized and scholastic practice, however, there is a middle ground. In the YS, for example, it is clear that meditation is not the only method involved in practice. The text itself is quite terse, intended to be memorized, therefore leading to the assumption that the foundation for the study of the YS lies in the commitment of the text to memory, a practice that in itself is surely transformational. This suggests a deeper psychological impact of memorization, perhaps even more so than usually found in conceptual thought, as "embodying" the text. Beyond the simple recitation of the text are a number of important ritual-based practices. The most notable example of this would probably be *tapas* and *svādhyāya*, both of which fall under the category of *niyama* "observances" (the second of the eight limbs of *aṣṭāṅgayoga*) in verse 32 of the *sādhanapāda* (YS II.32). While ritual and *śramaṇic* connotations of *tapas* are clear, the notion of *svādhyāya* is worth looking at a bit more closely. David Carpenter has noted the intimate link between the notion of *svādhyāya* in the context of Classical Yoga and the notions of recitation found in the Vedic tradition.[142] The term itself refers to the going over or "reciting to oneself" of Vedic compositions repeatedly in order to definitively memorize the texts, a practice understood to be a form of *tapas* itself.[143] It indicates an intimate link between Brahmanical ritualism and pedagogy, the development of the metaphorical use of ritual as being equal to or even superior to literal performance.[144] Carpenter also suggests that the association of the practices *tapas*, *svādhyāya*, and *samādhi* in the context of *niyama* suggests an appeal to a threefold model characteristic of Vedic religion.[145] It also is interesting to note that *svādhyāya* results in, according to Patañjali, "union with one's desired deity," *svādhyāyad iṣṭadevatāsaṃprayogaḥ* (YS II.44), a practice that suggests a numinous dimension to the development of the limbs of yoga. Clearly the study and practice as characterized in the YS is far from simply a description of how to meditate but also includes a range of practices that constitutes both opportunities for discursive analysis and a variety of ritual applications and observances. As we have seen, scholars such as Bronkhorst look at the YBh as a Sāṃkhya text that has effectively scholasticized Patañjali's more practice-oriented text. The important point here is that meditation is not antithetical to other types of religious practice in the Hindu or the Buddhist context. Rather, there is a strong sense of complementarity, one that deserves more attention than it has received in contemporary scholarship.

This complementary nature is further indicated by the notion of the functions of *abhyāsa* and *vairāgya* in the context of Classical Yoga, where effort and detachment are seen as the two foundational attitudes or approaches to bringing about the liberated state. *Abhyāsa* and *vairāgya* can be considered the seed forms of the development of *samādhi* as the connection of the *samāpatti* and *nirodha* dimension of *dhyāna*. Effort, *abhyāsa*, inclines toward attainment, *samāpatti*, and at a bare minimum it indicates the inclination toward action on the part of the yogin. Detachment, *vairāgya*, clearly parallels the notion of release or cessation, *nirodha*, attained through the elimination of ignorance and nonvirtuous activity. Just as *abhyāsa* and *vairāgya* are seen as being complementary aspects of yogic development, so are the *samāpatti* and *nirodha* aspects seen as being intimately related to the ultimate goal of yogic development. Both distinctions clearly tie into the distinction between the numinous and cessative, as we have discussed.

THE CONCEPT OF *SAMĀDHI*: THE CONJUNCTION OF THE NUMINOUS AND THE CESSATIVE

The development of the concepts of the numinous and cessative and the understanding of previous attempts to compare the Classical Yoga and Buddhist traditions provide an orientation toward textual sources that establishes a more sophisticated understanding of this relationship. When comparing the development of *samādhi* in Yoga and in Buddhism, it appears that two primary models emerge. In the first, the development of *samādhi* is analogous to the *dhyāna* states, sometimes with *asaṃprajñāta* being equivalent to the fourth *dhyāna* in the Buddhist system, due to the importance of the fourth *dhyāna* in the enlightenment accounts. In the second, the *samādhi* of Classical Yoga is related to both the development of *dhyāna* and to the notion of *nirodhasamāpatti*, or "the attainment of cessation." This second scheme can be further broken down to the degree that one asserts that in the *dhyāna-nirodha* scheme there should be the inclusion of the apocryphal states of the *ārūpya-dhyānas* associated with the attainment of cessation. The inclusion of the *ārūpya* states in the interpretation of the YS relies on the assignment of *ārūpya* status to *asaṃprajñāta samādhi*, and thereby a distinction between the *asaṃprajñāta* and *nirbija samādhi* states. Bronkhorst bases this assertion, as we have seen, upon the idea that the *ārūpyas* eliminate ideation and therefore have a strong thematic relationship with the conception of *asaṃprajñāta*. However, two primary difficulties emerge from this analysis. The first is that if one postulates such a parallelism, then there is difficulty in reconciling it with the fact that the commentary traditions suggest that *asaṃprajñāta* and *nirbija* are the same thing, not different practices. Second, whereas in the notion of *ārūpyasamāpatti* there is a distinct sense of progression through four levels, this analysis is not clearly present in the context of the YS, and therefore it has to be imposed on it.

It makes sense to emphasize the function of *nirodha* as being characteristic of the relationship between these traditions, as it does in the *samāpatti* dimension. The notions of both *nirodhasamāpatti* and *asaṃjñisamāpatti* are elaborated over time in Buddhist philosophical interpretations to refer to attainments of Buddhists and non-Buddhists that approximate liberation, therefore establishing, at minimum, an awareness of the role of *nirodha*-oriented meditative practices in both contexts. Even in Classical Yoga itself, we have the suggestion of inferior levels of meditation that do not constitute liberation, falling short of the noble goal. Vijñānabhikṣu, in his commentary to the YS and YBh, indicates how Vyāsa makes a critical distinction between the *asaṃprajñāta samādhi* of the one whose basis is method *(upāyapratyaya)* and the other whose basis is becoming *(bhavapratyaya)*.[146] Similarly, Buddhist sources, notably Vasubandhu in the *Abhidharmakośakārikā*, indicate a critical distinction between *asaṃjñisamāpatti* (an attainment contingent on the fourth *dhyāna* accessible to non-Buddhists) and *nirodhasamāpatti* (cessation as an extension of the fourth *samāpatti* attainable only by Buddhist practitioners).[147] We also should be aware that the polemical stance of Buddhism with respect to Hindu and likely Jaina sources may well have developed in a period prior to the formulation of the Classical Yoga tradition. Elements of the Classical Yoga system, or perhaps the YS itself, may well have been developed with those specific criticisms in mind, though its adaptations and development may have never been recognized by Buddhist polemicists. Over and above all, though, it is clear from the beginning of the YS, YS I.2 *yogaścittavṛttinirodhaḥ*, that *nirodha* is the goal of the tradition, and that this particular type of *nirodha*, with its cessative character, is central to the characterization of what liberation consists of and is therefore a critical if not *the* critical part of what is meant by *kaivalya*.

Several suggestions can be made about the import of the parallelism of *nirodha* found in the Classical Yoga system and Buddhism. The first is that if we accept the argument that Buddhism sought to distinguish itself from Brahmanical sources, then perhaps the steady syncretism of conceptions of *nirodha* into Hindu sectarian traditions pressed Buddhist scholastics to find new ways to express phenomenologically the experience of liberation that served a uniquely Buddhist interpretation. Second, what is likely even more prevalent here are either pan-Indian notions of meditative development and the possibility of developing unfruitful meditative states or specific Buddhist views that have been adapted to fight against anti-yoga polemics. One avenue of reconciling the issue of *nirodha* is to suggest that both Hinduism and Buddhism developed through several phases, in which both soteriological concerns and the relationship between these traditions and society went through significant changes. Though both numinous and cessative propensities existed in the *śramaṇic* and later in the mainstream currents of Indian religious thought, we would suggest the transformation of meditative practices over time to incorporate both greater conceptions of liberation in life and the realities of practicing religion in the context of society and not simply at its fringes.[148] This would suggest that as these traditions developed over time, their soteriological visions changed as well, from being *śramaṇic* to mainstream, transforming the role of both the numinous and the cessative at the same time. This is not to suggest that early Buddhism or Yoga was more authentic but rather to acknowledge the organic development of these traditions over time. As these traditions became integrated into mainstream society, the scholastic and ritual dimensions emerged naturally in the process of integrating the views into a larger system that recognized both the need to reach out to a larger society and to develop systems of authority that were based on firmer ground than charismatic virtuosity.

With the numinous dimension that we have characterized as the *samāpatti* element of yoga, it is extremely important to note the intimate relationship between the mythic elements of yoga and cosmology found in both Indian Buddhism and Classical Yoga. In fact, an answer to the problem of the role of the *ārūpya* states can be found in looking again at YS I.19, *bhavapratyayo videhaprakṛtilayānām*. These *videhas* and *prakṛtilayas* are considered the inferior *bhavapratyaya-yogins*, who are characterized by the respective qualities of being "bodiless" and "immersed in *prakṛti*." This may suggest that these inferior yogin are typified by their relationship to cosmology, that they may refer to a three-world conception that is characteristic of Buddhism, the division into desire, form, and formless realms. In this scheme, then, the inferior yogins would be characterized by their respective attainments of the cosmological level to which they have ascended. One can suggest that *videha* suggests "formlessness" and *prakṛtilaya* would then represent "form," or perhaps vice versa. However, to the degree that *videha* represents the denotation of a generic "god," it would make more sense to characterize the *videha* as being a desire realm deity in the Buddhist system. Whether there is a strict three-realm correlation or not, it is clear that in both the Classical Yoga context and in the context of Buddhist *śamatha* theory, there is a direct correlation between meditative attainments and future status as a divinity.[149]

Another context that further delineates the intimate relationship between *samādhi* and cosmology in the Classical Yoga tradition is in the YBh analysis of YS III.26, *bhuvanajñānam surye saṃyamāt*, "through *saṃyama* [meditative mastery] on the sun, [there is] knowledge of the world[s]." In his commentary to this *sūtra*, Vyāsa states that there are seven worlds, including three Brahmā worlds, worlds of Prajāpati, and worlds of Indra, among others, indicating the conception of hierarchical relationships of divinity and cosmology.[150] The Mahendra world includes *devas* such as the Tridaśas, Agniṣvāttas, Yāmyas, Tuṣitas, Aparinirmitavaśavartins, and Parinirmitavśavartins; the Prajāpatya worlds contain the Kamudas, Ṛbhavas, Pratardanas, Añjanābhas, and Pracitābhas; and the Brahmālokas contain the Brahmapurohitas, Barhmakāyikas, Brahmamahākāyikas, Ajarāmaras, Abhāsvaras, Mahābhāsvaras, Satyamahābhāsvaras, Achyuta, Śuddhanivāsa, Satyābhā, and Saṃjñāsaṃjñins.[151] In the context of the Brahmā realms, which have a direct parallelism to Buddhist conceptions of meditation and cosmology, the Acyutas are characterized by their practice of meditation with deliberation, the Śuddhanivāsas with reflection, and the Saṃjñsaṃjñins in the sense of ''I" or *asmitā*.[152] With the *videhas* and *prakṛtilayas*, Vyāsa states that such beings in a state of quasi-liberation do not belong to the world regions as characterized by the *sūtra*.[153] Vijñānabhikṣu notes that Vyāsa's description of the cosmos is based on a threefold division of *Bhu*, earth, *Bhuva*, between earth and the pole star, and *Sva*, the heavenly regions beyond.[154] This presentation would suggest, then, that the *videhas* and *prakṛtilayas* are "liminal" beings with respect to cosmology and can be said to bear some relationship with the break in Buddhism between the desire realm and the pair of the form and formless realms. It is clear that both traditions see an intimate relationship between the status of divinity and the progression of *samāpatti* states characterized here as the numinous dimension of *samādhi*. Though there is a vast difference between the simplicity of the *sūtra* itself and the elaboration that takes place in the *bhāṣya*, it is clear, at least in the context of the commentary, that yoga is situated within an elaborate system of cosmology and is not simply understood from the viewpoint of the manifestation of *prakṛti*.[155] The fact that the very names of the Brahma realms and the Brahmās themselves are identical in the YBh and in Abhidharma literature, such as that of the Brahmakāyika, Brahmapurohita, and so on, demonstrates a rootedness of the YS and of Buddhism in a common culture and, in particular, cosmology.[156]

The structure of *samādhi* can thus be understood to be more than simply an extension of a mental exercise, instead being understood to have significant karmic effects beyond the immediate effects on consciousness and perception. With another *sūtra*, III.51, *sthanyupanimantraṇe saṅgasmayākaraṇaṃ punaraniṣṭaprasaṅgāt*, detailing the invitations of the gods to enjoy the divine fruits of meditation, Vijñānabhikṣu identifies such deities as "Indra and the other gods" of classical Hindu mythos.[157] Similarly, Vyāsa tells of lovely women, fabulous elixirs, divine vehicles, wish-fulfilling trees, visions of sages, and so on in classical fashion, detailing the many numinous rewards of the development of proficiency in yogic *samādhi*.[158] Just as we have stated that yogic practice should not be excluded from the scholastic, so too we should emphasize that the cosmological and mythical elements of yogic *samāpatti*, its numinous characteristics, are another dimension that deserves significant recognition. This recognition is in line with getting beyond simplistic representations of these traditions as dry, philosophical traditions toward seeing them within a living nexus of philosophy and culture. What has been unrecognized and unexamined is the striking continuity between the numinous and cessative dimensions of Buddhism and Classical Yoga, representing a continuum or a continuity between extremes of activity and stasis, rooted in shared cosmological and mythical visions of reality.

THE TRANSFORMATION OF TRADITION: THE CHANGING NATURE OF *PRAXIS*

As we have argued, the development of *samāpatti* and *nirodha* in the pursuit of *samādhi* is characteristic of both Hindu and Buddhist notions of yoga. The extension of these characteristics into their philosophical and cultural contexts is here understood as the numinous and cessative dimensions of religious practice. Over time, these concepts have been interpreted and reinterpreted in numerous ways, reflecting attempts to ground these practices existentially in meditative *praxis* and analytically in scholasticism, shifting their significance in terms of their status as central and peripheral religious cults. It can be argued that the tension between central and peripheral cults is particularly important regarding the development of tantric forms of religious practice in both Hinduism and Buddhism. Tantric practice demonstrates an attempt to circumvent or transgress social and ethical norms, in part to access dimensions of psychological and spiritual life that are powerful and dangerous but, most notably, profoundly transformative. In the following chapter, we will examine how the tension between central and peripheral cults and between the numinous and cessative elements of Buddhist religious practice can be demonstrated powerfully in the development of tantric *sādhana*. It will be argued that the relationship between *bodhi* and *siddhi* in the tantric context represents the syncretic development of the *śamatha-vipaśyanā* paradigm and a shift toward the incorporation of numinous ideas of liberation into more mainstream notions of the cessative. It also will be demonstrated that the association of *śamatha* meditation with visualization and other numinous examples of Buddhist practice demonstrates the continuity between those dimensions in earlier formations of Buddhism and the development of the more elaborate forms found in late Indian Buddhism.

5

Traditions in Transition

Meditative Concepts in the Development of Tantric *Sādhana**

SĀDHANA AND MEDITATIVE CONCEPTS

The goal of this chapter is to examine the relationship between the development of Buddhist *sādhana* and broader conceptions regarding the nature of meditation theory and the place of tantra within the greater Buddhist cultus. It will be argued that Vajrayāna Buddhist *sādhana*, rather than divorcing itself from earlier Buddhist conceptions of meditation *(dhyāna)*, has adapted and expanded upon classical conceptions of meditative *praxis*. This thesis is rooted in the idea that the theory and practice of tantric *sādhana* are rooted in the "classical" Indian Buddhist division of meditation into "tranquility" (Skt. *śamatha*, Pali *samatha*) and "insight" (Skt. *vipaśyanā*, Pali *vipassanā*) forms of meditation, representing, respectively, the mastery over what can be termed the *numinous* and *cessative* dimensions of the Buddhist path. The connection between this earlier stratum of mediation theory and the practice of *sādhana* is exemplified in a number of different dimensions of tantric theory and practice. Tantric conceptions of liberation in many respects resemble "classical" conceptions of *nirodha* (cessation), developed philosophically through metaphors of dissolution and visually through imagery of dissolution. This basic connection is even more concrete in the contexts in which *śamatha* and *vipaśyanā* are understood to be indispensable prerequisites for the development of tantric practice. Furthermore, it will be shown how the series of Theravāda *samatha* meditation practices known as the "recollections" *(anussati)* can be considered a prototype for the visualization and identification processes that are at the heart of Vajrayāna conceptions of *sādhana*, demonstrating deep conceptual, if not developmental, connections between *samatha* in the Theravāda context and *śamatha* and *sādhana* in the Mahāyāna and Vajrayāna contexts.

The dynamics of this discussion will be brought out through the examination of a particular Vajrayāna deity, Vajrayoginī, and her representation in a key collection of Indian Vajrayāna *sādhana* instructions, the *Sādhanamālā*. In association with this, we will discuss how the tension between what will be called the *siddhi* "accomplishment" and *bodhi* "awakening" elements in tantric theory represents an extension of the numinous and cessative dimensions of the *śamatha-vipaśyanā* distinction. This discussion also will make evident how Vajrayāna imagery demonstrates the tension between mainstream and more liminal conceptions of religious *praxis*, lending to an understanding of the shifting place of tantra within the bounds of the mainstream and peripheral regions of Mahāyāna Buddhism. This aspect of the study will further demonstrate the power of Vajrayāna symbolism, its adaptation into the context of a monasticism that emphasizes the importance of *vinaya*, and its deep affinity for shamanic culture. The object of this chapter, then, will be to demonstrate how Vajrayāna *sādhana* conceptions incorporate and adapt the earlier strata of Buddhist meditation theory and how *sādhana* is tied into the tension between mainstream and esoteric Buddhism.

THE RISE OF TANTRA AND THE DEVELOPMENT OF TANTRIC *SĀDHANA*

The development of the Vajrayāna pantheon of buddhas, bodhisattvas, and deities mirrors that in Indian religion of an approach to religious practice based on the connection of the philosophical and esoteric. This combination of forms is characterized by the conjunction of numinous and cessative conceptions of religious practice or, in other words, the development of supernatural powers and abilities versus the knowledge and detachment that lead to the destruction of ignorance and affliction. This development of numinous and cessative orientations is deeply rooted in pan-Indian concepts concerning the practice of meditation, exemplified by conceptual divisions in meditation theory such as the *samāpatti-nirodha* and *śamatha-vipaśyanā* found in Hindu and Buddhist conceptions of religious discipline *(yoga)* and meditation *(dhyāna)*. The particular form of practice in the Vajrayāna that embodies the spirit of the conjunction of philosophical principles and their manifestations in numinous form (particularly as deities) is termed tantric *sādhana*. Through the development of Mahāyāna philosophy, scholasticism, and ritual in the centuries following the *parinirvāṇa* of Śākyamuni Buddha came the development of more sophisticated modes representing the numinous dimensions of Buddhism. The primacy of visualization, worship, and identification with numerous deities of varying character and demeanor in the practice of *sādhana* led to the development of complex images representative of the power inherent in Buddhist principles, a process mirrored in the development of elaborate tantric iconography and theory in the Hindu context.[1] In the Buddhist context, these images are intimately tied to the development of new forms of practice following earlier models of *śamatha-vipaśyanā*, in that they express a tension between the numinous and cessative conceptions of religious practice, a tension that is ultimately resolved in the context of Mahāyāna conceptions of buddhahood.

The development of tantra also can be considered a manifestation of peripheral cults in the greater scheme of Indian and Buddhist society.[2] As discussed earlier, Lewis has argued that in the context of shamanism, but not limited to it, religious phenomena can be characterized by their relationship to a particular level of social stability, ethical certainty or ambiguity, and degree of ecstatic intensity, among other dimensions.[3] Whereas central cults are tied into mainstream cultural mores and deeply rooted in ritual, peripheral cults often challenge the status quo or demonstrate ambiguity with respect to it, thriving on individual charisma and ecstasy rather than administrative authority. A cult's status in this system is constantly being reinterpreted and exists on a continuum between the center and the periphery of its socioreligious context.[4] The transgressive orientation of tantra, including the intentional breaking of social norms, is tied to conceptions of the development of a range of supernatural abilities and religious virtuosity. It is possible that we might view Buddhist tantra as being split regarding the peripheral and central status of tantric practices. Although the early monastic practice of tantra was likely considered transgressive, it can be argued that in both the Indian and Tibetan contexts, a key development in Mahāyāna practice is the adaptation of tantric practices to suit the monastic context, moving what were once peripheral practices and concepts toward central status. This would be opposed to lay tantric practice, which is characterized by its greater liminal status, being outside both monastic and mainstream society, and demonstrates the peripheral nature of the development of tantric charisma. The status of Vajrayāna in the spectrum of central to peripheral cults is exemplified by the physical form or iconography of its deities bearing characteristics that exemplify the tension inherent in both the *numinous-cessative* and *central-peripheral* relationships. It also is concretely demonstrated in the tension between the literal and figurative performance of tantric rituals, particularly those of a sexual or culturally transgressive nature.[5]

Structural Elements of Tantric *Sādhana*

Out of the standardization of deity images and the need for pedagogical tools in the monastic context of the Vajrayāna arose a class of texts delineating the central themes and images of the practice of *sādhana*. In these works, among which a twelfth-century Indian Buddhist text, the *Sādhanamālā*, will serve as a primary example here, elaboration is found of many of the technical aspects of what constitutes *sādhana* practice. Key among these are instructions on yogic discipline, mantra recitation, and worship and, perhaps most importantly, the description of iconographic images to be used in the visualization of tantric divinities. As a form of religious observance, *sādhana* is characterized by its integration of a number of threads of religious practice and philosophical thought, of both ritual and contemplation, including Mādhyamika and Yogācāra *śunyatā* theory, ritual propitiation of deities, yogic methods, and mantra formulas. Agehananda Bharati held that the character of *sādhana* itself is an emphasis on the practical, and he distinguished the tantric from the nontantric forms of Hindu and Buddhist religious practice on this basis.[6] He identified tantric *sādhana* as a type of radical "psycho-experimentalism" that attempts to get to the "bottom" of reality through the "anthropomorphism" of gods, goddesses, demons, and demonesses as the representation of mental or psychological realities.[7] This notion of "experimentalism," however, is largely contingent upon the notion that tantra is a "liminal" cult that thrives on the force of being away from the scholastic center of monastic life. Although this is characteristic of the "peripheral" dimensions of tantric practice, it should be pointed out that tantric theory is just as suitable to reinterpretation into "central status," or "ritualization," a process demonstrated extensively by Tibetan adaptations of Indian Vajrayāna theory to suit stricter conceptions of monasticism such as those found in the Kadampa and Gelukpa lineages.

Herrmann-Pfandt has suggested that the core of *sādhana* is systematic visualization that prepares the *sādhaka* for the "nondeliberate" and "nonwillful" vision of the nature of reality, bringing about deep esoteric knowledge of buddha nature, a process that is highly suggestive of a progression from numinous to cessative characteristics.[8] Furthermore, she argues that *sādhana* has a definitive set of phases—preparatory, developmental, and completion—that characterizes the process of development as such. The preparatory stage of meditation is that in which *śunyatā* is identified as the origin of all phenomena and the highest metaphysical reality. In the phase of development, through the help of mantra recitation, the visualization of a deity begins within the meditation space of the practitioner. The meditator then proceeds to identify with the deity visualized in the "buddha field" represented through a type of *unio mystica* in meditative absorption, while making sacrifices and offering praise to the deity. In the "phase of completion," the deity dissolves into the void again, leaving the *sādhaka* to contemplate the impermanence of all phenomena at the end of the *sādhana* process.[9]

Such a process indicates both numinous and cessative dimensions, employed in a fashion similar to classical accounts of *śamatha-vipaśyanā*, where the development of *dhyāna* and *samāpatti* culminates in the attainment of cessation, *nirodha*. Both the sense of dissolution and the frequently referred to notions of "skylike" mind arguably have a strong similarity to the characteristics given to the *ārūpyas* (formless meditations, *samāpattis*), such as *ākāśānantya*, "limitless space,"*vijñānāntaya*, "limitless consciousness," and *ākiṃcanya*, "nothingness," and to *nirodhasamāpatti*, "attainment of cessation." The process of first establishing the requisite level of numinous attainment, and that attainment finding its logical extension or end in the attainment of a state of cessation, is a familiar approach to the process of liberation. From a phenomenological viewpoint, the notion of a "skylike" nature of mind, an absolute sense of mind that encompasses all phenomena, resembles greatly the notion of a *puruṣa*, the indestructible consciousness principle in Classical Yoga and in Sāṃkhya. The key point to be made here, however, is that there is a tension between the conception of the visualization or the embodiment of the deity form that can be characterized as numinous as opposed to the tendency toward dissolution or *nirodha*, the cessative dimension of tantra. It also should be noted that the cessative can be an image represented by the dissolution of the deity form into primordial emptiness and can be represented more abstractly, as in the Mahāmudrā system's conceptions of the nature of mind.

Mircea Eliade, in a discussion of tantrism and yoga, defines *sādhana* foremost as "realization," noting the emphasis on the iconography of divine images in such practice:

> In tantric *sādhana*, iconography plays a role that, though of the greatest importance, is difficult to define in a few words. To be sure, divine images are "supports" for meditation, but not in exactly the sense of the Buddhist *kasinas*. Tantric iconography represents a "religious" universe that must be entered and assimilated. . . . This spiritual exercise comprises emerging from one's own mental universe and entering the various universes governed by the divinities.[10]

The establishment of such divine cosmologies, according to Eliade, is founded on the establishment of proper *mantra*, *mudrā*, yogic discipline, and micro-macrocosmic identification. The boundary between ritual worship and identification is primarily pedagogical—entrance into the *sādhana* of a particular deity often presupposes the development of a deep relationship with that figure, primarily as a devotee and subject in the fashion of *bhakti*. As Eliade also notes in giving an example from the *Sādhanamālā*, in order to emphasize the impermanence of the phenomenal flow, often a dynamic series of images is presented in which the objects of visualization appear in succession, building upon one another or arising from a seed state into a more developed form.[11]

Eliade also notes the necessity of the establishment of basic skill in *dhāraṇā* and *dhyāna* as foundational to *sādhana* establishment in both the Hindu and Buddhist contexts. Similarly, Alex Wayman has noted in the Vajrayāna context the role of the establishment of *samādhi* on deity images, and particularly on the Buddha, as the foundation for progress on tantric paths in the initiatory context.[12] Referring to the Tibetan *Mkhas grub rje's Fundamentals of the Buddhist Tantras*, Wayman elucidates the position that *śamatha* and *vipaśyanā*, namely, "calming" and "special insight," meditation are the two components of *samādhi* and the "backbone" of tantric practice.[13] *Śamatha* is understood to lead to the one-pointed grasping of images, mantras, and so on, while *vipaśyanā* is the analytic dimension of meditation out of which the cognition of *śūnyatā* arises. Joined as *śamathavipaśyanāyuganaddha*, "union of calm abiding and special insight," they can be said to be representative of the tantric vocation as bringing together opposed forces into the nondual state, ultimately exemplified by *maithuna* imagery. Wayman is particularly correct in noting the development of *śamatha* on buddha images as serving as a "gateway" of sorts to both Mahāyāna and in the context of tantric practice. It should be remembered that *śamatha* contains within itself a conception that attainments in meditation have cosmological and mythical analogues, and that the attainment of *śamatha* is more than simply the development of concentration. The powers that arise out of *śamatha* meditation are said to be intimately tied to developing mental states that are equivalent to those of deities at the levels of attainment, and rebirth in those realms is seen as one of the products of *śamatha* discipline. Clearly there is a deep connection between ideas of *śamatha* and the development of numinous imagery, both in terms of the nature of practice and the nature of the fruits of practice. As will be demonstrated later, the development of *śamatha* on a visualized image and the development of visualization in tantric *sādhana* have deep theoretical and historical roots in Buddhism.

The polarization and exemplification of the world of duality in tantra lend greatly to its development of a male-female dynamic, with their union representative of the ultimate, nondual state—the position of *śakti* in the Hindu tradition being mirrored by Buddhist *prajnā* figures. Bharati has argued that this fundamental characteristic of tantra is the foundation for the emphasis on sexual contact, whether real or imagined, as the central image of tantric *sādhana* in both traditions. The "coincidence of opposites" that is represented by the union of deities in the *yab-yum* or *maithuna* type of configuration may take precedence as being the most vivid example of the philosophical substratum of tantric theory. Representations of Vajrayāna iconography often do seem to be dominated by the embracing male and female figures, particularly in the Tibetan region. However, *sādhana* is by no means limited to these types of figures but is also greatly represented by individual figures in the fashion of deity yoga, in which the identification with a chosen deity (or, most notably, the Buddha) takes precedence as a supplement, a precursor, a preliminary to yoga tantra, and so on, or as a substitute for *maithuna* figurations. The emphasis on *maithuna* figurations may well obscure the greater range of practices and representations that is characteristic of the Vajrayāna throughout the Indo-Tibetan context. This distinction may well have its roots in the development of tantric forms in the tension between central and peripheral cults. *Maithuna* must have been a relatively liminal practice in the Indian religious context, particularly so to the degree that it presupposes transgressing caste and purity boundaries or monastic commitments. The full range of tantric practices accommodates the development of individual *sādhanas*, stressing identity or relationship with a deity in the fashion of *svādhyāya-īṣṭadevatā*, as found in the Classical Yoga tradition, for the development of visualized *maithuna*, and for the more controversial practices of literal tantric *maithuna*. It can be further added that the notion of having the *maithuna* pair represent "active" versus "passive" principles could be compared both to a distinction between the numinous and cessative, and the *enstatic* and *ecstatic*, though of course, as Bharati has noted, these polarities reverse across the Hindu-Buddhist boundary.

PROTO-*SĀDHANA* IN PRE-TANTRIC BUDDHISM

Though *sādhana* in name and form is a characteristic practice developed in the Indian tantric schools in the latter part of the first millennium C.E., it nevertheless has much in common with earlier Buddhist practices that are found in the Pali sources of the Theravāda. In the *Visuddhimagga* of Buddhaghosa, which dates closer to the middle of the first millennium, we find reference to a *samatha* meditation series called the "Six Recollections" *(anussati)*, which includes the recollections of the Buddha, Dhamma, Saṅgha, virtue, generosity, and deities. Among these six recollections, the "recollection of the Buddha" and the "recollection of deities" both bear a strong resemblance to the later tantric *sādhana* due to their emphasis on developing a mental image of the Buddha and numerous other deity forms with particular characteristics and powers. Falling into the section of the *Visuddhimagga* that is devoted to the development of *samādhi* (as opposed to *śīla* and *paññā*, the other two elements of the so-called "threefold training), the "Six Recollections" are stunning examples of a range of Buddhist practices far from the "dry" nature often attributed to the Theravāda. These practices demonstrate greatly the numinous side of Theravāda meditation theory and put to rest any idea that Theravāda is free from ideas of "imagery" and "visualization" that are so characteristic of the surviving Mahāyāna traditions. Rather, it makes sense that we see the importance of visualization and "embodiment" in Theravāda, in that they are characteristic of the tension between *samāpatti* and *nirodha*, or the *samatha-vipassanā* typology of meditation. Clearly in this context, Buddhaghosa is interested in portraying the *samatha* dimension of the Buddhist path as being of significant import, at bare minimum as a scholastic paradigm for understanding the Buddhist path and most notably the virtuous qualities of a buddha.

The recollection of the Buddha contains a complex set of Buddhist philosophical concepts that is integrated into the development of an image of the Buddha and his many accomplishments. Following Buddhaghosa, and presumably a teacher, a meditator is instructed to develop an image of the Buddha as being accomplished, fully enlightened, endowed with clear vision and virtuous conduct, sublime, the "knower" of worlds, the incomparable leader of men to be tamed, the teacher of gods and men, enlightened, and blessed.[14] Through subsequent contemplation of the manifold virtues of the Buddha, the monks build a mental image of the Buddha in all his glory that serves as a means of deepening their attainment of *samādhi* through *śamatha* meditation. This image then establishes an archetypal or a paradigmatic image of the Buddha in the eyes of the monks, making concrete and lucid exactly which virtues they are striving to attain themselves.

> When a *bhikkhu* is devoted to this recollection of the Buddha, he is respectful and deferential towards the Master. He attains fullness of faith, mindfulness, understanding, and merit. He has much happiness and gladness. He conquers fear and dread. He is able to endure pain. He comes to feel as if he were living in the master's presence. And his body, when the recollection of the Buddha's special qualities dwells in it, becomes as worthy of veneration as a shrine room. His mind tends towards the plane of the Buddhas.[15]

In the imagery of "identification" and in the inwardness of the visualization are found characteristics that bear a striking resemblance to elements of later Buddhist *sādhana*. The transformation of the body of the practitioner into a "pure vessel," one in which the qualities of the Buddha temporarily dwell, both exemplifies ideals that are characteristic of tantra and slightly suggests a type of "possession" or "embodiment" state. There is a strong sense that beyond the attainment of concentration characterized by *samatha* practice, the numinous qualities of the Buddha have permeated into the practice, giving it a quality far beyond the simple idea of concentration or mental focus.

Another example that is similar in this respect to the recollection of the Buddha is the "Recollection of Deities." As a subject for the development of *samatha* meditation, the recollection of deities, much like the recollection of the Buddha, demonstrates a strong degree of parallelism with *sādhana* exercises. This practice has as its foundation the idea of finding virtuous inspiration in contemplation of the "virtuous examples" made by the deities and their virtuous characteristics.[16] Developing an image of these beings, the practice follows thus:

> In the Sutta, however, it is said: "On the occasion, Mahānāma, on which a noble disciple recollects the faith, the virtue, the learning, the generosity, the understanding, that are both his own and those deities', on that occasion his mind is not obsessed by greed."[17]

Though it would be an overstatement to insist that this is an early example of a *sādhana* practice, it is clear that such a practice bears striking resemblance to some of the foundation conceptions of tantra and *sādhana* concerning the visualization and approximation of deity attributes.[18] Perhaps most compelling in this context is the sense in which the meditator is understood to participate or "share" in the blessedness and virtue of the object of visualization, whether it is the Buddha or a divine being. The development of deity images may well prefigure in some respects the deep and abiding emphasis in Mahāyāna and Vajrayāna on the development of deity yoga or *yidam* practice as the foundation for individual meditation practice. Again, as noted earlier, the early manifestations of such visualization practices also may be found in the context of Hindu yoga, particularly so in the Classical Yoga context, with its concepts of *svādhyāya*, and possibly also the notion of *īśvara-praṇidhāna*. In the development of Mahāyāna tantra, *śamatha* then becomes largely subsumed under the rubric of "deity yoga" types of practices. These *yidam* types of practices are a predominant medium for the development of both meditative stabilization, or *samādhi*, and the development of supernormal powers of action and perception, *siddhi*, both of which were characteristic elements of *śamatha* in the classical accounts of meditation theory.

Vajrayoginī as Tantric Paradigm

We now turn to a brief examination of a tantric figure of particular significance in both contemporary and premodern tantric Buddhism who demonstrates the dynamics of the numinous quality of tantric *sādhana*. Our subject is the Vajrayāna *prajñā* goddess known as Vajrayoginī, Sarvabuddhaḍākinī, or Vajraḍākinī, among other appellations. In the *Sādhanamālā*, or "Garland of Practices," a twelfth-century Indian Mahāyāna Buddhist text, this deity is portrayed in a number of *sādhanas*, with two primary variations. They demonstrate the distinctiveness of the *sādhana* form and the variety of images understood to be applicable to the terms *yoginī* and *ḍākinī* in this text, in a manner that is informative with respect to modern traditional representations. These goddesses are particularly significant in that they demonstrate how iconography serves as a nexus where philosophy and *praxis* come together in a dynamic and syncretic relationship with philosophical and religious currents. The "liminal" nature of these goddesses demonstrates their character as "peripheral" in origin, and the context, the *Sādhanamālā*, demonstrates the effort to bring tantric practice into the "center" of monastic practice. In addition, the development of these images also signifies the development of a greater subtlety regarding the representation of the psychophysical analogues of the numinous dimension of meditative *praxis*.

Yoginīs and *ḍākinīs* are deities common to both the Hindu and Buddhist cultus across the Indo-Tibetan region. They represent a wide range of characteristics, from the human to the divine, from wrathful and malevolent figurations to peaceful, boon-giving manifestations, though the emphasis appears to be on the wrathful manifestations. As such, they are, to a certain degree, similar to many female figures in the religions of South Asia, liminal figures who demonstrate the power of threshold and boundary situations and conceptions, such as processes of death and rebirth, or initiation, as found in the context of the cemetery and other places on the periphery of society, culturally and spatially.[19] The Hindu tradition appears to first and foremost have placed these divinities within the realm of the terrible and horrific. In literary sources such as the *Uttamacaritrakathānaka*, *Rājataraṅgini*, and *Kathasaritsāgara*, violence and dread surround the images of both classes of deities—they possess the power to move about in the air, consuming or reanimating corpses, stealing children, inhabiting cemeteries, and clad in skulls and glowing with a halo of light.[20] *Yoginīs* represent many levels of humanity and divinity, from the role of consort in *maithuna* rituals of tantric practitioners such as the Kaulas to ogresslike witches and demonesses to the highest manifestations of *śakti*.[21] Perhaps the most notable characteristic of the roles of *yoginīs* in Indian religious and cultural life is their "liminal" character. In contemporary popular Indian folk belief, there still remains a certain degree of fear and suspicion about *yoginīs* and their cultus. Ḍākinī figures appear to be secondary in the Hindu tradition, similar to the *yoginī* image of the "graveyard" spirit. However, the representations in the *yoginī* temples of northern India demonstrate an array of *yoginī* figures carrying at times classical representations of divinities and at other times strange and grotesque animal heads and other unusual forms reminiscent of Tibetan *ḍākinī* lore, demonstrating their hybrid and liminal nature.

The Vajrayāna representations of Vajrayoginī appear closely related to the depictions of the *yoginī* figures of eighth-century and later Indian temple art. In Vajrayoginī, we have a broad set of terminological identifications that indicates relationship if not identity among a number of female deities. Among these are the goddesses referred to as "Vajrayoginī," "Sarvabuddhaḍākinī," and "Vajravarāhī." Vajrayoginī is called "Naropa's Dakini" in the Tibetan tradition on the basis of her identification as the consort of Naropa. Sarvabuddhaḍākinī is representative of the consorts of all of the buddhas, and Vajravarāhī as the consort of Cakrasaṃvara, while Vajrayoginī proper is sometimes identified as the consort of Heruka. Vajravarāhī could possibly be an extension of a tantric *Yoginī* that bears the name of Varāhī, and even more distantly the ever-present member of the Matṛkas called "Varāhī." With the specific term *ḍākinī*, Janice Willis demonstrates key characteristics that show a parallelism, if not an identity, of the Buddhist ḍākinī with the Indian *Yoginī*.[22] Delineating the dynamics of the human and divine *ḍākinī* figures and their benevolent and malevolent images, she places the *ḍākinī* in an equivalency relationship with the *Yoginī*. She narrates the stories of numerous significant Vajrayāna lineage founders and their relationship with the *ḍākinīs*, such as Naropa, Tilopa, Padmasambhava, and so on. Clearly the term *ḍākinī* is considered equivalent to the term *yoginī* in the primary sense of a tantric consort, along with its other specific uses in conjunction with particular buddhas, bodhisattvas, and deities. These Mahāyāna conceptions of *yoginīs* and *ḍākinīs* and their integration into the greater Buddhist pantheon represent the integration of the liminal and peripheral dimensions of tantric practice with the highly systematic and syncretic approaches of Mahāyāna monasticism.

VAJRAYOGINĪ IN THE *SĀDHANAMĀLĀ*

The *Sādhanamālā* is a particularly useful work for understanding the character of the goddess Vajrayoginī in Indian Vajrayāna Buddhism and in the Tibetan traditions that grew out of the Indian traditions. The *Sādhanamālā* demonstrates the tension between Mahāyāna monasticism, exemplified by the *vinaya* and *samaya* precepts, and the more peripheral Vajrayāna culture that contains a tension between representations of wrathful and peaceful deities. Composed of the *sādhanas* of numerous authors, the *Sādhanamālā* presents a panoramic view of the diversity of Vajrayāna images available to tantric practitioners around the turn of the first millennium C.E. In the edition edited by Bhattacharya, which was based on eight different manuscripts, there are a total of 312 individual *sādhanas*.[23] Realizing the limitations of the accuracy of Bhattacharya's edition, we can nevertheless find much use in examining the representation of Vajrayoginī and similar deities.[24] Numbers 232–238 of Bhattacharya's text contain Vajrayoginī as a central figure in their *sādhanas*. In these *sādhanas* we find two primary images of Vajrayoginī, namely, the *ālīḍha*-posture, Vajrayoginī, and the Vajrayoginī with detached head, that is, "Severed Headed *Yoginī*," surrounded by two attendants. The references that are explicitly devoted to Vajrayoginī, numbers 232–238, demonstrate an overt identification of Vajrayoginī as sharing a number of different namesakes.[25] In numbers 232, 233, 234, and 236, Vajrayoginī is hailed as *sarvabuddhaḍākinī*, "consort of all of the buddhas." In nearly all of the *sādhanas*, Vajrayoginī also is identified as *vajraḍākinī*, "Vajra Ḍākinī," *śrīḍākinī*, "Auspicious Ḍākinī," or simply *ḍākinī*. A clear identification between iconography and Vajrayāna theory is exemplified in mantra formulas such as those that appeal to the *trikāya* theory, invoking the sequence of the *dharmakāya*, *saṃbhogakāya*, and *nirmāṇakāya*, or "truth body," "enjoyment body," and "manifestation body," respectively.[26]

The Vajrayoginī images that are presented in these *sādhanas* are of two kinds, as Bhattacharya has noted, a Vajrayoginī accompanied by two attendants, with an apparently self-decapitated head in one hand (thus the popular phrase "Severed-Headed Yoginī"), and another, alone and bearing the *khaṭvāṅga* staff.[27] The first figure is represented thus:

> The worshipper should conceive himself as Bhaṭṭārika Vajrayoginī . . . of yellow complexion, who carries in her left hand her own head severed by herself with her own Kartri held in her right hand; whose left hand is raised upwards while the right is placed below; who is nude, and whose right leg is stretched while the left is bent down. He (the worshipper) should also meditate on the streams of blood issuing out from the severed body as falling into her mouth and the mouths of the two *Yoginīs* on either side of her.[28]

Bhattacharya, along with De Mallman, notes the apparent iconographic equivalency between the "severed-headed" *Yoginī* figure and the goddess Cinnamastā, who is one of the ten Mahāvidyās of Hindu tantrism.[29] David Kinsley has suggested that, similar to our discussion of Vajravarāhī, there is a relationship with Cinnamastā and the Mātṛkās that is represented in her resemblance to another goddess, Koṭavī, speculating on a possible relationship to more ancient forms of goddess worship incorporated into "mainstream" Hinduism.[30] One can further question the more broad connotations of decapitation and "headlessness" that occur with reference to the *worship* of goddesses in folk tradition and in legend.[31] The horrific nature of this *Yoginī* figure demonstrates at once the cultural liminality of her figure, in that the shedding of such a culturally charged substance as blood is further extended by the fact that she and her devotees are *consuming* it, bringing the force of the image to greater heights. The deeply provocative image provides both for a deep emotive reaction such as may be intentionally cultivated for the purposes of meditation and a sense of transgression regarding religious and social purity.

Elisabeth Anne Benard has well demonstrated the intimate ties between Hinduism and Buddhism with the presentation of goddesses in this context. She notes how on several levels, including iconography, ritual, and philosophy, this goddess crosses the boundary between Hindu and Buddhist tantra. Particularly of relevance in this comparison is the correlation between Chinnamastā and Chinnamuṇḍā within the realm of ideas regarding the subtle body.[32] With yoga, this concept is particularly powerful, in that conceptions of the manipulation of the psychophysical body have arguably at this point in time entered the mainstream, through tantric sources. This would demonstrate another example of the way in which the drive toward numinous attainments becomes represented in physical form, just as we might find in other contexts with principles of impermanence, wisdom, and so on. In this system, then, the structure of psychological and physical functionality becomes represented by vivid and horrific imagery that seems much more characteristic of a shamanic cult than of monastic Buddhism or ascetic Hinduism. On one level, the horrific imagery itself provides for the encouragement of deep emotive reaction; on the other, it develops a sense of the movement of such energies in the context of conceptions regarding the subtle body and the energy channels represented in the body. One also can consider the possibilities of self-decapitation as being a metaphor for the removal of ego identity or of providing "nourishment" to others in a manner characteristic of *chöd* in the Tibetan context.[33]

The second Vajrayoginī figure of the Sādhanamālā is a red-colored yoginī figure, whose attributes include the *khaṭvaṅga and vajra*. This Vajrayoginī bears, as Bhattacharya notes, a strong resemblance to the goddesses Nairātmyā and Vajravārāhī. Traditional sources appear to be much more willing to actually identify these goddesses together under the rubric of *yoginī*, *ḍākinī*, or *prajñā*, though each has a particular role when placed in relationship to their male counterparts, that is, Heruka, Hevajra, and Saṃvara. This figure seems to be the one that has found the greatest affinity for the Tibetan context and provides more of a balance between the femininity of a *prajñā* type of goddess and the more wrathful manifestations found within the boundaries of Vajrayāna practice. It is a figure analogous to this that is prominently displayed throughout the Indo-Tibetan region as being representative of the *ḍākinī* as the female divinity *par excellence*. This figure too seems to have a form quite similar in demeanor and character to some of the more "peaceful" images found among the *yoginī* temples in India, including another familiar figure in the Indo-Tibetan region, the "bow-wielding *ḍākinī*." As in the case of the "severed-headed *yoginī*," her *sādhana* consists primarily of visualization of her form and "worship" in the form of mantras, with the presumption that the perfection *(siddhi)* of them confers upon the *sādhaka* powers and knowledge consistent with the tantric vehicle. It is not surprising that this slightly less aggressive and grandiose yet still wrathful image of Vajrayoginī would find parity in the context of a tantric monasticism that sought to reform tantra in such a way as to preserve some of its liminal or peripheral dimensions. The "severed-headed *yoginī*," in her horrific form, appears by virtue of her image to be a deity that is more difficult to reconcile with a more mainstream conception of religious practice. However, it is clear that even the more temperate *yoginī* figure bears the imprint of liminality. The development of tantric perfection *(siddhi)* is conferred, then, through the various *sādhanas* of Vajrayoginī, and, presumably, though secondarily, through insight into the nature of reality *(bodhi)*, the two contrasting yet complementary goals of tantric theory.[34]

THE POWER OF THE EMBODIED IMAGE

The practice of the Vajrayoginī *sādhanas*, as delineated in the *Sādhanamālā*, provides a complex set of visualizations and philosophical associations intended to help the *sādhaka* progress toward *siddhi* and *bodhi*. These two goals often appear in opposition to one another and are characterized by the numinous and cessative qualities discussed in previous pages, relating respectively to the perfection of manifestation and realization. The *siddhis*, or "perfections," give the practitioner power over a number of different facets of reality, particularly in the manner of supernormal powers of action and perception. Powers such as flight, longevity, manifesting oneself in multiple bodies, supernormal vision, and so on are some of the more mundane examples of tantric *siddhi* that are said to come about as an effect of *sādhana*. Bhattacharya notes that there is a range of attainments, culminating in expositions on powers such as the classic presentation of "eight *siddhis*."[35] The development of *bodhi* corresponds with the highest point of *siddhi* and involves the higher Buddhist truths regarding emptiness and the ultimate end of the bodhisattva course, the full and complete realization characteristic of buddhahood. It is often stated that the establishment of liberating knowledge based on insight into the nature of reality is the *sine qua non* of Buddhist soteriological thought and thus truly informs Buddhist practice—an interpretation that we found mirrored earlier in Hermann-Pfandt's interpretation of *sādhana*. However, it is difficult at times to assert the predominance of *bodhi* in viewing texts such as the *Sādhanamālā* that often seem centered on the attainment of exotic "worldly" *siddhis*. In many of the *sādhanas*, the performance of proper ritual activity, such as *pūjā* and mantra repetition, and the fruit of such ritual activity seem to be of more concern to the authors than liberating insight. This tension, however, is understandable in light of the fact that it is a manifestation of the numinous-cessative paradigm that is characteristic of the earlier formulations of meditation practice. If full buddhahood is classically understood in Mahāyāna as being the mastery of both the domains of *śamatha* and *vipaśyanā*, having the full range of both powers of concentration and insight, or numinous and cessative powers, then it makes sense that this dynamic would continue to play out in the tantric context. Also, it is clear that as a manner of practicing religion, tantra is, in many respects, the paradigm for what would be understood as a peripheral cult, in that its practices do not necessarily fit into mainstream morality and the powers that exemplify it are thoroughly ambiguous, lending to the predominance of *siddhi* over *bodhi*. However, to the degree to which tantric practices are reintegrated into the mainstream, they reflect the need to reconcile these dimensions together, a process greatly demonstrated in Tibetan attempts to provide systematic accounts of the role of tantra within traditional conceptions of the path.

Along these lines, we have noted at length that there are also obvious Theravāda parallels to the conceptions of *sādhana* practice that demonstrate a sense of continuity of concepts with the process of visualization between Theravāda and Mahāyāna sources. A strong belief in the power of the visualized image and an acute awareness of the proximity of visualization and identification, and thus embodiment, appear to be a characteristic of a range of Buddhist traditions, including the Theravāda and Sarvāstivāda, as well as the Mahāyāna and Vajrayāna. It may well be possible that visualizing and identifying with an image that shares anthropomorphic form with the practitioner may have a deeper psychic impact than dry philosophical argumentation and analysis, a concept at the heart of Bharati's theories regarding the "psycho-experimental" nature of tantra. Entering into a numinous reality or cosmos, as suggested in *sādhana* practice and in the development of *maṇḍala* images in the context of initiation, suggests that there are means of coming to know reality that are powerful and transformative in ways distinct from discursive, abstract knowledge. One can safely say that much of tantric theory rests on just such an assumption, with the added caveat that such methods are dangerous and not to be taken lightly. As an embodied being, it makes sense that conceptual issues would both take on a degree of reality as well as be in a more accessible medium for a practitioner, or *sādhaka*, as embodied images. In other words, the embodiment of truths in the visualized image and ultimately in oneself *concretizes* the theoretical domain and thus makes it a living reality. According to this theory, then, the "experience" of such truths is the manner of their ultimate verification and demonstrates how such principles operate in reality, and not simply in the realm of conceptuality. This fact is evident in that human self-transformation relies to some degree on the imaginative ability to envision or visualize an alternate reality and to transform that reality into an embodied one. As Janet Gyatso has stated, the development of tantric forms of experience renders such realties "discernable, transmissible, and intersubjective," allowing for both intimate exchange in initiatory contexts and for the performance of public ritual that bonds virtuoso and lay community.[36] It also demonstrates the intimate relationship between personal and social symbolism and the mediation of those domains, as is represented by Obeyesekere in his analysis of

Hindu and Buddhist ascetics.[37] Embodiment is particularly powerful in that embodiment can be considered the means of verifying, or testing, religious truth experientially. According to this logic, if a truth is capable of being embodied, then it must be consonant with reality on all levels, and not simply on the level of discursive knowledge. In this sense, we can view "practice" or "experience" as an affirmation of empiricism and objectivity, the "litmus test" of the veracity of philosophical understandings.

TANTRA, SHAMANISM, AND CULTURAL CONTINUITY

Having looked at the development of the tension between numinous and cessative features in the tantric context, it is clear that although the role of meditation in the Vajrayāna context has changed dramatically from Abhidharma presentations, the *śamatha-vipaśyanā* paradigm is still at work beneath the surface. Furthermore, it has been shown how, following Lewis's discussion of shamanism, Vajrayāna Buddhism serves as an ideal example of the tension between central and peripheral religious cults within the greater Buddhist context. The application of Lewis's system to tantra has both premodern and contemporary relevance on a number of planes, most notably with respect to the tension between central and peripheral cults within the context of the Tibetan four-school system. The Indo-Tibetan region offers many opportunities to demonstrate the proximity of shamanic and Buddhist dimensions of practice as well as culture. David Germano and Janet Gyatso have, for example, recently demonstrated how in the Tibetan Nyingma school the wrathful goddess, Vajravārāhi, and other deities play important religious roles in the context of possession as well as in visualization-oriented or internally cultivated tantra.[38] This is a clear example of the crossover between the numinous dimension of *sādhana* and the development of possession states as an approved form of Buddhist practice. The crossover of such methodologies is a fascinating subject, in that it leads one to wonder to what degree meditative methods are returning to their origin in shamanic phenomena, or to what degree shamanic phenomena are being syncretized into the Buddhist tradition through the common numinous ground they share. As we have endeavored to demonstrate, the development of *sādhana* is demonstrative of an ongoing, organic process, one that exists in the tension between the numinous qualities of virtuosity and charisma, so characteristic of shamanic authority, and the synthetic, socializing qualities characteristic of being integrated into the concerns of a larger society and a scholastic and ethically based culture. It also demonstrates the ongoing process of change and adaptation that can be said to be characteristic of meditative theory and practice, as found in both the Hindu and Buddhist contexts and particularly so in Vajrayāna Buddhism.

CONCLUSION

Meditation, Phenomenology, and the Concept of *Samādhi*

Redefining the Study of Meditation

Over the preceding pages two principal aims have been accomplished. The first was the development of a more satisfactory methodology for the study of meditation, and the second was the demonstration of the utility of such a methodology in concrete cases. The methodology developed in this study has been described as a new approach to phenomenology and has been applied at length to the practices of *dhyāna* and *samādhi* developed in the context of the Classical Yoga and Buddhist meditation systems. The concept of *samādhi* has been delineated as the conjunction of the meditative modalities of *samāpatti* and *nirodha*, paralleling our notions of numinous versus cessative religious phenomena in the broader context of yoga. The insights into the concept of *samādhi* obtained through this analysis demonstrate the validity and usefulness of integrating the psychological-phenomenological and the sociological approaches to the study of religious practice and experience. This development has had concrete ramifications in our understanding of the relationship between the Classical Yoga system of Patañjali and Indian Buddhism. This was demonstrated most notably through identifying common conceptions of the connection between meditation, cosmology, and divinity that have not been recognized previously—in particular, the relationship between the Brahmā divinities and meditative attainment found in both the Hindu and Buddhist contexts. We also have deepened our understanding of the manner in which meditation theory exists in a continuum between scholastic and yogic application and the manner in which text and tradition are adapted to suit a changing social and cultural context. A further element of significance that has emerged is the relationship between numinous and cessative conceptions of liberation in the meditative context and their formalization in religious ideals such as *kaivalya* and buddhahood. We have noted at length the manner in which the numinous dimensions of both Buddhism and Classical Yoga have played a significant, if not crucial, role in the development of meditative *praxis*, a reality that has been largely overlooked by scholarship in this area and that has great potential for future study.

It also has been noted that the role of meditation in both Hinduism and Buddhism, as well as in Jainism and in other *śramaṇa*-based traditions, is a complex one, a point that becomes clear in examining the dynamics of the role that meditation plays in both premodern and contemporary religious practice. As an extension of the early Indian religious context, in which the range of *śramaṇa* movements that yielded ideas of yoga in the Hindu, Buddhist, and Jaina traditions developed, the role and import of meditation have seen significant variations over time. The relationship between the larger traditions has not been a static one; rather, it demonstrates a continuity of influence, dialogue, and polemic over time. This book has helped weaken the notion that the Hindu, Buddhist, and Jaina traditions are autonomous and self-sufficient entities, an issue that has been addressed through the application of the idea of "tradition texts" to the development of meditative traditions. This has been further demonstrated through the examination of the boundary crossing and reinterpretation of yoga in light of the development of tantra, where sectarian autonomy can be said to give way to pan-Indian influences. As we have shown, in the context of Indian religion, meditation theory exists on a spectrum between pragmatic and scholastic interests, and as such, it demonstrates the tension between meditation as a central versus a peripheral phenomenon with the large religious and social order in which it exists.

We have defined *dhyāna* and *samādhi* as relating to the concepts of "meditation" and "absorption," respectively. Through an examination of the manner in which these terms play out in the path texts of the *Yogasūtras* and the *Bhāvanākrama*, we have sought to bring further subtlety to our understanding of the linguistic frame in which these terms operate. Noting the question of to what degree these texts are composite or syncretic in nature, it has been demonstrated how conceptions of *dhyāna* and *samādhi* show a tension between numinous and cessative qualities. These numinous and cessative qualities, termed *samāpatti* and *nirodha* in the context of Classical Yoga and *śamatha* and *vipaśyanā* in the Mahāyāna context, reflect a conception of the complementary operation of mental functions in the process of developing *samādhi*. As has been demonstrated, the numinous aspect of *samādhi* is tied to notions of attainment that are associated with the development of special powers of action and perception coexisting with cosmological conceptions of deity. The cessative aspect represents the drive toward detachment and release from the cosmological schema altogether. As Gonda has noted, the roots of *dhyāna* may be in conceptions of "vision." This is a notion that coheres with the idea that the development of *samādhi* is a numinous "seeing" that, by extension, leads to the liberated state and thus cessation. These complementary functions play out as well in the context of *bhāvanā*, which inherits and extends the notion of meditation being a process of visualization, cultivation, and a vehicle of soteriological purpose. Both *samāpatti* and *bhāvanā*, and thus *samādhi*, are understood to progress in a stepwise manner, and the development of *nirodha* can be understood either as complementary or as a radical disjunction from the *samāpatti* aspect, thus, out of this, questions arise about the primacy of one aspect of *samādhi* or another and, by extension, about where the liberated state lies on the spectrum. It has been argued that this tension can be understood to relate both to pragmatic and experiential concerns and to issues regarding the role that meditation plays in a particular religious context.

Constructivism, Context, and Experience

The notions of mysticism and religious experience have had a significant impact on conceptions of meditation in the Hindu and Buddhist traditions. Issues regarding core theories of mysticism have yielded interesting ideas regarding the nature of religious experience, from those of a fundamental "zero experience" to the distinction of mystical and numinous phenomena. Another key idea that bears an intimate relationship to our study is progression, the idea of a movement through a series of states that leads to some sort of culminating experience. A key point where such theoretical speculations have been challenged is in the idea that religious experience needs to be contextualized, and that there are no universal religious experiences. This position of constructivism is characterized by an emphasis on context in the formation of religious phenomenon and a concern with the problems inherent in talking about experiences comparatively. Though recognizing the validity of historical context, understood within the History of Religions as the condition of all religious experience, it has been argued that a strong or complete form of constructivism is problematic. It also has been argued that an incomplete form of constructivism provides for a more balanced perspective on religious phenomena, one that recognizes the subtle interplay between individual and environment. It has been noted as well that a number of proponents of what can be called a "common core theory of mysticism," such as Robert Forman and Agehananda Bharati, have observed the tentative relationship between religious experience and practice, understanding the catalytic function that *praxis* may or may not have. Furthermore, an important issue that is problematic for a complete constructivism is that it can be said to be in opposition theoretically to its own object of study, whether Classical Yoga, Theravāda or Mahāyāna Buddhism, Jainism, or any other tradition.

In arguing for a more satisfactory methodology, Robert Gimello's analysis of the practice of *śamatha* meditation and the role of discursive thought in Buddhist theory has illuminated a number of important issues. His conception that *śamatha* itself is a constructivist enterprise is a useful way of approaching the manner in which *dhyāna* and *samādhi* are understood to be cultivated across the scope of South Asian religion. Gimello does an excellent job in drawing out what we term the *numinous* qualities that arise from *śamatha* and, by extension, *samādhi*. The connection of the numinous and experiential side of the spectrum with *śamatha*, and the cessative and nonexperiential side of the spectrum with *nirvāṇa*, or *nirodha*, is a conception of *samādhi* that is paradigmatic to Classical Yoga as well as Buddhism. This tension is further reflected in conceptions regarding the ethical status of meditation, the nature of the soteriological process, and the nature of the state of liberation. It sets up a dynamic spectrum within which different conceptions of the religious life and different attitudes toward the world about liberation operate. In the Tibetan context, this has been shown to relate both to notions of *śamatha-vipaśyanā* and to questions of mediated versus unmediated experience. The idea that the direct perception of truth is beyond conceptuality is a point that plays out in the YS as well, in the distinction between the type of wisdom arising from experience versus scriptural and inferential knowledge.[1] This difference is a critical part of the soteriological conceptions of the meditative traditions of both Hinduism and Buddhism, in that there is a claim to a unique type of knowledge that is not simply the subordination of one conceptual schema to another.

We also have examined arguments that claim that studies centered on ideas of meditation in the Hindu and Buddhist context have misconstrued the role of religious experience in these traditions. The expanding recognition of inaccurate representations of Hindu and Buddhist culture in the academic study of religion is an issue of great relevance and import. In this context, it has been argued that a discriminating approach is one that recognizes the fact that meditation plays a different role in different contexts, but that it is nevertheless a critical element of these religious traditions. The fact that meditation is and has been associated with ritual and scholasticism demonstrates the range of roles that meditation concepts can play. Janet Gyatso has offered a number of significant points in this discussion, most notably the idea that experience, particularly *embodied* experience, is a critical part of Tibetan Buddhist self-understanding. She also notes the fact that this idea of experience is one that recognizes a relationship between conceptuality and nonconceptuality, the former preceding the latter. We have demonstrated how this can be interpreted as an incomplete constructivism in which conceptuality is the basis, but not the content, of experience, a position in line with the interpretation provided in this study.

From a psychological standpoint, this fundamental tension can be said to represent the tendencies toward narrowing the field of awareness and broadening it, thereby having immediate effects on the relative proportions of what is in conscious awareness versus that which is unconscious. It makes sense in this context that *samāpatti* types of meditation are referred to as "stabilizing," and the *nirodha* types are called "insight" or "discrimination," as they respectively refer to control over the contents of consciousness and the perception and release of unconscious psychological content. As Obeyesekere has noted, the yogin both establishes control over reality and confronts the fearsome aspects of it as well.[2] Traditional yogic conceptions follow this closely, noting the danger of falling prey to the lure of powers arising from yogic practices and the danger of falling into a state of pseudo-liberation that represents only temporary liberation. We have noted as well that the tension between the individual and environment is reflected in the manner in which meditative methods engage the psychological, cosmological, and mythical levels of reality through the conjunction of numinous and cessative qualities.

Bridging the Gap: *Enstasis*, *Ecstasis*, and a New Phenomenology

As we have argued, Eliade's development of the conceptions of *enstasis* and *ecstasis* provides a useful background for further exploring the conception that *samādhi* is a function of complementary methodologies characterized by numinous and cessative qualities. Though Eliade's distinction is useful in understanding some of the important distinctions between yoga and shamanism, it can be expanded and adapted in a number of ways to provide a more nuanced understanding of yoga practices in Hinduism and Buddhism. The numinous qualities of Theravāda Buddhism that parallel shamanic contemplations of death demonstrate what are more *ecstatic* qualities of Buddhist conceptions of yoga and hint at the even greater complexity of the numinous dimensions of tantric practice. In terms of conceptions of meditative ascension, it has been demonstrated how the development of *samādhi* in both Classical Yoga and Buddhist accounts might be better understood as the conjunction of *enstatic* and *ecstatic* modalities rather than simply as one or the other. The fact that *samādhi* is both a cognitive function and is connected to cosmological ideas is an issue that Eliade recognizes in the Buddhist context and one that should be extended to our understanding of the Classical Yoga system as well. It also can be tied into questions regarding the nature of liberation that arise out of the tension between *enstatic* and *ecstatic* conceptions of *kaivalya* and *jīvanmukti*. As we have seen, the import of numinous conceptions becomes clear in examining the yoga practitioner as a "psychopomp," in examining the language of illness and cure in the Hindu and Buddhist contexts, and in analyzing the emphasis on embodied images in the tantric context.

It has been further suggested that the expansion of the phenomenological approach to incorporate both psychological and sociological conceptions may shed further insight into the practice of yoga and meditation. As we have shown, Eliade's conceptions of religious experience and mysticism are valuable in uncovering a number of different dimensions of religious practice. However, it has been suggested that phenomenological theory needs to be expanded to better represent the dynamic relationship between person and environment. This theory is in line with the concept of an incomplete constructivism, one that recognizes the validity of understanding from the perspective of autonomy and from the position of context. The conceptions of *enstasis* and *ecstasis* and those of the *numinous* and *cessative* have been compared to Lewis's conceptions regarding central and peripheral cults in ecstatic religion. This has led to the establishment of another dynamic relationship, one between a central and a peripheral cult status and the numinous and cessative qualities of practice and experience. It can be argued as well that these dimensions are never completely separate so much as they are on a spectrum.

This new phenomenological approach immediately finds a degree of impact in examining the tension between pragmatic and scholastic approaches in meditation. This context may demonstrate the manner in which formerly peripheral dimensions of religion become part of the mainstream through a process of becoming ritualistic and scholastic. We have discussed this process with respect to the *śramaṇic* traditions, where earlier charismatic authority and an emphasis on yogic practice become, over time, integrated into mainstream cultural conceptions and form a foundation for ritual observance. Another example is tantra, which, as a peripheral cult, challenged key philosophical doctrines of mainstream religion and provided new types of *praxis*, only to be integrated back into mainstream conceptions of philosophy and ethics. We have postulated that the tension between a peripheral and a central cult may be tied into conceptions of the *numinous* and *cessative*, that the idea of meditative attainment, *samāpatti*, represents both psychologically and socially the individualization of power, and that *nirodha* represents its flowing out to the environment on both the psychological and social levels. Particularly interesting is the question of where differing conceptions of soteriology exist on this spectrum. These would include, among them, Upaniṣadic conceptions of *mokṣa*, Hindu and Jaina conceptions of *kaivalya*, Vedāntic conceptions of *mokṣa* and *jīvanmukti*, and Theravāda, Mahāyāna, and Vajrayāna conceptions of *nirvāṇa* and buddhahood.

Issues of Influence and Comparison

In order to better understand questions regarding the origin and development of meditative methods and to demonstrate the validity of the methodological approach proposed in this study, we have examined the question of influence in the relationship of Classical Yoga and Buddhism. In particular, we have examined the manner in which a number of notable scholars have approached this subject, including Emile Sénart, Louis de la Vallée Poussin, Herman Oldenburg, Mircea Eliade, Winston King, and others. Out of this discussion ideas emerge regarding the shared theoretical conceptions of the nature of *samādhi* and the methods for developing this state as found in the Hindu and Buddhist traditions. This brings up important questions such as that of superstructure and whether there can be a technical skill in meditation that is separable from greater metaphysical and soteriological concerns. Though this question has been addressed only briefly, it can be argued that it is clear that these techniques are being adapted to suit different contexts, but at the same time these contexts are not radically different from one another with respect to a number of foundational soteriological issues.

In the context of the comparison of the Pātañjala Yoga system and selected schools of Indian Buddhism, it is clear that notions of *samādhi* have been developed in dialogue and discussion with one another, sharing both pragmatic and philosophical conceptions. Nearly all of the scholars who have approached this subject have noted the intimate relationship between the development of meditative ideas in the *śramaṇic* context and in the Vedic context. Though there is some dispute over the primacy of Vedic versus non-Vedic traditions and questions regarding the primacy of meditative concepts in Upaniṣadic versus Buddhist contexts, it is clear that the body of knowledge regarding ascetic techniques is represented systematically, as yoga had a wide dissemination in the ancient Indian context. Eliade and King have noted how this question of influence may have played out in the context of a tension between scholars and practitioners, or in questions about the relative importance of yogic attainments and the power of analysis and discursive thought. We have noted how this tension is representative of the relationship between central and peripheral cults, characterized by the development of mainstream scholastic interpretations and the shift from the charismatic authority of the *śramaṇa* context toward the monastic and scholastic authority of mainstream Hinduism and Buddhism. Scholastic practice, however, should not necessarily be understood to be bereft of an idea of *praxis* either, however, and it is clearly the case, as Zahler and Cox have noted, that the boundary between scholasticism and meditation may be a fluid one in some contexts.

The work of Bronkhorst, Larson, Yamashita, and others has expanded our understanding of the context in which the Classical Yoga tradition was formed in the early centuries of the Common Era. The question of whether or not Classical Yoga was ever an autonomous tradition of its own and whether or not the YS itself is a composite text remains a challenge to seeing Classical Yoga as a unique tradition. If Bronkhorst and Larson are followed, then it would make more sense to understand the Classical Yoga tradition as the attempt of Sāṃkhya philosophers to wrestle with the challenge of Buddhist Abhidharma sources and the development of new philosophical trends emerging from this engagement. However, the question of the roots of the Classical Yoga system in the Upaniṣadic context, in the *śramaṇa* context, and in the early development of the Indian philosophical systems still remains unclear. One element of this that needs further investigation and elaboration is the question of proto-YS texts, such as that attributed to Hiraṇyagarbha. Another key issue that may yield further insights, and that has been pursued to some degree by Bronkhorst and Chapple, is the possibility of differentiating the viewpoints of the YS and the YBh. This may help clarify to what degree the YBh stands for a further development of the thought of the YS and to what degree these two texts are at parity with one another. Further research clearly needs to be done in examining both the YS and YBh in light of the contents of the *Abhidharmakośa* and its *bhāṣya*. Such a study will bring considerably more light to the common vocabulary of these traditions. As Chakravarti has noted, the relationship between the development of Abhidharma theory and conceptions in Sāṃkhya remains a subject that may offer considerable revelations about the influence and pervasion of different theories in Indian philosophy.

It also has been argued that the numinous dimensions of the Classical Yoga tradition need more attention and exposition. The further development of the Vedic concepts of *tapas* and *svādhyāya* indicates that the Yoga tradition did not see itself as simply a philosophy of liberation or as simply instruction in a meditative process. Both the inclusion of Īśvara as being the prototypical yogin and the conception of the idea of an *īṣṭadevatā* indicate that the YS is not simply reiterating a rationalist, philosophical theory. The complementary nature of the *abhyāsa-vairāgya* distinction further underlines the dynamic relationship between the numinous and cessative approaches to liberation. The idea of *nirodhasamāpatti* can be said to signify the point at which such approaches come together. Clearly both traditions contain notions that there can be such an attainment as well as other attainments, such as *asaṃjñisamāpatti*, that closely approximate but are not equivalent to such a state. What is most striking, however, is that upon closer investigation, it becomes clear that the cosmological connections that are made with *samāpatti* in Buddhism are closely followed in the context of Classical Yoga as well. Whether or not the cosmology of Classical Yoga is identical to the three-realm system of Buddhism, it is clear that the levels of *samāpatti* are understood to be identical to the states of consciousness of the deities (the

Brahmās). Beyond the explicit cosmological associations are many conceptions in the YBh that situate the practice of yoga within the numinous dimension of all sorts of mythical beings, magical powers, and mythical objects of delight. Perhaps it can be further said that chapter 3 of the YS, *vibhūtipāda*, which often seems like an appendage in light of the soteriological concerns of the text, makes more sense within a vision of the YS that understands the import of the numinous dimension of meditation theory.

Issues in Tantrism

The role of the meditative concepts in the development of tantric *sādhana* has further demonstrated the utility of the numinous-cessative paradigm in understanding both the philosophical and social dimensions of the Buddhist tradition in the Indo-Tibetan region. It was established that rather than being a concept that had been abandoned in the development of tantra, the concept of *samādhi* was reinterpreted in light of these new trends in religious thought. Thus the distinctions of *samāpatti-nirodha* and *śamatha-vipaśyanā* can be understood as the foundation upon which tantric theory was built, and as a result, *sādhana* demonstrates similar dynamics in its philosophical applications and its role within its cultural context. Tantra emphasizes the numinous dimension of religious practice, the relationship and identity with mythical figurations, and the peripheral quality of challenging mainstream conceptions of religion and ethics. However, the adaptation of tantra within the monastic context makes clear that tantra was suitable for interpretation and integration into the tradition as a central cult that was more focused on the cessative dimension, such as that which occurred in the late Indian and Tibetan contexts.

Playing on conceptions such as manifestation and dissolution, the attainment or approximation of powers of deities, and notions regarding the liberated state using the language of spaciousness, tantra demonstrates the extension of the dynamic relationship of attainment and cessation characteristic of its predecessors. In the Buddhist context, this relationship may or may not be directly associated with the *śamatha-vipaśyanā* distinction that plays such a critical role in classical accounts of the means to liberation. This can extend even farther through the development of *maithuna* imagery, where the tension inherent in the soteriological vision of tantra is represented in the form of male and female divinities. The practice of visualization and identification, however, has deep roots in the Buddhist tradition, demonstrated by the Theravāda conceptions of *anussati* centered on the Buddha, deities, and other objects. The relationship between meditation and divinity is one that demonstrates significant continuity, whether we speak about the types of yoga practiced in the *śramaṇic* context, those found in the classical period of development in both Hinduism and Buddhism, or those that developed under the influence of tantric theory. In the tantric context, the example of Vajrayoginī has served the purpose of demonstrating the vivid imagery of the tantric Buddhist pantheon and the liminal status of such tantric deities, which plays into both conceptions of the numinous and of tantra as a peripheral cult. This further brings to light the important connection between the numinous qualities of enlightened beings, referred to as *siddhi*, and the cessative qualities, referred to as *bodhi*, underlying the tantric conception of liberation as an embodied state characterized by both dimensions.

CONCLUSION

The application of the methodological approach proposed in this work offers much promise for expanding our understanding of the internal dynamics of the practice of meditation and the manner in which such practices inform and are informed by the religious and cultural contexts in which they are situated. In this respect, it can be understood as an extension of the ideals of the History of Religions methodology and an inherently comparative approach to the study of religion. The immediate value of such a comparative approach is that it moves us beyond orientalist conceptions of Hinduism, Buddhism, and Jainism, through understanding their continuity within the greater scope of Indian culture, as opposed to seeing them as isolated entities. The conception of the *numinous-cessative* distinction provides for an incomplete constructivism that values both comparison and contextuality in the study of meditation. This offers a context in which to understand both the experiential dimension of meditation and its reality as a foundation for scholasticism and ritual, dimensions of meditation that often have been viewed as being at odds with one another in contemporary scholarship. It also has ramifications in how ideas of liberation are understood on both philosophical and social levels, whether it is considered a state of absolute separation from the world or one that is described as an embodied state of liberation within the world. As a new form of phenomenology, this methodology has sought to bring together psychological and sociological approaches in order to better grasp the relationship between experience and context, or between autonomy and environment. As has been demonstrated, this approach has much to offer to the study of meditation in the context of the religions of India and provides a foundation for the further development of the History of Religions methodology in the study of religion.

Notes

Introduction

1. For a discussion of these issues, see J. J. Clarke, *Oriental Enlightenment: The Encounter between Asian and Western Thought* (New York: Routledge, 1997); Mark C. Taylor, ed., *Critical Terms for Religious Studies* (Chicago: University of Chicago Press, 1998); Richard King, *Orientalism and Religion: Postcolonial Theory, India, and "The Mystic East"* (New York: Routledge, 1999); Kimberly C. Patton and Benjamin C. Ray, eds., *A Magic Still Dwells: Comparative Religion in the Postmodern Age* (Berkeley: University of California Press, 2000).

2. See Mircea Eliade, *The Sacred and the Profane: The Nature of Religion*, trans. Willard R. Trask (New York: Harcourt Brace Jovanovich, 1959), 201–13.

3. Ibid.

4. Robert Ellwood, *Alternative Altars: Unconventional and Eastern Spirituality in America* (Chicago: University of Chicago Press, 1979), 20–64.

5. Frits Staal, *Exploring Mysticism: A Methodological Essay* (Berkeley: University of California Press, 1975), 168–89.

6. Ellwood, *Alternative Altars*, 57–58. Ellwood notes the separation of "religion" from "spirituality," which can be said to provide for the possibility of a *liminal* space between the interior and exterior of a religious community.

7. Erica Bourguignon, *Religion, Altered States of Consciousness, and Social Change* (Columbus: Ohio State University Press, 1973), 340–56.

8. Gananath Obeyesekere, *The Work of Culture: Symbolic Transformation in Psychoanalysis and Anthropology* (Chicago: University of Chicago Press, 1990), 51–68.

9. Gavin Flood provides a concise exposition on this tension in the study of religion in his recent work *Beyond Phenomenology: Rethinking the Study of Religion* (New York: Cassell, 1999).

10. This will be examined at length later with respect to Robert Sharf's discussion of the impact of orientalism on Hindu and Buddhist self-representation. See Robert H. Sharf, "Buddhist Modernism and the Rhetoric of Meditative Experience,"

Numen 42 (1995): 228–93; "Experience," in *Critical Terms for Religious Studies*, ed. Mark C. Taylor (Chicago: University of Chicago Press, 1998), 94–116.

11. This tension might be said to be exemplified in the work of Bryan Rennie and Russell McCutcheon regarding Eliade's phenomenology and in Huston Smith's recent text on the study of religion and popular culture. The positions of Rennie and McCutcheon are illustrated in Bryan Rennie, ed., *Changing Religious Worlds: The Meaning and End of Mircea Eliade* (Albany: State University of New York Press, 2001). Smith's reflections, which are aimed more at a mainstream audience, are represented in his *Why Religion Matters: The Fate of the Human Spirit in an Age of Disbelief* (San Francisco: Harper San Francisco, 2000).

12. Post-orientalist scholarship has demonstrated how religious ideas become part of this process, becoming "commodities" in a "spirituality market," only faintly resembling their manifestation in historical and cultural contexts. While this is a significant critique of our culture's ability to commodify and invert meanings, it has led to an unwarranted cynicism regarding the ideals expressed in the Indian and Tibetan traditions and meditation more generally. These issues are demonstrated in Donald S. Lopez, *Prisoners of Shangri-La* (Chicago: University of Chicago Press, 1998) and in the range of criticism it has drawn. See the series of review essays by David Germano, Tsering Shakya, and Robert A. F. Thurman and a subsequent response by Lopez in *Journal for the American Academy of Religion* 69:1 (2001): 163–213.

13. The growing emphasis on ethnography and on culturally situating text can be said to represent an understanding of social dynamics as the focus of postmodern thought. For a discussion of the reorientation of the study of religion in light of postmodernism, see Taylor, *Critical Terms for Religious Studies*, 1–19. On the need to balance generic (phenomenological) and specific (anthropological) aspects in the study of religion, see William E. Paden, "Elements of a New Comparativism," in *A Magic Still Dwells: Comparative Religion in the Postmodern Age*, ed. Patton and Ray (Berkeley: University of California Press, 2000), 182–92.

14. Clarke, *Oriental Enlightenment*, 211–12.

15. George Kalamaras, "The Center and Circumference of Silence: Yoga, Poststructuralism, and the Rhetoric of Paradox," *International Journal of Hindu Studies* 1:1 (1997): 4–5.

16. Ibid., 3–4.

17. Ibid., 4.

18. Ibid., 5–6.

19. King identifies the propensity to separate the "mystical" from the "rational" as one of the underlying themes of both modernist and, by extension, orientalist approaches to the study of religion. This dichotomy, as King notes, is by no means applicable to Indian philosophical and religious literature, as the Indian tradition demonstrates the full spectrum of such thinking. See King, *Orientalism and Religion*, 7–34.

20. King, *Orientalism and Religion*, 161–86.

21. Kalamaras, "The Center and Circumference of Silence," 7–11. For a discussion of issues regarding the relationship of *samādhi* and *dhyāna* to Vedāntic conceptions of liberation, see Jonathan Bader, *Meditation in Śaṅkara's Vedanta* (New Delhi: Aditya Prakashan, 1990), and Michael Comans, "The Question of the Importance of *Samādhi* in Modern and Classical Advaita Vedānta," *Philosophy East & West* 43:1 (1993): 19–38.

22. On Gadamer's thesis of interpretation, see Hans H. Penner, "Interpretation," in *Guide to the Study of Religion*, ed. Willi Braun and Russell T. McCutcheon (London: Cassell, 2000), 57–71.

23. King, *Orientalism and Religion*, 74.

24. Mircea Eliade, *The Quest: History and Meaning in Religion* (Chicago: University of Chicago Press, 1969b), 62. Gadamer's notion of dialogue might be contrasted with a more insight-oriented understanding, which would be a point of divergence between the two scholars' approaches to text. See Clarke, *Oriental Enlightenment*, 189–90. Beyond demonstrating the dialogic character of Gadamer's interpretation, Clarke also notes how scholars such as Halbfass and Turner have demonstrated that the process of interpretation is in significant operation *within* what we would characterize as a single culture and tradition, weakening Gadamer's case regarding comparison (183–84). On the issue of the comparison of Eliade's and Gadamer's thought, see Bryan S. Rennie, *Reconstructing Eliade: Making Sense of Religion* (Albany: State University of New York Press, 1996), 228–29.

25. Eliade, *The Quest*, 63–64. For an extended discussion of the question of the relationship of Eliade's theory to postmodernism, see Rennie, *Reconstructing Eliade*, 215–41.

Chapter 1

1. Gerald Larson, "Classical Yoga as Neo-Sāṃkhya: A Chapter in the History of Indian Philosophy," *Asiatische Studien* 53:3 (1999): 723–32. It might be asked as well to what degree such a "tradition text" could be considered to precede the formation of sectarian traditions, an issue tied closely to the debate regarding the origins of yoga.

2. See Tenzin Gyatso (H. H. the Dalai Lama), *Stages of Meditation*, trans. Geshe Lobsang Jordhen, Lobsang Choephel Ganchepa, and Jeremy Russell (Ithaca, N.Y.: Snow Lion Press, 2001). The BK has been used in recent years by the Dalai Lama in the context of teaching meditation seminars to Buddhist groups throughout the United States. Another version of the text that has been used in this context is Ācārya Kamalaśīla, *The Stages of Meditation Middle Volume (Bhāvanākrama II)*, trans. Ven. Geshe Lhundub Sopa, Ven. Elvin W. Jones, and John Newman (Madison, Wis.: Deer Park Books, 1998).

3. Paul Williams, *Mahāyāna Buddhism: The Doctrinal Foundations* (New York: Routledge, 1989), 196–97.

4. Johannes Bronkhorst, "Patañjali and the Yoga Sūtras," *Studien zur Indologie und Iranistik* 10 (1985): 191–212.

5. Johannes Bronkhorst, "Yoga and Seśvara Sāṃkhya," *Journal of Indian Philosophy* 9 (1981): 309–20. It should be pointed out that this "malleability" has been part of the reason the YS is seen as such an important *practice* text, and not simply a source for Sāṃkhya philosophy.

6. See Staal, *Exploring Mysticism*, 86–91.

7. For a discussion of alternate scenarios regarding this debate, see Herbert Guenther, "Meditation Trends in Early Tibet," in *Early Ch'an in China and Tibet*, ed. Whalen Lai and Lewis R. Lancaster (Berkeley, Calif.: Asian Humanities Press, 1983), 351–56.

8. Lewis Gomez has noted problems in viewing the sudden-gradual debate as being fundamentally an issue of Indian versus Chinese understandings of Buddhism. See his article "Indian Materials on the Doctrine of Sudden Enlightenment," in *Early Ch'an in China and Tibet*, 425–26.

9. D. S. Ruegg, *Buddha-Nature, Mind, and the Problem of Gradualism in a Comparative Perspective: On the Transmission and Reception of Buddhism in India and Tibet* (London: School of Oriental and African Studies, 1989), 111–12.

10. YS II.29, *yamaniyamāsanaprāṇāyāmapratyāhāradhāraṇādhyānasamādhayo' ṣṭāvaṅgānī.*

11. YS I.39; YS II.11.

12. YS IV.6.

13. YBh, III.2.

14. Jan Gonda, *The Vision of the Vedic Poets* (The Hague, the Netherlands: Mouton & Co., 1963), 289.

15. Ibid.

16. Ibid., 18.

17. Ibid., 289–95.

18. Ibid., 296.

19. Ibid., 298.

20. Bader, *Meditation in Śaṅkara's Vedanta*, 40–44.

21. Gonda, *Vision of the Vedic Poets*, 299–300.

22. Bader, *Meditation*, 25.

23. Ibid., 26.

24. Ibid.

25. Ibid., 28.

26. Ibid., 29.

27. Ibid., 32.

28. YS II.34, *vitarkā hiṃsādayaḥ kṛtakāritānumoditā lobhakrodhamohapurvakā mṛdumadhyādhimātrā duḥkhājñānānantaphalā iti pratipakṣabhāvanam.*

29. Ācārya Gyaltsen Namdol, ed., *Bhāvanākramaḥ of Ācārya Kamalaśīla: Tibetan Version, Sanskrit Restoration, and Hindi Translation* (Sarnath: Central Institute of Higher Tibetan Studes, 1985), 181.

30. Ibid., 223.

31. Ibid., 227.

32. Ian Whicher, *The Integrity of the Yoga Darśana: A Reconsideration of Classical Yoga* (Albany: State University of New York Press, 1998a), 181–90.

33. Ibid., 202.

34. Ibid., 216.

35. Sir M. Monier-Williams, *A Sanskrit-English Dictionary* (Oxford: Oxford University Press, 1899), 1161. Monier-Williams specifically refers to the YS for a series of definitions.

36. Franklin Edgerton, *Buddhist Hybrid Sanskrit Grammar and Dictionary, Volume II: Dictionary* (New Haven, Conn.: Yale University Press, 1953), 569–70.

37. YS III.4, *trayamekatra saṃyamaḥ*.

38. Whicher, *The Integrity of the Yoga Darśana*, 184.

39. Ibid., 182–83.

40. Paramananda Sharma, trans., *Bhāvanākrama of Kamalaśīla* (New Delhi: Aditya Prakashan, 1997), 55.

41. Namdol, *Bhāvanākramaḥ*, 204.

42. Mircea Eliade, *Yoga: Immortality and Freedom* (Princeton: Bollingen, 1990), 101–38.

43. Eliade, *Yoga*, 236.

44. Jean Filliozat, *Religion, Philosophy, Yoga* (Delhi: Motilal Banarsidass, 1991), 379.

45. David M. Knipe, *In the Image of Fire: Vedic Experiences of Heat* (Delhi: Motilal Banarsidass, 1975), 53–54 passim.

46. Edward Crangle, *The Origin and Development of Early Indian Contemplative Practices* (Wiesbaden: Harrassowitz, 1994), 274.

47. Winston King, *Theravāda Meditation: The Buddhist Transformation of Yoga* (Delhi: Motilal Banarsidass, 1992).

48. Henepola Gunaratana, *The Path of Serenity and Insight: An Explanation of the Buddhist Jhānas* (Delhi: Motilal Banarsidass, 1985), 3.

49. Ven. Geshe Lhundub Sopa, "*Śamathavipaśyanāyuganaddha:* The Two Leading Principles of Buddhist Meditation," in *Mahāyāna Buddhist Meditation: Theory and Practice*, ed. Minoru Kiyota (Honolulu: University Press of Hawaii, 1978), 52.

50. Gunaratana, *The Path of Serenity and Insight*, 136. Buddhaghosa refers to momentary concentration *(khaṇika-samādhi)* and the "bare-insight worker" *(sukkha-*

vipassaka) a number of times in the *Visuddhimagga*. An interesting point is that in the discussion of cessation, Buddhaghosa notes that bare-insight workers are classed among those individuals who *cannot* attain cessation. See Bhikku Nyanamoli, trans., *The Path of Purification (Visuddhimagga)* (Colombo: A. Semage, 1964), 778–82, 824–83.

51. L. S. Cousins, "Buddhist *Jhāna*: Its Nature and Attainment according to the Pali Sources," *Religion* 3 (1973): 115–31; Paul Griffiths, "Concentration or Insight: The Problematic of Theravāda Buddhist Meditation-Theory," *Journal of the American Academy of Religion* 49:4 (1981): 605–24; Martin Stuart-Fox, "*Jhāna* and Buddhist Scholasticism," *Journal of the International Association of Buddhist Studies* 12:2 (1989): 79–105; Roderick S. Bucknell, "Reinterpreting the *Jhānas*," *Journal of the International Association of Buddhist Studies* 16:2 (1993): 374–409.

52. On modern interpretations of *samatha-vipassanā*, see George D. Bond, *The Buddhist Revival in Sri Lanka: Religious Tradition, Reinterpretation, and Response* (Columbia: University of South Carolina Press, 1988).

53. Leah Zahler, "The Concentrations and Formless Absorptions in Mahāyāna Buddhism: Ge-Luk Tibetan Interpretations" (Ph.D. dissertation, University of Virginia, 1994), 21–42.

CHAPTER 2

1. Agehananda Bharati, *The Light at the Center* (Santa Barbara, Calif.: Ross-Erikson, 1976), 25.

2. Ninian Smart, "Understanding Religious Experience," in *Mysticism and Philosophical Analysis*, ed. Steven T. Katz (New York: Oxford University Press, 1978), 10–21.

3. Robert K. C. Forman, "Mysticism, Constructivism, and Forgetting," in *The Problem of Pure Consciousness* (New York: Oxford University Press, 1990), 3–49.

4. Ibid.

5. Ibid., 10.

6. Bharati, *The Light at the Center*, 87–111.

7. This was an informal comment made during a panel discussion on the subject of mysticism at the Annual Meeting of the American Academy of Religion, Nashville, Tennessee, November 18–21, 2000.

8. Ibid.

9. King, *Orientalism and Religion*, 161–86.

10. Ibid., 178–80.

11. Ibid.

12. Ibid., 180.

13. Ibid., 181. King also notes the significance of the work of philosopher Bhartṛhari, who appears to have held a "constructivist" position of sorts with respect to religious phenomena.

14. Ibid., 183. King demonstrates how postmodern theory can be applied in a *positive* sense in uncovering presuppositions of scholarship that presumptively undercut the truth claims of the traditions studied.

15. Robert Gimello, "Mysticism and Meditation," in *Mysticism and Philosophical Analysis*, ed. Steven T. Katz (New York: Oxford University Press, 1978), 170–99.

16. A key issue of import here is the distinction between knowledge and experience regarding the meditative process. At issue is the manner in which experience is "created" through the internalizaiton of the meditative discipline. However, it might be argued that though consciousness is being informed or shaped by the discipline, nevertheless the perception of the meditative subject *(ālambana)* is thought to be a direct and clear perception, not "constructed." Likewise, the modes of higher perception *(abhijñā)* and manifestation *(nirmāṇa)* that result from advanced *śamatha* are said to be phenomenally real and not simply mental constructions or perceptions.

17. Ibid., 181. An error that Buddhist sources often claim to be characteristic of non-Buddhist traditions as well.

18. Ibid., 183.

19. Ibid., 184. This might be argued to be a very *sūtra*-oriented interpretation of Mahāyāna soteriology.

20. In Vajrayāna, this becomes more problematic to argue, due to the breaking down of the distinction between the *sādhaka* and the deity. The stress on the impermanence of the figure does not take away from the fact that the goal of Mahāyāna and Vajrayāna is buddhahood and the subsequent ability to manifest oneself in myriad forms.

21. Ibid., 185.

22. Smart, "Understanding Religious Experience." Smart, however, would likely argue that the experiences characterized as mystical are those characterized by cessation, as opposed to those of the numinous, that is, the powers coming out of *śamatha*. Another interpretation would be that his distinction hinges upon the nature of the religious object as either "self" or "other."

23. Ibid., 13.

24. Ibid.

25. Ibid., 20.

26. Gimello, "Mysticism and Meditation," 187. Following the development of *dharmamegha samādhi*, described in YS IV.29, IV.30, and IV.31, are, respectively, *tataḥ kleśakarmanivṛttiḥ*, "From that point, there is the cessation of the activity of the afflictions," and *tadā sarvāvaraṇamalāpetasya jñānasyānantyājjñeyamalpam*, "Then, due to the endless knowledge free from the impurity of all obstructions, little is to be known."

27. T. S. Rukmani argues that a key tension in the YS exists between *vyutthāna* and *nirodha*, "manifestation" and "cessation." Although this opposition would seem to counter an idea conjunction of *samāpatti* and *nirodha* in the YS, it ultimately indicates the equivocal nature of *samāpatti*. On the one hand, *samādhi* is the basis for the development of the range of *siddhis* documented in the *vibhūtipāda* (chapter 3) of the YS, and on the other hand, as it states in YS III.37, *te samādhau upasargāḥ siddhayaḥ*, "these [*prātibha*, special forms of perception, referred to in III.36] are perfections in manifestation, impediments for [*nirbija*] *samādhi*." See T. S. Rukmani, "Tension between *Vyutthāna* and *Nirodha* in the *Yoga-Sūtras*," *Journal of Indian Philosophy* 25 (1997): 613–28.

28. Ibid., 189.

29. Robert Gimello, "Mysticism in Its Contexts," in *Mysticism and Religious Traditions*, ed. Steven T. Katz (New York: Oxford University Press, 1983), 61–88.

30. Ibid., 72.

31. YS II.34.

32. See Williams, *Mahāyāna Buddhism*, 29–33, 49–54.

33. Anne C. Klein, *Knowledge and Liberation: Tibetan Buddhist Epistemology in Support of Transformative Religious Experience* (Ithaca, N.Y.: Snow Lion Publications, 1986).

34. Ibid., 13.

35. Ibid., 18.

36. Gimello, "Mysticism and Meditation," 72.

37. Anne C. Klein, "Mental Concentration and the Unconditioned," in *Paths to Liberation: The Mārga and Its Transformation in Buddhist Thought*, ed. Robert E. Buswell Jr. and Robert M. Gimello (Honolulu: University of Hawaii Press, 1992), 270.

38. Ibid., 271.

39. Ibid., 281.

40. Ibid., 284. Tilmann Vetter states that this "contradiction in terms" is such that it should lead to the questioning of Buddhist assertions of soteriology about the notion of such discrimination. This issue leads Vetter to offer the hypothesis that the nondiscursive experience of the fourth *dhyāna* attained by the Buddha was tantamount to his liberation, and that later tradition superimposed the discursive element upon his teachings and his life narrative. See Tilmann Vetter, *The Ideas and Meditative Practices of Early Buddhism* (New York: E. J. Brill, 1988), xxi–xxxvi, 3–6.

41. Ibid., 295.

42. Lloyd Pflueger, "Discriminating the Innate Capacity," in *The Innate Capacity: Mysticism, Psychology, and Philosophy*, ed. Robert K. C. Forman (New York: Oxford University Press, 1998), 47.

43. Ibid., 48.

44. Ibid., 52.

45. Ibid., 54.

46. Ibid., 55.

47. Ibid., 56.

48. Ibid., 59.

49. Larson, "Classical Yoga as Neo-Sāṃkhya," 730–32.

50. Ibid., 69.

51. Ibid.

52. In this context, John Dunne has demonstrated how Dharmakīrti and Chandrakīrti struggled with finding a way to reconcile what can be referred to as the *numinous* and *cessative* characteristics of the Buddha, the fact that according to Mahāyāna, the Buddha was at once utterly transcendent and a compassionate guide. It appears that one of the things that characterizes and differentiates these traditions is to what degree they have attempted to reconcile the numinous and cessative dimensions of their soteriology, or where they exist on that spectrum. Mario D'Amato also has noted that from the viewpoint of the *Mahāyānasūtrālamkāra*, the most significant characteristic of the Mahāyāna is that it leads to buddhahood, as opposed to non-Buddhist paths and the paths of the so-called Hīnayāna, demonstrating the central import of competing ideas of soteriology. On these issues, see John D. Dunne, "Thoughtless Buddha, Passionate Buddha," *Journal of the American Academy of Religion* 64:3 (1993): 525–55; Mario D'Amato, "The Mahāyāna-Hīnayāna Distinction in the *Mahāyānasūtrālamkāra*: A Terminological Analysis" (Ph.D. dissertation, University of Chicago, 2000), 134. The complex range of philosophical and pragmatic issues that embodied liberation present in Indo-Tibetan Buddhism is dealt with extensively in John J. Makransky, *Buddhahood Embodied: Sources of Controversy in India and Tibet* (Albany: State University of New York Press, 1997).

53. Sharf, "Buddhist Modernism," 94–116.

54. Ibid., 229.

55. Ibid., 231.

56. Ibid.

57. Ibid., 236.

58. Ibid., 237–39.

59. Ibid.

60. Ibid. As noted earlier, on this point see King, *Orientalism and Religion*, 178–80.

61. Ibid., 269.

62. Ibid., 243.

63. Ibid., 261–62.

64. Ibid.

65. Janet Gyatso, "Healing Burns with Fire: The Facilitations of Experience in Tibetan Buddhism," *Journal of the American Academy of Religion* 67:1 (1999): 113–47.

66. YS I.5.

67. Another problem with Sharf's theory arises in the context of his arguing more broadly against the conception of experience. In doing so, he misconstrues experience and memory, claiming that inconsistencies in people's memory of certain experiences demonstrate the constituted nature of experience. In fact, all this observation does is reveal the constituted and impermanent nature of *memory*, that our understanding of experience and our engagement with the world are contingent to some degree upon our perspective in time and space. Memory tends to be less clear over time, and therefore interpretation and interpolation may well be active parts of dealing with hazy or long-forgotten memories. Common experiences are likely to be reported in divergent ways the farther away in time from the event, and this should be no surprise. People are more likely to agree about a shared experience if they are closer in spatial and temporal proximity to the actual event. The experience itself may be understood differently by the various perceiving subjects, but certain aspects should approximate each other. The epistemology of Classical Yoga might be invoked here to talk about this distinction, that memory and direct perception are both modes of experience (*smṛti* and *pratyakṣa*) but distinct in form and function. It also should be noted that both Classical Yoga and Buddhism allow for direct types of perception that are at different levels of clarity and different levels of consistency regarding the actual nature of reality. See Sharf, "Experience," 107–14.

68. Gyatso, "Healing Burns with Fire," 115.

69. Ibid., 116.

70. Ibid., 138.

71. Ibid., 138–39.

72. Ibid., 120, 126.

73. Mircea Eliade, *Myths, Dreams, and Mysteries: The Encounter between Contemporary Faiths and Archaic Realities* (New York: Harper & Row, 1960), 47–56.

74. The notion of spaciousness has particular relevance in the Buddhist context as representative of ideas regarding the "skylike" nature of mind found in systems such as Mahāmudrā.

75. Gananath Obeyesekere, *Medusa's Hair: An Essay on Personal Symbols and Religious Experience* (Chicago: University of Chicago Press, 1981), 180.

76. Ibid., 180–81.

77. Ibid.

78. Obeyesekere, *The Work of Culture*, 68.

79. Ibid.

80. Ibid., 52.

81. Ibid., 65–67.

82. Speculations on the relationship of neurophysiology to shamanism can be found in Michael Winkelman, *Shamanism: The Neural Ecology of Consciousness and Healing* (Westport, Conn.: Bergin & Garvey, 2000).

83. Frits Staal, *Rules without Meaning: Rituals, Mantras, and the Human Sciences* (New York: Peter Lang, 1989).

84. It is interesting to note that this view is easily inverted, in arguing that particular types of religious practice are "anti-evolutionary" and result in "primitive" modes of consciousness or awareness.

85. Eliade, *Yoga*, 66–67.

86. The topic of the *siddhis* or *vibhūtis* offered by Pātañjala Yoga has been discussed at length by Yohanan Grinshpon in *Silence Unheard: Deathly Otherness in Pātañjala Yoga* (Albany: State University of New York Press, 2002), 32–35 passim. Grinshpon offers a number of provocative theories regarding the *vibhūtis* and of *kaivalya*, linking liberation to the concept of near-death states in a creative manner. Though he situates the *vibhūtis* in a more central position, which is in agreement with our discussion, he nevertheless postulates an ultimate state of *kaivalya* that is more *cessative* than *numinous* in its character, as the "dying yogin" passes ultimately beyond the world into complete isolation, the "deathly otherness."

87. Staal, *Exploring Mysticism*, 168–89.

CHAPTER 3

*This chapter is a revised, expanded version of the article "*Enstasis* and *Ecstasis*: A Critical Appraisal of Eliade on Yoga and Shamanism," *Journal for the Study of Religion* 15:1 (2002): 21–37.

1. Eliade, *Yoga*, 320.

2. Ibid.

3. I. M. Lewis, *Ecstatic Religion: A Study in Shamanism and Spirit Possession* (New York: Routledge, 1995), 121.

4. Birgitte Sonne, "The Professional Ecstatic in His Social and Ritual Position," in *Religious Ecstasy, Based on Papers Read at the Symposium on Religious Ecstasy Held at Ebo, Finland, on the 26th-28th of August 1981*, ed. Nils Holm (Stockholm: Almqvist & Wiksell International, 1982), 128–50.

5. Eliade, *Yoga*, 321–26.

6. Approaching this subject in the context of Jainism also would be appropriate. See Padmanabh S. Jaini, *The Jaina Path of Purification* (Berkeley: University of California Press, 1979), 251–58.

7. George Bond, "Theravāda Buddhism's Mediations on Death and the Symbolism of Initiatory Death," *History of Religions* 19 (1980): 254.

8. Ibid., 252.

9. See Liz Wilson, *Charming Cadavers: Horrific Figurations of the Feminine in Indian Buddhist Hagiographic Literature* (Chicago: University of Chicago Press, 1996). Wilson documents the power and ambiguity found in the relationship between the body, death, and wisdom in the post-Aśokan Buddhist context. Theravāda conceptions of the transformative potential of the cremation ground also can be said to greatly foreshadow the extensive elaboration on such themes and imagery in Hindu and Buddhist tantra.

10. Eliade, *Yoga*, 326–30.

11. Mircea Eliade, *Shamanism: Archaic Techniques of Ecstasy* (Princeton: Bollingen, 1972), 403.

12. Eliade, *Shamanism*, 406.

13. Ibid.

14. The relationship of liberation to *nirodha* in the Buddhist meditative context, in particular to *nirodhasamāpatti*, "the attainment of cessation," is a problematic one, due to ambiguity in Buddhist sources. Paul Griffiths has discussed a number of issues related to this problem in "Indian Buddhist Meditation-Theory: History, Development and Systematization" (Ph.D. dissertation, University of Wisconsin-Madison, 1983), and in *On Being Mindless: Buddhist Meditation and the Mind-Body Problem* (LaSalle: Open Court, 1986). It also should be noted that a yogin can traverse the states of *dhyāna* while alive, and that such ascension does not require physical death, though meditative attainments may have implications for future rebirth.

15. See YS I.19, *bhavapratyayo videhaprakṛtilayānām*, "for the *videhas* and *prakṛtilayas*, the basis is becoming."

16. Staal, *Exploring Mysticism*, 86–91.

17. The strong parallelism between the development of *samādhi* in the context of Indian Buddhism and in Classical Yoga, particularly notions of the conjunction of *samāpatti* and *nirodha* elements, suggests otherwise. Both the Indian Buddhist and Classical Yoga traditions recognize cooperation and tension in this relationship.

18. Whicher, *The Integrity of the Yoga Darśana*, 201–204.

19. Larson, "Classical Yoga," 730–31.

20. Robert Forman, *Mysticism, Mind, Consciousness* (Albany: State University of New York Press, 1999), 4–6.

21. Obeyesekere, *Medusa's Hair*, 169–82.

22. Louis de la Vallée Poussin, "Le Bouddhisme et le Yoga de Patañjali," *Mélanges chinois et boudddhiques* 5 (1936–1937b): 223–42.

23. Eliade, *Yoga*, 326–27; *Shamanism*, 406–407.

24. Eliade, *Yoga*, 339.

25. Karel Werner criticizes Eliade's thought on this distinction, noting what he believes is an "evolutionary" bias in Eliade's analysis. See Karel Werner, ed., "The Long-haired Sage of Ṛg Veda 10, 136; A Shaman, a Mystic, or a Yogi?," in *The Yogi and the Mystic: Studies in Comparative Mysticism* (London: Curzon, 1989), 33–53.

26. This is an issue that arguably plays out in the tension between Theravāda, Hīnayāna, and Mahāyāna conceptions of soteriology as well.

27. Whicher, *The Integrity*, 289–300.

28. Rukmani, "Tension between *Vyutthāna* and *Nirodha* in the *Yoga-Sūtras*," 613–28; "Sāṅkhya and Yoga: Where They Do Not Speak in One Voice," *Asiatische Studien* 53:3 (1999): 733–53.

29. Eliade, *Shamanism*, 418–20.

30. Ibid., 216–17.

31. YS, II.12–17. For an extensive exploration of the relationship between yoga and tantra and therapeutic modalities, see Gregory P. Fields, *Religious Therapeutics: Body and Health in Yoga, Āyurveda, and Tantra* (Albany: State University of New York Press, 2001).

32. Vetter, *Ideas*, 14–16.

33. Bharati, *The Light at the Center*, 144–45. Bharati furthermore believes that the "mystic type" may exist within shamanic traditions much in the sense that it does in more *enstatic* or *cessative* types, but that it may be that because the social aspects of shamanism take such precedence within the aboriginal context, "mystical" types of experiences, characterized by an emptiness of content, may be deemphasized.

34. Robert Beck, "Some Proto-Psycho-Therapeutic Elements in the Practice of the Shaman," *History of Religions* 2 (1962): 330–47.

35. Eliade, *Shamanism*, 8.

36. Ibid., 265.

37. Douglas Allen, *Myth and Religion in Mircea Eliade* (New York: Garland, 1998); "Recent Defenders of Eliade: A Critical Evaluation," *Religion* 24 (1994): 333–51.

38. David Cave, *Mircea Eliade's Vision for a New Humanism* (New York: Oxford University Press, 1993).

39. Carl Olson, "Mircea Eliade, Postmodernism, and the Problematic Nature of Representational Thinking," *Method and Theory in the Study of Religion* 11:4 (1999): 357–85; *The Theology and Philosophy of Eliade* (New York: St. Martin's Press, 1992).

40. Rennie, *Reconstructing Eliade: Making Sense of Religion.*

41. Ivan Strenski, *Religion in Relation* (Columbia: University of South Carolina Press, 1993).

42. Robert Segal, "Misconceptions of the Social Sciences," *Zygon* 25:3 (1990): 264–78.

43. Ansgar Paus, "The Secret Nostalgia of Mircea Eliade for Paradise: Observations on the Method of the 'History of Religions,'" *Religion* 19 (1989): 137–49.

44. Russell T. McCutcheon, *Manufacturing Religion: The Discourse on Sui Generis Religion and the Politics of Nostalgia* (New York: Oxford University Press, 1997); *Critics Not Caretakers: Redescribing the Public Study of Religion* (Albany: State University of New York Press, 2001).

45. Kimberly C. Patton and Benjamin C. Ray, eds., *A Magic Still Dwells: Comparative Religion in the Postmodern Age* (Berkeley: University of California Press, 2000).

46. Rennie, *Changing Religious Worlds*.

47. Ibid., 8–9.

48. Along with the aforementioned *Ecstatic Religion*, see also I. M. Lewis, *Religion in Context: Cults and Charisma* (Cambridge: Cambridge University Press, 1996).

49. Holm, ed., *Religious Ecstasy*.

50. Lewis, *Ecstatic Religion*, 22.

51. David Yamane and Megan Polzer, "Ways of Seeing Ecstasy in Modern Society: Experiential-Expressive and Cultural-Linguistic Views," *Sociology of Religion* 55:1 (1994): 1–25.

52. Ibid., 23.

53. Bourguignon, *Religion*, 340–52.

54. Lewis, *Ecstatic Religion*, 28.

55. Ibid.

56. Ibid., 29–30.

57. Ibid., 43.

58. Ibid., 49.

59. Ibid., 43–50.

60. Ibid., 155.

61. Ibid.

62. Ibid., 156.

63. Ibid., 163.

64. Ibid., 164.

65. Ibid., 171.

66. Larson also discusses the formation of the *śramaṇa* traditions at significant length, noting the social and psychological dimensions at work in the formation of yoga and meditation methodologies. See Gerald Larson, *India's Agony over Religion* (Albany: State University of New York Press, 1995), 65–75, 170–77.

67. On this point, see W. King, *Theravāda Meditation*; Gunaratana, *The Path of Serenity and Insight*; Sopa, "*Śamathavipaśyanāyuganaddha*."

68. Johannes Bronkhorst, "Yoga and Seśvara Sāṃkhya," *Journal of Indian Philosophy* 9 (1981): 309–20.

69. YS IV.7.

70. YS II.31.

71. Sudhir Kakar, *Shamans, Mystics, and Doctors: A Psychological Inquiry into India and Its Healing Traditions* (Chicago: University of Chicago Press, 1982), 122.

72. Ibid.

73. YS I. 29–31.

74. Stephen R. Wilson, "Becoming a Yogi: Resocialization and Deconditioning as Conversion Processes," *Sociological Analysis* 45:4 (1984): 310–23.

75. Obeyesekere notes this ambiguity in discussing the relationship between what he terms the three modes of *enstasis*, *ecstasis*, and possession with the analysis of Buddhist biographical material and conceptions of meditation. See Gananath Obeyesekere, *Imagining Karma: Ethical Transformation in Amerindian, Buddhist, and Greek Rebirth* (Berkeley: University of California Press, 2002), 164–68.

Chapter 4

1. Emile Sénart, "Bouddhisme et Yoga," *Revue de l'Histoire des Religions* 21 (1900): 345–46.

2. Ibid., 349–50; see also YS I.20.

3. Ibid., 348.

4. Ibid., 346.

5. Ibid., 346–47.

6. Ibid., 348. The issue of the relationship between the Sāṃkhya system and Classical Yoga is one of significant contention. A collection of recent articles on this subject by Ian Whicher, T. S. Rukmani, Gerald Larson, and others can be found in *Asiatische Studien* 53:3 (1999).

7. Ibid.

8. Sénart, "Bouddhisme et Yoga," 349–52.

9. Ibid., 353–54.

10. Ibid., 355, 361.

11. Ibid., 362.

12. Ibid., 349.

13. Ibid., 349–50.

14. Ibid.

15. Ibid.

16. Ibid.

17. Ibid.

18. Ibid., 352.

19. Ibid.

20. De la Vallée Poussin, "Le Bouddhisme et le Yoga de Patañjali," 223–42.

21. Ibid., 224, 226–27.

22. Ibid., 225.

23. Ibid., 226.

24. Ibid., 227–28.

25. Ibid., 229–42.

26. Ibid., 242.

27. Ibid.

28. Ibid., 230.

29. Ibid.

30. Ibid., 229.

31. Ibid., 225. De la Vallée Poussin argues that the legends of Arāḍa and Udraka are not convincing in terms of factually grounding the conception of the "non-Buddhist" origin of the meditation system. Instead, he argues that the *ārūpyas* are more indicative of the "pure yoga" orientation of early Buddhism, a point that is in disagreement with more recent scholarship, such as that of Bronkhorst, which postulates a non-Buddhist origin for the *ārūpyas*. See Johannes Bronkhorst, *The Two Traditions of Meditation in Ancient India* (Delhi: Motilal Banarsidass, 1993b), 78–95.

32. Pulinbihari Chakravarti, *Origin and Development of the Sāṃkhya School of Thought* (New Delhi: Oriental Books Reprint Corp., Munshiram Manoharlal, 1975), 69–73.

33. References to Hiraṇyagarbha in the *Śvetāsvatara Upaniṣad* suggest the continuity between the Vedic and *sūtra* traditions, possibly implying that the appellation is, like Vyāsa, a way of engendering authority by appeal to mythic figuration. However, the symbolic role of Hiraṇyagarbha in the Upaniṣadic context may well provide clues about the relationship between mythical conceptions of creation and the doctrines developed in yoga.

34. Hermann Oldenburg, *The Doctrine of the Upaniṣads and Early Buddhism*, trans. Shridhar B. Shrotri (Delhi: Motilal Banarsidass, 1991). In the *Śvetāsvatara Upaniṣad* many issues are found relevant to the current discussion. These include reference to *nirodha* in chapter 3 and references to Sāṃkhya and yoga in chapter 6, as well as important connections between light, luminosity, and liberation. Further examples of interest include references to mythical figures, making connections, such as that of Brahman-Śiva-Rudra, which demonstrate the numinous dimension of Upaniṣadic con-

templation. See Patrick Olivelle, *The Early Upaniṣads: Annotated Text and Translation* (New York: Oxford University Press, 1998), 413–33.

35. Oldenburg, *The Doctrine of the Upaniṣads*, 170–71. In the *Maitrī Upaniṣad*, ascetic practices take greater precedence, with intimations of Vedānta and tantric conceptions of physiology coming to the fore. The portrayal of the supreme self as manifested in many forms is reminiscent of the *Bhagavadgītā*, and the many references to light and the association with the sun are reminiscent of the *Śvetāsvatara Upaniṣad*. Continuity with conceptions of sacrifice is particularly important as well, for example, references to key Vedic rituals such as the *Agnihotra* and *Agniṣṭoma*. See Robert Ernest Hume, trans., *The Thirteen Principal Upaniṣads* (Madras: Oxford University Press, 1965); Rai Bahdur Srisa Vidyarnava and Pandit Mohan Lal Sandal, trans., *The Maitri Upaniṣat*, Sacred Books of the Hindus, vol. 31, pt. 2 (Allahabad: Bhuvaneswari Asram, 1926).

36. Oldenburg, *Doctrine of the Upaniṣads*, 171.

37. Ibid., 186–87.

38. Ibid., 191–92.

39. Ibid., 207.

40. Ibid., 208–209.

41. Ibid.

42. Ibid., 209–10.

43. Ibid., 210.

44. Ibid., 210–11.

45. Ibid., 213.

46. Friedrich Heiler, *Die Buddhistische Versenkung: Eine Religionsgeschichtliche Untersuchung* (Munchen: Verlag von Ernst Reinhardt, 1922), 46–47.

47. Ibid., 48–49.

48. Eliade, *Yoga*, 371. Eliade also notes the counterarguments of Prasad and Dasgupta, who assert that the fourth *pāda* was not part of the original text.

49. Heiler, *Die Buddhistische Versenkung*, 46.

50. Gerhard Oberhammer, *Strukturen Yogischer Meditation*, Veröffentlichungen der Kommission für Sprachen und Kulturen Südasiens, vol. 13 (Vienna: Verlag der Osterreichischen Akademie der Wissenschaften, 1977), 145–50.

51. De la Valleé Poussin, 224.

52. Ibid., 242.

53. Ibid., 370–72.

54. Ibid., 372.

55. Ibid., 162–99.

56. Ibid., 162.

57. Ibid., 165.

58. Ibid., 169.

59. Ibid., 173–74. Eliade refers to de la Vallée Poussin as the authority on this issue, particularly in the context of Poussin's article "Musila et Nārada," *Mélanges chinois et bouddiques* 5 (1936–1937a): 189–222. A more recent and engaging discussion of this problem also can be found in Ruegg's *Buddha-Nature, Mind, and the Problem of Gradualism in a Comparative Perspective: On the Transmission and Reception of Buddhism in India and Tibet*, 191–92.

60. Ibid., 174.

61. Eliade, *Yoga*, 174–75.

62. Eliade, *Yoga*, 175. Eliade prefaces this statement as follows: "But in the first stage of Buddhism, the problem that arose was the same problem that had arisen for Sāṃkhya-Yoga: which has the primacy, 'intelligence' or 'experience?'"

63. Ibid., 177.

64. Zahler, "The Concentrations," 12–14.

65. Zahler, "The Concentrations," 31–38; Collett Cox, "Attainment through Abandonment: The Sarvāstivādin Path of Removing Defilements," in *Paths to Liberation*, 63–105.

66. Eliade, *Yoga*, 198–99.

67. King, *Theravāda Meditation*, 6–10.

68. Ibid., 15.

69. Ibid., 42.

70. Ibid., 14–17.

71. Ibid.

72. Ibid., 16–17.

73. Ibid., 15.

74. Ibid.

75. Ibid., 111.

76. See Cousins, "Buddhist *Jhāna*;" Griffiths, "Concentration or Insight."

77. King, *Theravāda Meditation*, 111.

78. L. S. Cousins, "*Vitakka/Vitarka* and *Vicāra*: The Stages of *Samādhi* in Buddhism and Yoga," *Indo-Iranian Journal* 35:2–3 (1992): 137–55.

79. Ibid., 137.

80. Ibid., 152–53.

81. Ibid., 147–49.

82. Ibid., 156, n. 69. Cousins also notes the use of *ajjhattaṃ sampasādanaṃ* in the context of *jhāna* and its affinity for the *adyātma-prasādaḥ* of YS I.47.

83. Ibid., 149.

84. Ibid., 149–50.

85. Ibid., 149.

86. See Whicher, *The Integrity*, 253 passim.

87. Crangle, *Origin and Development*, 24–35.

88. Ibid., 66–69, 93.

89. Ibid., 267–74.

90. Ibid., 295.

91. Ibid.

92. Ibid., 288.

93. Ibid., 292.

94. Bronkhorst, *The Two Traditions of Meditation in Ancient India*, 22–23.

95. Ibid., 44.

96. Ibid., 45–53.

97. Ibid., 70.

98. Ibid., 71.

99. Ibid., 74–75.

100. Ibid., 74.

101. Ibid., 91–92.

102. Ibid., 110–11, 119–21. This view also finds support from Vetter, xxi–xxvi passim. As we have noted, Vetter argues that liberation in Buddhism in the earliest context represented the attainments of insight at the level of the fourth *dhyāna*, as opposed to what he believes are later schemes based upon the ideas of *saññavedayitanirodha* and of separating oneself into the five components through insight.

103. Ibid., 122–23.

104. Bronkhorst, "Yoga and Seśvara Sāṃkhya," 309.

105. Ibid., 310–15.

106. Ibid., 316.

107. Ibid., 317.

108. Bronkhorst, "Patañjali and the Yoga Sūtras," 191–212.

109. Ibid., 193–200.

110. Ibid., 203–208.

111. Ibid., 203.

112. Ibid., 209.

113. Christopher Key Chapple, "Reading Patañjali without Vyāsa," *Journal of the American Academy of Religion* 62:1 (1994): 85–103.

114. Koici Yamashita, *Pātañjala Yoga Philosophy with Reference to Buddhism* (Calcutta: Firma KLM Private Limited, 1994), 77.

115. Ibid., 46–55.

116. Ibid.

117. Ibid., 65–82.

118. Chakravarti, *Origin and Development*, 93–99.

119. Ibid., 99.

120. David J. Kalupahana, *The Principles of Buddhist Psychology* (Albany: State University of New York Press, 1987), 61.

121. Bronkhorst, *The Two Traditions of Meditation*, 68–77.

122. Kalupahana, *The Principles of Buddhist Psychology*, 62.

123. Yamashita, *Pātañjala Yoga Philosophy with Reference to Buddhism*, 120–21.

124. Ibid., 124.

125. Ibid., 125. This point is also noted by Eliade in *Yoga*, 173.

126. Ruegg, *Buddha-Nature*, 198; YS I.37. Similarly, the presence of *dharmamegha* as a Mahāyāna *Bodhisattvabhūmi*, the tenth and culminating member, and the use of the term in YS IV.29 to indicate the point at which discriminating perception overcomes the accumulation of afflictions, and immediately before referring to the destruction of obscuration leading to endless knowledge. YS IV.31, *tadā sarvāvaraṇamalāpetasyā jñānasyānantyajjñeyamalpam*, can be translated as "Then, on account of the limitlessness of knowledge free from all obstructive substrata, [there remains] little to be known."

127. Gerald Larson, "An Old Problem Revisited: The Relation between Sāṃkhya, Yoga, and Buddhism," *Studien zur Indologie und Iranistik* 15 (1989): 129–46.

128. Ibid., 131–32.

129. Ibid., 133–35.

130. Ibid., 135–36.

131. Larson, "Classical Yoga as Neo-Sāṃkhya," 723–32.

132. Ibid., 726–27.

133. Ibid., 729.

134. Ibid., 727–30.

135. Ibid., 730–31. In this context, Frits Staal has argued that there is a great deal of ambiguity in how philologists (including Oberhammer and Hauer) have broken down the YS into component parts, particularly the *samāpatti* and *nirodha* aspects. Staal calls into question the degree to which the aspects understood as incompatible by these scholars from a textual viewpoint might not be quite compatible on the level of pragmatics, and argues that the reconsideration of these positions with regard to the YS

might offer some new insights into its relationship with Buddhism. See Staal, *Exploring Mysticism*, 71–91.

136. Ibid., 731.

137. Eliade, *Yoga*, 174.

138. Stuart-Fox, *Jhāna*, 104.

139. This distinction plays out strongly in Theravāda with forest monasticism, which may offer a more profound opportunity for renunciation and for meditative praxis, becoming a *vanavāsin* (forest dweller) as opposed to a *grāmavāsin* (village dweller). See Obeyesekere, *Imagining Karma*, 144–49.

140. Another suggestion might be that the numinous dimension of *samāpatti* was sublimated into the *vipassanā* practice, in the manner of the progression from "gross" to "subtle" that one finds in the development of the four foundations of mindfulness and other key *vipassanā*-type practices in the Theravāda context. On the process of adaptation and syncretism in Theravāda, see Stanley J. Tambiah, *Buddhism and the Spirit Cults in North-East Thailand* (Cambridge: Cambridge University Press, 1970), and *The Buddhist Saints of the Forest and the Cult of Amulets: A Study in Charisma, Hagiography, Sectarianism, and Millennial Buddhism* (New York: Cambridge University Press, 1984); George D. Bond, *The Buddhist Revival in Sri Lanka: Religious Tradition, Reinterpretation, and Response* (Columbia: University of South Carolina Press, 1988); Richard Gombrich and Gananath Obeyesekere, *Buddhism Transformed: Religious Changes in Sri Lanka* (Princeton: Princeton University Press, 1988).

141. Griffiths, *Meditation-Theory*, 334 passim.

142. David Carpenter, "Practice Makes Perfect: The Role of Practice *(Abhyāsa)* in Pātañjala Yoga" (paper presented at the annual meeting of the American Academy of Religion, Nashville, Tennessee, November 18–21, 2000), 5–6.

143. Ibid. See also David M. Knipe, "Becoming a Veda in the Godavari Delta," *India and Beyond: Aspects of Literature, Meaning, Ritual, and Thought, Essays in Honor of Frits Staal*, ed. Dick van der Meij (New York: Kegan Paul International, 1997), 306–32. The issue of "embodiment" of text is a notion that demonstrates the affinity between Vedic and *sūtra* literature and, by extension, between *śruti* and *smṛti* as oral traditions in the domain of Hinduism.

144. Carpenter, "Practice Makes Perfect," 6.

145. Ibid., 4. In another context, Gonda has identified, following Gopinath Kaviraj, another possible example of a threefold system carried over from Vedic sources into both the Classical Yoga and Buddhist contexts. This is the connection between the Vedāntic and Yoga sources with regard to conceptions found in Buddhist formulations of the nature of *prajñā* as twofold, as a means *(hetubhūta)* and as an end *(phalabhūta)*. *Hetubhūta* is broken down into three parts, *śruta, cintā*, and *bhāvanā*, roughly "listening," "thinking," and "meditating." Vācaspatimiśra argues that these three are synonymous with the Vedāntic group of *śravana*, *manana*, and *nididhyāsana*, and the Classical Yoga system's *āgama*, *anumāna*, and *dhyānābhyāsa*. See Gonda, *Vision of the Vedic Poets*, 304–305. In arguing for the continuity between conceptual knowledge

and religious experience, Gimello cites Kamalaśīla's Bhāvanākrama as representing authoritatively this particular doctrine in the context of Mahāyāna Buddhism. See Gimello, "Mysticism in its Contexts," 71–72.

146. T. S. Rukmani, *Yogavārttika of Vijñānabhikṣu: Text with English Translation and Critical Notes along with the Text and English Translation of the Pātañjala Yogasūtras and Vyāsabhāṣya* (New Delhi: Munshiram Manoharlal, 1981), 1: 113–18.

147. Ruegg, *Buddha-Nature*, 199.

148. For a discussion of some of the difficulties of reconciling yogic *nirodha* with the concept of *jīvanmukti*, see Rukmani, "*Vyutthāna* and *Nirodha*," 620–23. See also Whicher, *Yoga Darśana*, 259–300, for a discussion of the ramifications of yogic *kaivalya*, the textual perspectives on *jīvanmukti*, and the question of the relationship of *prakṛti* and *puruṣa* to liberation.

149. One way to answer this question more extensively might be to look at relationships between the *trailokya* concept in comparison to *Sāṃkhya* conceptions of cosmology. In the context of the YS, we might look at YS II.19 with its division of *viśeṣa-aviśeṣa-liṅgamātra-aliṅga* (distinct, indistinct, mark only, and unmarked) as the states of the *gunas* possibly representing the relationship of *prakṛti* to liberation, the first three representing the desire, form, and formless realms and the fourth representing *prakṛti* and its *gunas* at the moment of libertation, as withdrawn, *pratiprasava*. See YS IV.34. Another comparison of significance is with the Vedic conception of dividing the world into three divisions of the earth, atmosphere, and celestial regions. This "threefold" breakdown may follow another Vedic pattern, to the degree that the postulation of *nivāṇa* "the fourth realm," ultimately leads to the postulation of a fifth, *apratiṣṭhita-nirvāṇa*. David Knipe has argued that in the Vedic context, threefold systems are ascensional, fourfold systems are horizontal, and fivefold systems are the integration of these models together in "communication and *correspondence*." See David Knipe, "One Fire, Three Fires, Five Fires: Vedic Symbols in Transition," *History of Religions* 11 (1972): 35. We might suggest then, that the "fourth" state of *prakṛti* would have to yield a fifth in order to deal with the state of the *jivanmukti*. For an examination of the cosmological correlates of the Buddhist *dhyānas* and *samāpattis* in the Tibetan Mahāyāna as an extension of those found in *Abhidharmakośa* and *Abhidharmakośabhāṣya*, see Leah Zahler, "Meditation and Cosmology: The Physical Basis of the Concentrations and Formless Absorptions according to dGe-lugs Tibetan Presentations," *Journal of the International Association for Buddhist Studies* 13:1 (1990): 53–78.

150. Rukmani, *Yogavārttika of Vijñānabhikṣu*, 3: 109–10. See also Knut A. Jacobsen, *Prakṛti in Sāṃkhya-Yoga: Material Principle, Religious Experience, Ethical Implications* (New York: Peter Lang, 1999), 283–88.

151. Rukmani, *Yogavārttika of Vijñānabhikṣu*, 3: 112–13.

152. Ibid., 3: 113. The central point here is that Buddhist conceptions regarding the identity of *dhyāna* states with Brahmā realms are paralleled by similar conceptions of the Brahmā realms found in yoga. It is very likely that a significant number of details in this relationship would find similar parity if examined further.

153. Ibid.

154. Ibid.

155. One also might consider the manner in which the identification of yogin and deity functions in a manner analogous to the identification of the qualities of kingship to divinity in the Vedic context. See Jan Gonda, *Ancient Indian Kingship from the Religious Point of View* (Leiden: E. J. Brill, 1969), 24–70.

156. On the Buddhist cosmology and related terminology, see Akira Sadakata, *Buddhist Cosmology: Philosophy and Origins* (Tokyo: Kosei, 1997), 63–67; Randy Kloetzli, *Buddhist Cosmology: From Single World System to Pure Land: Science and Theology in the Images of Motion and Light* (Delhi: Motilal Banarsidass, 1983), 23–50; Henepola Gunaratana, *The Path of Serenity and Insight*, 139–41, 223–24.

157. Rukmani, *Yogavārttika of Vijñānabhikṣu*, 3: 191.

158. Ibid., 3: 189.

Chapter 5

*This chapter is a revised and an updated version of the article "Traditions in Transition: Meditative Concepts in the Development of Tantric *Sādhana*," *International Journal of Tantric Studies* 6:1 (2002), available online at http://www.asiatica.org/ijts/.

1. The investigation of the roots of tantric attitudes in the Vedic context is a subject of considerable importance but outside the scope of this book. For example, chapter 4 of the *Bṛhadāraṇyaka Upaniṣad* offers an extensive exposition on issues of male-female union that might be considered paradigmatic for tantric notions of *maithuna*. See Olivelle, *The Early Upaniṣads*, 155–63. See also Crangle's discussion of the subject of *upāsanā* in Crangle, *Origin and Development*, 59–65, which demonstrates the import of visualization as a critical component of the development of yoga and meditation in the Upaniṣads.

2. Lewis, *Ecstatic Religion*, 28.

3. Ibid.

4. Ibid., 54.

5. The more specifically social and political dimensions of these distinctions, such as that of lay versus monastic *tanrikas*, are dealt with at length in Ronald Davidson, *Indian Esoteric Buddhism: A Social History of the Tantric Movement* (New York: Columbia University Press, 2002). Though many of our points here will be at parity with Davidson's presentation, our goal is to demonstrate continuity between tantra and earlier meditative traditions and to link these developments to cultural trends, a broader methodological process. Davidson's notions of the deification of the *tantrika* and the relationship that this has to issues regarding royal consecration can be tied to our earlier discussions about the numinous effects of meditation and the embodiment of divinity by the king in the Vedic context.

6. Agehananda Bharati, *The Tantric Tradition* (London: Rider & Co. 1965), 17.

7. Ibid., 20–21.

8. Adelheid Herrmann-Pfandt, *Ḍākinīs: Zur Stellung und Symbolik des Weiblichen im Tantrischen Buddhismus* (Bonn: Indica et Tibetica, 1992), 127–30.

9. Ibid.

10. Eliade, *Yoga*, 207.

11. Ibid., 208–10.

12. Alex Wayman, *Buddhist Tantras: Light on Indo-Tibetan Esotericism* (New York: Samuel Weiser, 1973), 57–59.

13. Ibid., 110–11.

14. Nyanamoli, *Path of Purification*, 206.

15. Ibid., 230.

16. Ibid., 233.

17. Ibid., 244. This is a citation of Aṅguttara Nikāya, III.

18. On this topic, see also Ria Kloppenborg and Ronald Poelmeyer, "Visualizations in Buddhist Meditation," in *Effigies Dei: Essays on the History of Religions*, ed. Dirk Van Der Plas (New York: E. J. Brill, 1987), 83–96. The authors point out the relevance of examples such as *buddhānusmṛti* for understanding later tantra and demonstrate "intermediate" forms of visualization in Sarvāstivāda sources.

19. For a discussion of "liminality" in the context of tantric goddesses in the Hindu Tradition, see David Kinsley's *Tantric Visions of the Divine Feminine: The Ten Mahāvidyās* (Berkeley: University of California Press, 1997), 233–52.

20. Vidya Dehejia, *Yoginī: Cult and Temples* (New Delhi: National Museum, 1986), 13–17; R. K. Sharma, *Temple of Chansatha-yogini at Bheraghat* (Delhi: Agam Kala Prakashan, 1978), 29–30.

21. Dehejia, *Yoginī*, 11–39.

22. Janice Willis, *Feminine Ground: Essays on Women and Tibet* (Ithaca, N.Y.: Snow Lion Press, 1987), 57–75.

23. Benoytosh Bhattacharya, *Sādhanamālā*, vols. 1 and 2 (Baroda: Oriental Institute, 1968).

24. Gudrun Bühnemann, *Sādhanaśataka and Sādhanaśatapañcāśikā: Two Buddhist Sādhana Collections in Sanskrit Manuscript* (Wien: Arbeitskreis für Tibetische und Buddhistische Studien Universität Wien, 1994), 18–19. Bühnemann argues that Bhattacharya's *Sādhanamālā* contains a number of errors due to his lack of awareness of relevant textual resources, such as several *sādhanas* that are actually from another text altogether, the *Sādhananatapañcāsikā*. She states that comparison to viable Tibetan sources also would provide corrections to Bhattacharya's edition that were not possible for Bhattacharya at the time of editing due to his limited resources.

25. Bhattacharya, *Sādhanamālā*, 2: 452–58.

26. Bhattacharya, *Sādhanamālā*, 2: 455, *oṃ dharmakāya vajrapuṣpe svāha, oṃ sambhogakāya puṣpe svāhā, oṃ nirmāṇakāya puṣpe svāhā, madhye, oṃ mahāsukhavajrapuṣpe svāhā.*

27. Benoytosh Bhattacharya, *The Indian Buddhist Iconography: Mainly Based on the Sādhanamālā and Other Cognate Tantric Texts of Rituals* (New Delhi: Asian Educational Services, 1993), 156–57.

28. Ibid., 156.

29. Marie-Therese de Mallman, *Introduction a l'Iconographie du Tantrisme Boddhique* (Paris: Bibliotheque du Centre de Recherches sur l'Asia Centrale et la Hause Asie, 1975), 431–33.

30. Kinsley, *The Ten Mahāvidyās*, 144–47.

31. See Kathleen M. Erndl, *Victory to the Mother: The Hindu Goddess of Northwest India in Myth, Ritual, and Symbol* (New York: Oxford University Press, 1993); Kinsley, *The Ten Mahāvidyās*, 146, 151–52.

32. Elisabeth Anne Benard, *Cinnamastā: The Aweful Buddhist and Hindu Tantric Goddess* (Delhi: Motilal Banarsidass, 1994), 86–116.

33. See Kinsley, *The Ten Mahāvidyās*, 149–50, 161–63.

34. For an extensive treatment of Vajrayoginī and her *sādhanas*, see Elizabeth English, *Vajrayoginī: Her Visualizations, Rituals, and Forms* (Boston: Wisdom, 2002).

35. Bhattacharya, *Sādhanamālā*, 2: lxxxv. See also Sir M. Monier-Williams, *A Sanskrit-English Dictionary* (Oxford: Oxford University Press, 1899), 1216. The list is represented in Monier-Williams as *animā laghimā prāptiḥ prākāmyam mahimā tathā, īśitvaṃ ca vaśitvaṃ ca tathā kāmāvasāyitā*, "smallness, lightness, obtaining, irresistible will, greatness, supremacy, self-mastery, and suppression of desire."

36. Gyatso, "Healing," 141.

37. Gananath Obeyesekere, *Medusa's Hair*, 169–82.

38. See David Germano and Janet Gyatso, "Longchenpa and the Possession of the Ḍākinīs," in *Tantra in Practice*, ed. David Gordon White (Princeton: Princeton University Press, 1998), 239–65.

Conclusion

1. YS 1.49, *śrutānumānaprajñābhyāmanyaviṣayā viśeṣārthatvāt.*

2. Obeyesekere, *The Work of Culture*, 68.

Bibliography

Allen, Douglas. "Recent Defenders of Eliade: A Critical Evaluation." *Religion* 24 (1994): 333–51.

———. *Myth and Religion in Mircea Eliade*. New York: Garland, 1998.

Allen, N. J. "The Indo-European Prehistory of *Yoga*." *International Journal of Hindu Studies* 2:1 (1998): 1–20.

Anacker, Stefan. *Seven Works of Vasubandhu: The Buddhist Psychological Doctor*. Delhi: Motilal Banarsidass, 1984.

Āraṇya, Swāmi Hariharānanda. *Yoga Philosophy of Patañjali*. Albany: State University of New York Press, 1983.

Aronson, Harvey B. *Love and Sympathy in Theravāda Buddhism*. Delhi: Motilal Banarsidass, 1980.

Bader, Jonathan. *Meditation in Śaṅkara's Vedānta*. New Delhi: Aditya Prakashan, 1990.

Banerji, Sures Chandra. *Studies in Origin and Development of Yoga from Vedic Times, in India and Abroad, with Texts and Translations of Patañjala Yogasūtra and Haṭhayoga-Pradīpikā*. Calcutta: Punthi Pustak, 1995.

Beck, Robert. "Some Proto-Psycho-Therapeutic Elements in the Practice of the Shaman." *History of Religions* 2 (1962): 330–47.

Bedekar, V. M. "Dhyānayoga in the Mahābhārata." *Bharatiya Vidya Bhavan* 20–21 (1960–1961): 116–25.

Benard, Elisabeth Anne. *Cinnamastā: The Aweful Buddhist and Hindu Tantric Goddess*. Delhi: Motilal Banarsidass, 1994.

Bharati, Agehananda. *The Ochre Robe*. London: George Allen & Unwin, 1961.

———. *The Tantric Tradition*. London: Rider & Co., 1965.

———. *The Light at the Center*. Santa Barbara, Calif.: Ross-Erickson, 1976.

Bhattacharya, Benoytosh. *Sādhanamālā*. Vols. 1 and 2. Baroda: Oriental Institute, 1968.

———. *The Indian Buddhist Iconography: Mainly Based on the Sādhanamālā and Other Cognate Tantric Texts of Rituals*. New Delhi: Asian Educational Services, 1993.

Bond, George D. *The Buddhist Revival in Sri Lanka: Religious Tradition, Reinterpretation, and Response*. Columbia: University of South Carolina Press, 1988.

Bourguignon, Erica. *Religion, Altered States of Consciousness, and Social Change*. Columbus: Ohio State University Press, 1973.

Braun, Willi, and Russell T. McCutcheon. *Guide to the Study of Religion*. London: Cassell, 2000.

Bronkhorst, Johannes. "Yoga and Seśvara Sāṃkhya." *Journal of Indian Philosophy* 9 (1981): 309–20.

———. "Patañjali and the Yoga Sūtras." *Studien zur Indologie und Iranistik* 10 (1985): 191–212.

———. "Remarks on the History of Jaina Meditation." In *Jain Studies in Honour of Jozef Deleu*, edited by Rudy Smet and Kenji Watanab, 151–62. Tokyo: Hon No Tomosha, 1993a.

———. *The Two Traditions of Meditation in Ancient India*. 2d ed. Delhi: Motilal Banarsidass, 1993b.

———. *The Two Sources of Indian Asceticism*. 2d ed. Delhi: Motilal Banarsidass, 1998.

Bucknell, Roderick S. "Reinterpreting the *Jhānas*." *Journal of the International Association of Buddhist Studies* 16:2 (1993): 374–409.

Bühnemann, Gudrun. *Sādhanaśataka and Sādhanaśatapañcāśikā: Two Buddhist Sādhana Collections in Sanskrit Manuscript*. Wien: Arbeitskreis für Tibetische und Buddhistische Studien Universität Wien, 1994.

Buswell, Robert E. Jr., and Robert M. Gimello. *Paths to Liberation: The Mārga and Its Transformation in Buddhist Thought*. Studies in East Asian Buddhism, vol. 7. Honolulu: University of Hawaii Press, 1992.

Carpenter, David. "Practice Makes Perfect: The Role of Practice *(Abhyāsa)* in Pātañjala Yoga." Paper presented at the annual meeting of the American Academy of Religion, Nashville, Tennessee, Novermber 18–21, 2000.

Cave, David. *Mircea Eliade's Vision for a New Humanism*. New York: Oxford University Press, 1993.

Chakravarti, Pulinbihari. *Origin and Development of the Sāṃkhya System of Thought*. 2d ed. New Delhi: Oriental Books Reprint Corp., Munshiram Manoharlal, 1975.

Chapple, Christopher Key. "Reading Patañjali without Vyāsa." *Journal of the American Academy of Religion* 62:1 (1994): 85–103.

———. "Living Liberation in Sāṃkhya and Yoga." In *Living Liberation in Hindu Thought*, edited by Andrew O. Fort and Patricia Y. Mumme, 115–34. Albany: State University of New York Press, 1996.

———. "Haribhadra's Analysis of Pātañjala and Kula Yoga in the *Yogadṛṣṭasamuccaya*." In *Open Boundaries: Jain Communities and Cultures in Indian History*, edited by John E. Cort, 15–30. Albany: State University of New York Press, 1998.

Chapple, Christopher Key, and Yogi Anand Viraj (Eugene P. Kelly Jr.), trans. *The Yoga Sūtras of Patañjali: An Analysis of the Sanskrit with Accompanying English Translation.* Delhi: Sri Satguru, 1990.

Chaudhuri, Sokomal. *Analytical Study of the Abhidharmakośa.* Calcutta: Firma KLM Private Limited, 1983.

Clarke, J. J. *Oriental Enlightenment: The Encounter between Asian and Western Thought.* New York: Routledge, 1997.

Comans, Michael. "The Question of the Importance of *Samādhi* in Modern and Classical Advaita Vedānta." *Philosophy East & West* 43:1 (1993): 19–38.

Conze, Edward. *Buddhist Meditation.* New York: Harper & Row, 1956.

Cort, John E., ed. *Open Boundaries: Jain Communities and Cultures in Indian History.* Albany: State University of New York Press, 1998.

Cousins, L. S. "Buddhist Jhāna: Its Nature and Attainment according to the Pali Sources." *Religion* 3 (1973): 115–31.

———. *Buddhist Studies in Honour of I. B. Horner.* Edited by L. Cousins, A. Kunst, and K.R. Norman. Boston: Reidel, 1974.

———. "*Vitakka/Vitarka* and *Vicāra*: The Stages of *Samādhi* in Buddhism and Yoga." *Indo Iranian Journal* 35:2–3 (1992): 137–55.

Coward, Harold. *Jung and Eastern Thought.* Albany: State University of New York Press, 1985.

———. Yoga and Psychology: Language, Memory, and Mysticism. Albany: State University of New York Press, 2002.

Cox, Collett. "Attainment through Abandonment: The Sarvāstivādin Path of Removing Defilements." In *Paths to Liberation: The Mārga and Its Transformation in Buddhist Thought,* edited by Robert E. Buswell Jr. and Robert M. Gimello, 63–105. Honolulu: University of Hawaii Press, 1992.

Crangle, Edward. *The Origin and Development of Early Indian Contemplative Practices.* Wiesbaden: Harrassowitz, 1994.

D'Amato, Mario. "The Mahāyāna-Hīnayāna Distinction in the *Mahāyānasūtrālamkāra*: A Terminological Analysis." Ph.D. dissertation, University of Chicago, 2000.

Dasgupta, Surendranath. *Yoga as Philosophy and Religion.* New York: Kennikat Press, 1924.

Davidson, Ronald. *Indian Esoteric Buddhism: A Social History of the Tantric Movement.* New York: Columbia University Press, 2002.

Dehejia, Vidya. *Yoginī: Cult and Temples.* New Delhi: National Museum, 1986.

de Mallman, Marie-Therese. *Introduction a l'Iconographie du Tantrisme Boddhique.* Paris: Bibliotheque du Centre de Recherches sur l'Asia Centrale et la Hause Asie, 1975.

Dixit, K. K. *Yogabindu of Ācārya Haribhadrasūri.* Ahmedabad: Lalbhai Dalpatbhai Sanskriti Vidyamandira, 1968.

Dunne, John D. "Thoughtless Buddha, Passionate Buddha." *Journal of the American Academy of Religion* 64:3 (1993): 525–56.

Dvivedi, M. N., trans. *The Yoga-Sūtras of Patañjali*. Madras: Theosophical, 1930.

Edgerton, Franklin. *Buddhist Hybrid Sanskrit Grammar and Dictionary, Volume II: Dictionary*. New Haven, Conn.: Yale University Press, 1953.

Eliade, Mircea. *The Sacred and the Profane*. New York: Harvest, 1959.

———. *Myths, Dreams, and Mysteries: The Encounter between Contemporary Faiths and Archaic Realities*. New York: Harper & Row, 1960.

———. *Patañjali and Yoga*. New York: Funk & Wagnalls, 1969a.

———. *The Quest: History and Meaning in Religion*. Chicago: University of Chicago Press, 1969b.

———. *Shamanism: Archaic Techniques of Ecstasy*. Princeton: Princeton University Press, 1972.

———. *Yoga: Immortality and Freedom*. 2d ed. Princeton: Bollingen, 1990.

Ellwood, Robert. *Alternative Altars: Unconventional and Eastern Spirituality in America*. Chicago: University of Chicago Press, 1979.

———. *Mysticism and Religion*. Englewood Cliffs, N.J.: Prentice Hall, 1980.

English, Elizabeth. *Vajrayoginī: Her Visualizations, Rituals, and Forms*. Boston: Wisdom, 2002.

Erndl, Kathleen M. *Victory to the Mother: The Hindu Goddess of Northwest India in Myth, Ritual, and Symbol*. New York: Oxford University Press, 1993.

Falk, Maryla. *Nāma-Rūpa and Dharma-Rūpa*. Calcutta: University of Calcutta Press, 1943.

Feuerstein, Georg. *The Yoga-Sūtra of Patañjali: A New Translation and Commentary*. Rochester, Vt.: Inner Traditions International, 1979.

———. *Yoga: The Technology of Ecstasy*. Los Angeles: J. P. Tarcher, 1989.

———. *The Philosophy of Classical Yoga*. Rochester, Vt.: Inner Traditions International, 1996.

Fields, Gregory P. *Religious Therapeutics: Body and Health in Yoga, Āyurveda, and Tantra*. Albany: State University of New York Press, 2001.

Filliozat, Jean. *Religion, Philosophy, Yoga*. Delhi: Motilal Banarsidass, 1991.

Flood, Gavin. *An Introduction to Hinduism*. Cambridge: Cambridge University Press, 1996.

———. *Beyond Phenomenology: Rethinking the Study of Religion*. New York: Cassell, 1999.

Forman, Robert K. C. "Mysticism, Constructivism, and Forgetting." In *The Problem of Pure Consciousness*, edited by Robert K. C. Forman, 3–49. New York: Oxford University Press, 1990.

———. *Mysticism, Mind, Consciousness*. Albany: State University of New York Press, 1999.

Forman, Robert K. C., ed. *The Problem of Pure Consciousness*. New York: Oxford University Press, 1990.

———, ed. *The Innate Capacity: Mysticism, Psychology, and Philosophy*. New York: Oxford University Press, 1998.

Fort, Andrew O., and Patricia Y. Mumme. *Living Liberation in Hindu Thought*. Albany: State University of New York Press, 1996.

Frauwallner, Erich. *Studies in Abhidharma Literature and the Origins of Buddhist Philosophical Systems*. Translated by Sophie Francis Kidd and Ernst Steinkellner. Albany: State University of New York Press, 1995.

Geertz, Armin W., and Russell T. McCutcheon, eds. *Perspectives on Method and Theory in the Study of Religion*. Adjunct Proceedings of the 17th Congress of the International Association for the History of Religions, Mexico City, 1995. Boston: Brill, 2000.

Germano, David. "Encountering Tibet: The Ethics, Soteriology, and Creativity of Cross-Cultural Interpretation." *Journal of the American Academy of Religion* 69:1 (2001): 165–82.

Germano, David, and Janet Gyatso. "Longchenpa and the Possession of the *Ḍākinīs*." In *Tantra in Practice*, edited by David Gordon White, 239–65. Princeton: Princeton University Press, 1998.

Gier, Nicholas F. *Spiritual Titanism: Indian, Chinese, and Western Perspectives*. Albany: State University of New York Press, 2000.

Gimello, Robert. "Mysticism and Meditation." In *Mysticism and Philosophical Analysis*, edited by Steven T. Katz, 170–99. New York: Oxford University Press, 1978.

———. "Mysticism in Its Contexts." In *Mysticism and Religious Traditions*, edited by Steven T. Katz, 61–88. New York: Oxford University Press, 1983.

Gokhale, Pradeep P. *Yoga: Its Philosophy and Practice*. Pune: Datta Lakshmi Trust, 1995.

Gombrich, Richard, and Gananath Obeyesekere. *Buddhism Transformed: Religious Changes in Sri Lanka*. Princeton: Princeton University Press, 1988.

Gomez, Lewis. "Indian Materials on the Doctrine of Sudden Enlightenment." In *Early Ch'an in China and Tibet*, edited by Whalen Lai and Lewis R. Lancaster, 393–434. Berkeley, Calif.: Asian Humanities Press, 1983.

Gonda, Jan. *The Vision of the Vedic Poets*. The Hague, the Netherlands: Mouton & Co., 1963.

———. *Ancient Indian Kingship from the Religious Point of View*. Leiden: E. J. Brill, 1969.

Goudriaan, Teun, ed. *Ritual and Speculation in Early Tantrism: Studies in Honor of André Padoux*. Albany: State University of New York Press, 1992.

Griffiths, Paul. "Concentration or Insight: The Problematic of Theravāda Buddhist Meditation-Theory." *Journal of the American Academy of Religion* 49:4 (1981): 605–24.

———. "Indian Buddhist Meditation-Theory: History, Development, and Systematization." Ph.D. dissertation, University of Wisconsin-Madison, 1983.

———. *On Being Mindless: Buddhist Meditation and the Mind-Body Problem.* LaSalle: Open Court, 1986.

Grinshpon, Yohanan. *Silence Unheard: Deathly Otherness in Pātañjala-Yoga.* Albany: State University of New York Press, 2002.

Guenther, Herbert. "Meditation Trends in Early Tibet." In *Early Ch'an in China and Tibet*, edited by Whalen Lai and Lewis R. Lancaster, 351–66. Berkeley, Calif.: Asian Humanities Press, 1983.

Gunaratana, Henepola. *The Path of Serenity and Insight: An Explanation of the Buddhist Jhānas.* Delhi: Motilal Banarsidass, 1985.

Gyatso, Janet. "Healing Burns with Fire: The Facilitations of Experience in Tibetan Buddhism." *Journal of the American Academy of Religion* 67:1 (1999): 113–48.

Gyatso, Tenzin (H. H. the Dalai Lama). *Stages of Meditation.* Translated by Geshe Lobsang Jordhen, Lobsang Choephel Ganchepa, and Jeremy Russell. Ithaca, N.Y.: Snow Lion Press, 2001.

Hacker, Paul. "Śaṅkara der Yogin und Śaṅkara der Advaitin: Einige Beobachtungen." *Beitrfge zur Geistesgeschichte Indiens: Festschrift E. Frauwallner: Wiener Zeitschrift für die Kunde Süd-und Ostasiens und Archiv für indische Philosophie* 12–13 (1968): 119–48.

Hallisey, Charles. "Roads Taken and Not Taken in the Study of Theravāda Buddhism." In *Curators of the Buddha: The Study of Buddhism under Colonialism*, edited by Donald Lopez, 31–61. Chicago: University of Chicago Press, 1995.

Harper, Katherine Anne, and Robert L. Brown. *The Roots of Tantra.* Albany: State University of New York Press, 2002.

Hauer, J. W. *Der Yoga: Ein Indischer Weg Zum Selbst.* Stuttgart: W. Kohlhammer Verlag, 1958.

Heiler, Friedrich. *Die Buddhistische Versenkung: Eine Religionsgeschischtliche Untersuchung.* Muchen: Verlag von Ernst Reinhardt, 1922.

Hermann-Pfandt, Adelheid. *Ḍākinīs: Zur Stellung und Symbolik des Weiblichen im Tantrischen Buddhismus.* Bonn: Indica et Tibetica, 1992.

Holm, Nils, ed. *Religious Ecstasy, Based on Papers Read at the Symposium on Religious Ecstasy Held at Èbo, Finland, on the 26th–28th of August 1981.* Stockholm: Almqvist & Wiksell International, 1982.

Hopkins, E. Washburn. "Yoga-Technique in the Great Epic." *Journal of the American Oriental Society* 22 (1901): 333–79.

Hume, Robert Ernest. *The Thirteen Principal Upaniṣads.* Madras: Oxford University Press, 1965.

Iyengar, B. K. S. *Light on the Yoga Sūtras of Patañjali*. San Francisco: HarperCollins, 1993.

Jacobsen, Knut A. *Prakṛti in Sāṃkhya-Yoga: Material Principle, Religious Experience, Ethical Implications*. New York: Peter Lang, 1999.

Jaini, Padmanabh S. "On the Sarvajñātva (Omniscience) of Mahāvīra and the Buddha." In *Buddhist Studies in Honor of I. B. Horner*, edited by L. Cousins, A. Kunst, and K. R. Norman, 71–90. Boston: Reidel, 1974.

———. *The Jaina Path of Purification*. Berkeley: University of California Press, 1979.

Jhaveri, Indukalaben H. *The Sāṅkhya-Yoga and the Jain Theories of Pariṇāma*. Ahmedabad: Gujarat University, 1990.

Kakar, Sudhir. *Shamans, Mystics, and Doctors: A Psychological Inquiry into India and Its Healing Traditions*. Chicago: University of Chicago Press, 1982.

Kalamaris, George. *Reclaiming the Tacit Dimension: Symbolic Form in the Rhetoric of Silence*. Albany: State University of New York Press, 1994.

———. "The Center and Circumference of Silence: Yoga, Poststructuralism, and the Rhetoric of Paradox." *International Journal of Hindu Studies* 1:1 (1997): 3–18.

Kalupahana, David J. *The Principles of Buddhist Psychology*. Albany: State University of New York Press, 1987.

Kast, Verena. *Joy, Inspiration, and Hope*. Translated by Douglas Whitcher. New York: Fromm International, 1994.

Katz, Steven T. *Mysticism and Philosophical Analysis*. New York: Oxford University Press, 1978.

———. *Mysticism and Religious Traditions*. New York: Oxford University Press, 1983.

———. *Mysticism and Language*. New York: Oxford University Press, 1992.

Kesarcodi-Watson, Ian. "Samādhi in Patañjali's Yoga-Sūtras." *Philosophy East and West* 32:1 (1982): 77–90.

King, Richard. *Orientalism and Religion: Postcolonial Theory, India, and the "Mystic East."* New York: Routledge, 1990.

———. *Indian Philosophy: An Introduction to Hindu and Buddhist Thought*. Edinburgh: Edinburgh University Press, 1999.

King, Winston L. *Theravāda Meditation: The Buddhist Transformation of Yoga*. Delhi: Motilal Banarsidass, 1992.

Kinsley, David. *Tantric Visions of the Divine Feminine: The Ten Mahāvidyās*. Berkeley: University of California Press, 1997.

Klein, Anne C. *Knowledge and Liberation: Tibetan Buddhist Epistemology in Support of Transformative Religious Experience*. Ithaca, N.Y.: Snow Lion Publications, 1986.

———. "Mental Concentration and the Unconditioned." In *Paths to Liberation: The Mārga and Its Transformation in Buddhist Thought*, edited by Robert E. Buswell Jr. and Robert M. Gimello, 269–308. Honolulu: University of Hawaii Press, 1992.

Kloetzli, Randy. *Buddhist Cosmology: From Single World System to Pure Land: Science and Theology in the Images of Motion and Light.* Delhi: Motilal Banarsidass, 1983.

Kloppenborg, Ria, and Ronald Poelmeyer. "Visualizations in Buddhist Meditation." In *Effigies Dei: Essays on the History of Religions*, edited by Dirk Van Der Plas, 83–96. New York: E. J. Brill, 1987.

Klostermaier, Klaus K. "*Dharmamegha Samādhi:* Comments on Yoga IV.29." *Philosophy East and West* 36:3 (1986): 253–62.

Knipe, David M. "One Fire, Three Fires, Five Fires: Vedic Symbols in Transition." *History of Religions* 11 (1972): 35.

———. *In the Image of Fire: Vedic Experiences of Heat.* Delhi: Motial Banarsidass, 1975.

———. "Becoming a Veda in the Godavari Delta." In *India and Beyond: Aspects of Literature, Meaning, Ritual, and Thought, Essays in Honor of Frits Staal*, edited by Dick van der Meij, 306–22. New York: Kegan Paul International, 1997.

Kochumuttom, Thomas A. *A Buddhist Doctrine of Experience: A New Translation and Interpretation of the Works of Vasubandhu the Yogācārin.* Delhi: Motilal Banarsidass, 1982.

Koelman, Gaspar M. *Pātañjala Yoga: From Related Ego to Absolute Self.* Poona: Papal Athenaeum, 1970.

Lai, Whalen, and Lewis R. Lancaster. *Early Ch'an in China and Tibet.* Berkeley, Calif.: Asian Humanities Press, 1983.

Lamrimpa, Gen (Ven. Jampal Tenzin). *Calming the Mind: Tibetan Buddhist Teachings on Cultivating Meditative Quiescence.* Translated by B. Alan Wallace. Edited by Hart Sprager. Ithaca, N.Y.: Snow Lion Publications, 1992.

Larson, Gerald. *Classical Sāmkhya.* Delhi: Motilal Banarsidass, 1969.

———. "An Old Problem Revisited: The Relation between Sāṃkhya, Yoga, and Buddhism." *Studien zur Indologie und Iranistik* 15 (1989): 129–46.

———. *India's Agony over Religion.* Albany: State University of New York Press, 1995.

———. "Classical Yoga as Neo-Sāṃkhya: A Chapter in the History of Indian Philosophy." *Asiatische Studien* 53:3 (1999): 723–32.

La Vallée Poussin, Louis de. "Musila et Nārada." *Mélanges chinois et bouddiques* 5 (1936–1937a): 189–222.

———. "Le Bouddhisme et le Yoga de Patañjali." *Mélanges chinois et bouddhiques* 5 (1936–1937b): 223–42.

———. *Abhidharmakośabhāṣyam*. Translated by Leo M. Pruden. Berkeley, Calif.: Asian Humanities Press, 1988.

Leggett, Trevor. *Śaṅkara on the Yoga-sūtra-s (Vol. I: Samādhi)*. London: Routledge & Kegan Paul, 1983a.

———. *Śaṅkara on the Yoga-sūtra-s (Vol II: Means)*. London: Routledge & Kegan Paul, 1983b.

Lester, Robert. *Rāmānuja on the Yoga*. Madras: Adyar Research Center, 1976.

Lewis, I. M. *Ecstatic Religion: A Study of Shamanism and Spirit Possession*. New York: Routledge, 1995.

———. *Religion in Context: Cults and Charisma*. Cambridge: Cambridge University Press, 1996.

Lopez, Donald S. *Prisoners of Shangri-La Tibetan Buddhism and the West*. Chicago: University of Chicago Press, 1998.

———. "Jailbreak: Author's Response." *Journal of the American Academy of Religion* 69:1 (2001): 203–13.

Lopez, Donald S., ed. *Curators of the Buddha: The Study of Buddhism under Colonialism*. Chicago: University of Chicago Press, 1995.

Lordrö, Geshe. *Walking through Walls: A Presentation of Tibetan Meditation*. Translated and edited by Jeffrey Hopkins, Anne C. Klein, and Leah Zahler. Ithaca, N.Y.: Snow Lion Press, 1992.

———. *Calm Abiding and Special Insight: Achieving Spiritual Transformation through Meditation*. Translated and edited by Jefferey Hopkins, Anne C. Klein, and Leah Zahler. Ithaca, N.Y.: Snow Lion Press, 1998.

Luigi Suali, ed. *Haribhadrasuri's Yogabindu with Commentary*. Bhavnagar: Jain Dharma Prasaraka Sabha, 1911.

Makransky, John J. *Buddahood Embodied: Sources of Controversy in India and Tibet*. Albany: State University of New York Press, 1997.

Matilal, B. "Mysticism and Reality: Ineffability." *Journal of Indian Philosophy* 3 (1975): 217–52.

McCutcheon, Russell T. *Manufacturing Religion: The Discourse on Sui Generis Religion and the Politics of Nostalgia*. New York: Oxford University Press, 1997.

———. *Critics Not Caretakers: Redescribing the Public Study of Religion*. Albany: State University of New York Press, 2001.

McGovern, William Montgomery. *A Manual of Buddhist Philosophy: Cosmology*. London: Routledge, 2002.

Monier-Williams, Sir M. *A Sanskrit-English Dictionary*. Oxford: Oxford University Press, 1899.

Namdol, Ācārya Gyaltsen, ed. *Bhāvanākramaḥ of Ācārya Kamalaśīla: Tibetan Version, Sanskrit Restoration, and Hindi Translation*. Sarnath: Central Institute of Higher Tibetan Studies, 1985.

Nyanamoli, Bhikku, trans. *The Path of Purification (Visuddhimagga)*. Colombo: A. Semage, 1964.

Oberhammer, Gerhard. "Meditation und Mystik im Yoga des Patañjali." *Wiener Zeitschrift für die Kunde Süd-und Ostasiens und Archiv für indische Philosophie* 9 (1965): 98–118.

———. *Strukturen Yogischer Meditation*. Veröffentlichungen der Kommission für Sprachen und Kulturen Südasiens, vol. 13. Vienna: Verlag der Österreichischen Akademie der Wissenschaften, 1977.

Obeyesekere, Gananath. *Medusa's Hair: An Essay on Personal Symbols and Religious Experience*. Chicago: University of Chicago Press, 1981.

———. *The Work of Culture: Symbolic Transformation in Psychoanalysis and Anthropology*. Chicago: University of Chicago Press, 1990.

———. *Imagining Karma: Ethical Transformation in Amerindian, Buddhist, and Greek Rebirth*. Berkeley: University of California Press, 2002.

Oldenburg, Hermann. *Buddha: His Life, His Doctine, His Order*. Translated by William Hoey. London: Williams and Norgate, 1882.

———. *Ancient India: Its Language and Religions*. Calcutta: Punthi Pustak, 1962.

———. *The Doctrine of the Upaniṣads and Early Buddhism*. Translated by Shridhar B. Shrotri. Delhi: Motilal Banarsidass, 1991.

Olivelle, Patrick. *The Early Upaniṣads: Annotated Text and Translation*. New York: Oxford University Press, 1998.

Olson, Carl. *The Theology and Philosophy of Eliade*. New York: St. Martin's Press, 1992.

———. "Mircea Eliade, Postmodernism, and the Problematic Nature of Representational Thinking." *Method and Theory in the Study of Religion* 11:4 (1999): 357–85.

Patton, Kimberly C., and Benjamin C. Ray, eds. *A Magic Still Dwells: Comparative Religion in the Postmodern Age*. Berkeley: University of California Press, 2000.

Paus, Ansgar. "The Secret Nostalgia of Mircea Eliade for Paradise: Observations on the Method of the 'History of Religions.'" *Religion* 19 (1989): 137–49.

Penner, Hans H. "Interpretation." In *Guide to the Study of Religion*, edited by Willi Braun and Russell T. McCutcheon, 57–71. London: Cassell, 2000.

Pflueger, Lloyd. "Discriminating the Innate Capacity." In *The Innate Capacity: Mysticism, Psychology, and Philosophy*, edited by Robert K. C. Forman, 45–81. New York: Oxford University Press, 1998.

Pickering, John, ed. *The Authority of Experience: Essays on Buddhism and Psychology*. Surrey: Curzon Press, 1997.

Prasāda, Rāma, trans. *Patañjali's Yoga Sutras: With the Commentary of Vyāsa and the Gloss of Vācaspati Miśra*. The Sacred Books of the Hindus. Edited by Major B. D. Basu. Allahabad: Bhuvaneswari Asram, 1912.

Rennie, Bryan. *Reconstructing Eliade: Making Sense of Religion.* Albany: State University of New York Press, 1996.

Rennie, Bryan, ed. *Changing Religious Worlds: The Meaning and End of Mircea Eliade.* Albany: State University of New York Press, 2001.

Rinbochay, Lati, and Denma Locho Rinbochay. *Meditative States in Tibetan Buddhism.* Translated by Jeffrey Hopkins and Leah Zahler. Edited by Leah Zahler. Boston: Wisdom, 1987.

Ruegg, David Seyfort. *Buddha-Nature, Mind, and the Problem of Gradualism in a Comparative Perspective: On the Transmission and Reception of Buddhism in India and Tibet.* London: School of Oriental and African Studies, 1989.

Ruegg, David Seyfort, and Lambert Schmithausen, eds. *Earliest Buddhism and Madhyamaka.* New York: E. J. Brill, 1990.

Rukmani, T. S., trans. *Yogavārttika of Vijñānabhikṣu: Text with English Translation and Critical Notes along with the Text and English Translation of the Pātañjala Yogasūtras and Vyāsabhāṣya.* Vols. 1–4. New Delhi: Munshiram Manoharlal, 1981–1989.

———. "Śaṅkara's Views on Yoga in the Brahmasūtrabhāṣya." *Journal of Indian Philosophy* 21 (1993): 395–404.

———. "Tension between *Vyutthāna* and *Nirodha* in the Yoga-Sūtras." *Journal of Indian Philosophy* 25 (1997): 613–28.

———. "Sāṅkhya and Yoga: Where They Do Not Speak in One Voice." *Asiatische Studien* 53:3 (1999): 733–53.

Sadakata, Akira. *Buddhist Cosmology: Philosophy and Origins.* Translated by Gaynor Sekimori. Tokyo: Kosei, 1997.

Sarbacker, Stuart. "*Enstasis* and *Ecstasis*: A Critical Appraisal of Eliade on Yoga and Shamanism." *Journal for the Study of Religion* 15:1 (2002a): 21–37.

———. "Traditions in Transition: Meditative Concepts in the Development of Tantric *Sādhana*." *International Journal of Tantric Studies* 6:1 (2002b).

Sastri, Asoke Chatterjee. *Upaniṣadyoga and Patañjalayoga—A Comparative Approach.* Calcutta: University of Calcutta Press, 1989.

Segal, Robert. "Misconceptions of the Social Sciences." *Zygon* 25:3 (1990): 264–78.

Senart, Emile. "Bouddhisme et Yoga." *Revue de l'Histoire des Religions* 21 (1900): 345–64.

Shakya, Tsering. "Who Are the Prisoners?" *Journal of the American Academy of Religion* 69:1 (2001): 183–89.

Shapiro, Deane H., Jr., and Roger N. Walsh, eds. *Meditation: Classic and Contemporary Perspectives.* New York: Aldine, 1984.

Sharf, Robert. "Buddhist Modernism and the Rhetoric of Meditative Experience." *Numen* 42 (1995): 228–83.

———. "Experience." In *Critical Terms for Religious Studies*, edited by Mark C. Taylor, 94–116. Chicago: University of Chicago Press, 1998.

Sharma, Parmananda, trans. *Bhāvanākrama of Kamalaśila.* New Delhi: Aditya Prakashan, 1997.

Sharma, R. K. *Temple of Chansatha-Yogini at Bheraghat.* Delhi: Agam Kala Prakashan, 1978.

Shastri, Siddhesvar Varma, trans. *The Svetasvatara Upanisad.* The Sacred Books of the Hindus, vol. 18, pt. 2. Edited by Major B. D. Basu. Allahabad: Bhuvaneswari Asram, 1916.

Shastri, Suvrat Muni. *Jaina Yoga in the Light of the Yogabindu.* Delhi: Nirmal, 1995.

Shastri, Swami Dwarikadas. *Abhidharmakośa & Bhāṣya of Ācārya Vasubandhu with Sphutārthā Commentary of Ācārya Yaśomitra.* Part IV (VII and VII Kośasthāna). Varanasi: Bauddha Bharati, 1973.

Shukla, Karunesha. *Śrāvakabhūmi of Ācārya Asaṅga.* Patna: K. P. Jayaswal Research Institute, 1973.

Smart, Ninian. *Doctrine and Argument in Indian Philosophy.* London: George Allen and Unwin, 1964.

———. *The Yogi and the Devotee.* London: George Allen and Unwin, 1968.

———. "Understanding Religious Experience." In *Mysticism and Philosophical Analysis*, edited by Steven T. Katz, 10–21. New York: Oxford University Press, 1978.

Smith, Huston. *Why Religion Matters: The Fate of the Human Spirit in an Age of Disbelief.* San Francisco: Harper San Francisco, 2000.

Snellgrove, David L. *Indo-Tibetan Buddhism: Indian Buddhists and Their Tibetan Successors.* London: Serindia, 1987.

Sonne, Birgitte. "The Professional Ecstatic in His Social and Ritual Position." In *Religious Ecstasy, Based on Papers Read at the Symposium on Religious Ecstasy Held at Ebo, Finland, on the 26th–28th of August 1981*, edited by Nils Holm, 128–50. Stockholm: Almqvist & Wiksell International, 1982.

Sopa, Ven. Geshe Lhundub. "*Śamathavipaśyanāyuganaddha:* The Two Leading Principles of Buddhist Meditation." In *Mahāyāna Buddhist Meditation: Theory and Practice*, edited by Minoru Kiyota, 46–65. Honolulu: University Press of Hawaii, 1978.

Sopa, Ven. Geshe Lhundub, Ven. Elvin W. Jones, and John Newman, trans. *The Stages of Meditation Middle Volume (Bhāvanākrama II).* Madison, Wis.: Deer Park Books, 1998.

Staal, Frits. *Exploring Mysticism: A Methodological Essay.* Berkeley: University of California Press, 1975.

———. *Rules without Meaning: Rituals, Mantras, and the Human Sciences.* New York: Peter Lang, 1989.

Strenski, Ivan. *Religion in Relation*. Columbia: University of South Carolina Press, 1993.

Stuart-Fox, Martin. "*Jhāna* and Buddhist Scholasticism." *Journal of International Association of Buddhist Studies* 12:2 (1989): 79–110.

Tambiah, Stanley J. *Buddhism and the Spirit Cults in North-East Thailand*. Cambridge: Cambridge University Press, 1970.

———. *The Buddhist Saints of the Forest and the Cult of Amulets: A Study in Charisma, Hagiography, Sectarianism, and Millennial Buddhism*. New York: Cambridge University Press, 1984.

Tandon, S. N. *A Re-Appraisal of Patanjali's Yoga-Sutras in the Light of the Buddha's Teaching*. Igatpuri: Vipassana Research Institute, 1995.

Tatia, Nathmal. *Jaina Meditation Citta-Samādhi: Jaina-Yoga*. Ladnun: Jain Vishva Bharati, 1986.

Taylor, Mark C., ed. *Critical Terms for Religious Studies*. Chicago: University of Chicago Press, 1998.

Thurman, Robert A. F. "Critical Reflections on Donald S. Lopez Jr.'s *Prisoners of Shangri-La: Tibetan Buddhism and the West*." *Journal of the American Academy of Religion* 69:1 (2001): 191–201.

Tripāṭhī, Rāma Śaṅkara, ed. *Bauddha Tathā Anya Bhāratīya Yoga Sādhanā*. Varanasi: Sampurnanand Sanskrit Vishvavidyalaya, 1981.

Tucci, Giuseppe. *Minor Buddhist Texts, Part II*. Rome: Instituto Italiano Per Il Medio Ed Estremo Oriente, 1958.

———. *Minor Buddhist Texts, Part III*. Rome: Instituto Italiano Per Il Medio Ed Estremo Oriente, 1971.

Vajirañāṇa, Paravahera Mahāthera. *Buddhist Meditation in Theory and Practice: A General Exposition according to the Pāli Canon of the Theravāda School*. Colombo: M. D. Gunasena & Co., 1962.

Vetter, Tilmann. *The Ideas and Meditative Practices of Early Buddhism*. New York: E. J. Brill, 1988.

Wallace, B. Alan. *The Bridge of Quiescence: Experiencing Tibetan Meditation*. Chicago: Open Court, 1998.

Vidyarnava, Rai Bahadur Srisa, and Pandit Mohan Lal Sandal, trans. *The Maitri Upanisat*. Sacred Books of the Hindus, vol. 31, pt. 2. Edited by Major B. D. Basu. Allahabad: Bhuvaneswari Asram, 1926.

Walsh, Roger. "Phenomenological Mapping and Comparison of Shamanic, Buddhist, Yogic, and Schizophrenic Experiences." *Journal of the American Academy of Religion* 61:4 (1993): 739–69.

Wayman, Alex. *Analysis of the Śrāvakabhūmi Manuscript*. Berkeley: University of California Press, 1961.

———. *Buddhist Tantras: Light on Indo-Tibetan Esotericism.* New York: Samuel Weiser, 1973.

———. *Calming the Mind and Discerning the Real: Buddhist Meditation and the Middle View.* New York: Columbia University Press, 1978.

———. *Buddhist Insight: Essays by Alex Wayman.* Edited by George Elder. Delhi: Motilal Banarsidass, 1984.

———. *Untying the Knots in Buddhism: Selected Essays.* Delhi: Motilal Banarsidass, 1997.

Werner, Karel. "Religious Practice and Yoga in the Time of the Vedas, Upaniṣads, and Early Buddhism." *Annals of the Bhandarkar Oriental Research Institute* 61 (1975): 179–94.

———. *Yoga and Indian Philosophy.* Delhi: Motilal Banarsidass, 1977.

———. "The Long-haired Sage of Ṛg Veda 10, 136; A Shaman, a Mystic, or a Yogi?" In *The Yogi and the Mystic: Studies in Comparative Mysticism*, edited by Karel Werner, 33–53. London: Curzon, 1989.

West, Michael A. *The Psychology of Meditation.* Oxford: Clarendon Press, 1987.

Whicher, Ian. "Cessation and Integration in Indian Philosophy." *Asian Philosphy* 5:1 (1995): 47–58.

———. "The Mind *(Citta)*: Its Nature, Structure, and Functioning in Classical Yoga (1)." *Saṃbhāṣa (Nagoya Studies in Indian Culture and Buddhism)* 18 (1997a): 35–62.

———. "Nirodha, Yoga *Praxis*, and the Transformation of the Mind." *Journal of Indian Philosophy* 25:1 (1997b): 1–67.

———. *The Integrity of the Yoga Darśana: A Reconsideration of Classical Yoga.* Albany: State University of New York Press, 1998a.

———. "The Mind *(Citta)*: Its Nature, Structure, and Functioning in Classical Yoga (2)." *Saṃbhāṣa (Nagoya Studies in Indian Culture and Buddhism)* 19 (1998b): 1–50.

———. "Yoga and Freedom: A Reconsideration of Patañjali's Classical Yoga." *Philosophy East and West* 48:2 (1998c): 272–322.

———. "Classical Sāṃkhya, Yoga, and the Issue of Final Purification" *Asiatische Studien* 53 (1999): 779–98.

White, David Gordon. *The Alchemical Body: Siddha Traditions in Medieval India.* Chicago: University of Chicago Press, 1996.

White, David Gordon, ed. *Tantra in Practice.* Princeton: Princeton University Press, 2000.

Williams, Paul. *Mahāyāna Buddhism: The Doctrinal Foundations.* New York: Routledge, 1989.

Williams, R. *Jaina Yoga: A Survey of the Medieval Śrāvakācāras.* Delhi: Motilal Banarsidass, 1991.

Willis, Janice. *Feminine Ground: Essays on Women and Tibet.* Ithaca, N.Y.: Snow Lion Press, 1987.

Wilson, Liz. *Charming Cadavers: Horrific Figurations of the Feminine in Indian Buddhist Hagiographic Literature.* Chicago: University of Chicago Press, 1996.

Wilson, Stephen R. "Becoming a Yogi: Resocialization and Deconditioning as Conversion Processes." *Sociological Analysis* 45:4 (1984): 310–23.

Winkelman, Michael. *Shamanism: The Neural Ecology of Consciousness and Healing.* Westport, Conn.: Bergin & Garvey, 2000.

Woods, James H., trans. *The Yoga System of Patañjali.* Harvard Oriental Series, vol. 17. Cambridge: Harvard University Press, 1914.

Yamane, David, and Megan Polzer. "Ways of Seeing Ecstasy in Modern Society: Experiential-Expressive and Cultural-Linguistic Views." *Sociology of Religion* 55:1 (1994): 1–25.

Yamashita, Koichi. *Pātañjala Yoga Philosophy with Reference to Buddhism.* Calcutta: Firma KLM Private Limited, 1994.

Yardi, M. R. *The Yoga of Patañjali.* Bhandarkar Oriental Series No. 12. Poona: Bhandarkar Oriental Research Institute, 1979.

Zahler, Leah. "Meditation and Cosmology: The Physical Basis of the Concentrations and Formless Absorptions according to dGe-lugs Tibetan Presentations." *Journal of the International Association of Buddhist Studies* 13:1 (1989): 53–78.

———. "The Concentrations and Formless Absorptions in Mahāyāna Buddhism: Geluk Tibetan Interpretation." Ph.D. dissertation, University of Virginia, 1994.

Zimmer, Heinrich. *Artistic Form and Yoga in the Sacred Images of India.* Translated and edited by Gerald Chapple and James B. Lawson, in collaboration with J. Michael McKnight. Princeton: Princeton University Press, 1984.

Index